Learning and Persuasion in the German Middle Ages

A Dominican teaching (miniature from the third book of Vincent of Beauvais), courtesy of Giraudon.

Learning and Persuasion in the German Middle Ages

Ernst Ralf Hintz

LONDON AND NEW YORK

First Published 1997 by Garland

Published 2013 by Routledge
2 Park Square, Milton Park, Abingdon, Oxfordshire OX14 4RN
711 Third Avenue, New York, NY 10017

First issued in paperback 2016

Routledge is an imprint of the Taylor & Francis Group, an informa business

Copyright © 1997 by Ernst Ralf Hintz
All rights reserved

Library of Congress Cataloging-in-Publication Data

Hintz, Ernst Ralf.
  Learning and persuasion in the German Middle Ages / by Ernst Ralf Hintz.
       p.   cm. — (Garland studies in medieval literature ; v. 15) (Garland reference library of the humanities ; vol. 1958)
    Includes bibliographical references and index.
    ISBN 0-8153-2182-1
    1. Christian education—Germany—History. 2. Germany—Church history—843-1517.   3. German literature—Old High German, 750-1050—History and criticism. 4. German literature—Middle High German, 1050-1500—History and criticism. 5. Christian literature, German—History and criticism. 6. Education, Medieval—Germany.   I. Title. II. Series. III. Series: Garland reference library of the humanities ; vol. 1958.
    BV1517.G3H56 1997
    268'.0943'0902—dc21   97-12532
                                                                                                        CIP

ISBN 13: 978-1-138-97957-4 (pbk)
ISBN 13: 978-0-8153-2182-8 (hbk)

General Editors' Foreword

Garland Studies in Medieval Literature (GSML) is a series of interpretative and analytic studies of the Western European literatures of the Middle Ages. It includes both outstanding recent dissertations and book-length studies, giving junior scholars and their senior colleagues the opportunity to publish their research.

In accordance with GSML policy the general editors have sought to welcome submissions representing any of the various schools of criticism and interpretation. Western medieval literature, with its broad historical span, multiplicity and complexity of language and literary tradition, and special problems of textual transmission and preservation as well as varying historical contexts, is both forbidding and inviting to scholars. It continues to offer rich materials for virtually every kind of literary approach that maintains a historical dimension. In establishing a series in an eclectic literature, the editors acknowledge and respect the variety of texts and textual possibilities and the "resisting reality" that confronts medievalists in several forms: on parchment, in mortar, or through icon. It is no mere imitative fallacy to be eclectic, empirical, and pragmatic in the face of this varied literary tradition that has so far defied easy formulation. The cultural landscape of the twentieth century is littered with the debris of broken monomyths predicated on the Middle Ages, the autocratic Church and the Dark Ages, for example, or conversely, the romanticized versions of love and chivalry.

The openness of the series means in turn that scholars, and particularly beginning scholars, need not pass an a priori test of "correctness" in their ideology, method, or critical position. The studies published in GSML must be true to their premises, complete within their articulated limits, and accessible to a multiple readership. Each study will advance the knowledge of the literature under discussion, opening it up for further consideration and creating intellectual value. It is also hoped that each volume, while bridging the gap between contemporary perspective and past reality, will make old texts new again. In this way the literature will remain primary, the method secondary.

In this fifteenth volume of the series, Ernst Ralf Hintz sketches key ideas of early Christian education and shows how these ideas affected both early German vernacular literature and also select Middle High German poems. What unites this focused literary history and the works examined is the common theme, call to Judgment. Hintz begins with a survey of formative Christian works on education by Augustine, Gregory the Great, and Hrabanus Maurus. As every medievalist knows, Augustine's *De doctrina christiana* is the major theoretical document for medieval Christian culture, establishing as it does a fusion of late Antique notions about rhetoric and truth with Christian ideas about the Bible and wisdom and concluding in Book IV with, arguably, the first manual for preaching. Hintz highlights major Augustinian themes, found also in Augustine's *De catechizandis rudibus,* such as exegesis, purification, wisdom, and *timor Dei,* and links them to Gregory's *Regula pastoralis,* that widely circulated "bishop's book" on how to teach and preach. Many surveys might end here, but Hintz brings forward into the discussion Hrabanus Maurus, the ninth-century *praeceptor Germaniae,* who continues the Augustinian-Gregorian program.

This first chapter is a most useful survey for any reader who wants an up-to-date treatment of early medieval theory on education. Hintz applies his survey to the *Muspilli,* an Old High German poem found in the margin of a St. Emmeram codex of (likely) the late ninth century, treating it as an instructional text and then as within the manuscript context, for it is related to an accompanying work, *Sermo de Symbolo contra Iudaeos.* Hintz reads the poem to show that it continues the major themes of Christian education with a rhetorical strategy appropriately drawn from these foundational texts. Hintz then shows how an eleventh-century work, Noker's *Memento Mori,* offers a balanced presentation of rational arguments and controlled emotional intensity to achieve that conversion that leads to salvation; thus, the tradition can show a variety of rhetorical strategies to attain the same end. This variety and adaptability continues in the early twelfth-century poems of Frau Ava. Reflecting in part the changes in Christian religion, Frau Ava considers the individual learner to be part of a community and guides the individual to take the moral initiative to attain salvation. The call to Judgment in the three-part *Von den Letzten Dingen (Der Linzer Entecrist)* exhibits a teaching strategy that reveals in this late-twelfth-century work a linear pattern of purification and ascent to wisdom. Hintz sees a narrative pattern with retarding elements that help establish a tension leading to forceful persuasion. All in all, Hintz demonstrates, as he puts it in his coda, that there is "the continuity of fundamental concepts of learning and teaching" that is identical with "the continuity of strategies of persuasion that shaped religious literature of the German Middle Ages."

The editors are happy to welcome this volume to the series. They furthermore wish to express their appreciation to Dr. Hintz for his cooperation and his collegiality.

Christopher Kleinhenz
University of Wisconsin-Madison

Paul E. Szarmach
Western Michigan University

For David Binke and Ruth Neville

Es war vor beinahe tausend Jahren. Die Welt wußte weder von Schießpulver noch von Buchdruckerkunst. Über dem Hegau lag ein bleischwerer Himmel, doch war von der Finsternis, die bekanntlich über dem ganzen Mittelalter lastete, im einzelnen nichts wahrzunehmen.

Ekkehard,
Joseph Viktor von Scheffel

CONTENTS

	Acknowledgments	ix
	Preface	xi
1.	Concepts of Learning and Teaching from Augustine to Hrabanus Maurus	3
2.	The Lesson of the *Muspilli*	43
3.	Christian Education in the *Memento Mori:* The Call to Judgment in the Late Eleventh Century	79
4.	Persuasion and Pedagogy in the Works of Frau Ava	103
5.	The Call to Judgment in *Von den Letzten Dingen (Der Linzer Antichrist)*	139
	Conclusion	181
	Bibliography	185
	Index	199

ACKNOWLEDGMENTS

In the course of this work, I have benefitted, in particular, from the advice and generosity of Francis G. Gentry and Paul E. Szarmach. Their wit and encouragement helped me to complete the laborious process of research and revision. I also wish to thank Fannie LeMoine, Douglas Kelly, Michael Leff, and William Courtenay for their interest in the early stages of this work. My thanks to Robert Crotty, who always found time to share his expertise in Early Church History with me during my stay in Australia. I am also indebted to my teachers in Germany, especially Gert Kaiser, who first kindled my interest in the German Middle Ages. Finally, I received unflagging moral support from my parents, my sister Karen, Edda Schrader-Gentry, Günter Helmes, Walter Tschacher, and Aliona Kosloff. My thanks, as well, to Cherene Holland, Ray Liddick Jr., and Patricia Mitchell for their successful efforts in putting my computer copy into publishable form. And special thanks to Rilla, whose enjoyment of life buoys me still.

PREFACE

This study examines Christian education in early vernacular texts of the German Middle Ages on the basis of Latin traditions of learning and teaching from Late Antiquity. The point of departure for the study will be Augustine's *De doctrina christiana.* In this work, Augustine not only consolidated Christian and pagan traditions, but combined them into a program of Christian education that disseminated its pedagogical theory and practice in the medieval period. I will look at the continuity of these traditions in the late sixth century in Gregory the Great's treatise on pastoral care, *Regula pastoralis,* and in the early ninth-century work of Hrabanus Maurus, *De institutione clericorum.*

In the chapters that follow I trace the continuity of traditional concepts of learning and teaching in the Old High German poem, the *Muspilli,* from the ninth century, then in the Middle High German works, the *Memento Mori* from the late eleventh century, and the poems of Frau Ava and *Von den Letzten Dingen* dating from the early and late twelfth century, respectively. These works, though far from encompassing all medieval German religious literature, lend themselves to examination because of their short to moderate length, which accentuates their narrative and teaching strategies. But more important, all works examined in this study provide a common ground for comparative analysis due to their common theme: the Call to Judgment.

I have provided the reader of this book with translations of the Latin and early German texts. For comparison, translations generally appear together with a version of their original texts. And, as in all translations, there is a measure of interpretation and poetic license.

E. R. H.
Hays, Kansas
August 1996

Learning and Persuasion in the German Middle Ages

1

CONCEPTS OF LEARNING AND TEACHING FROM AUGUSTINE TO HRABANUS MAURUS

In an age when an awareness of death and imminent accountability at judgment pervaded daily life, acquiring knowledge in matters of faith bound the learner to pass it on.[1] Even cloistered contemplatives offered instruction by their lives and dedication to a spiritual ideal. When Christians sought wisdom in the canon of Church literature, learning was oriented to practice.[2] The bishop was to be both exegete and teacher; and Christian parents were expected to see to the religious upbringing of their children. The acquisition and dissemination of Christian thought went hand in hand.

In the transitional period of the fifth century, the laity still commented on Scripture and participated in doctrinal discussion together with the clergy.[3] Although the duties of both *laicus* and *clericus* became increasingly distinct and institutionalized throughout the early medieval period, the fundamental attitude toward the importance of learning and communicating Christian moral tenets remained a constant imperative to all who professed the faith. The efforts of the Western Church to clarify and defend its doctrine against heretical threats to its authority—along with extensive missionary campaigns to expand ecclesiastical influence—required guidelines for instruction; yet the most prevalent pedagogical activity was in the area of routine pastoral duties within the Christian community itself.

The purpose of this book is to show how the reader and listener learned, were taught, and subsequently taught others in early medieval times. This study begins by examining sources of Christian education, namely, treatises on methods of biblical study and teaching, which passed from one generation of monastic and clerical scholars to the next during the four centuries from Late Antiquity to the Carolingian period. The following works provide a frame of reference for the development of medieval learning and teaching in this area: Augustine's *De doctrina christiana*, his *De magistro*, and his *De catechizandis rudibus;* Gregory the Great's *Liber regulae pastoralis;* and Hrabanus Maurus's *De clericorum institutione.*

Augustine began his *De doctrina christiana* in 396; three decades were to pass before he completed it. In his *Retractationes,* written toward the end of his life, Augustine not only reaffirms the importance of the first three books of *De doctrina,* but perceives the need for a fourth and final book. His decision to interrupt his work on the *Retractationes* to finish the third book (sect. 35) and to write the fourth affirms the importance that he attributed to this completion. And yet, Augustine long felt that the initial installment of *De doctrina* was adequate for the task, namely, of presenting guidelines for biblical study. Hence the fourth book offers more than hermeneutical and homiletic instruction; it complements the guidelines of the first three books by showing how the results of biblical study—the exegetical message—is to be taught to the listener and reader.

Viewed in its entirety, *De doctrina christiana* marks a shift in Augustine's evaluation of nonbiblical literature, pagan and Christian alike. In his early work, *De ordine,* written shortly after his conversion, Augustine documented the instruction that he gave during his pedagogically active retreat at Cassiciacum. Augustine still adhered to the Hellenistic program, yet raised the same objections as Cicero once did against the neglect of philosophy and the over-emphasis on rhetoric. Augustine's willingness to search allegorically for a Christian *sensus spiritualis* is revealed in his initial acceptance of pagan literature—the preoccupation of his student Licentius.[4] Only when his pupil's enthusiasm for the lovers' tale of *Pyramus and Thisbe* became an obsession did the teacher direct him toward the study of Scripture.

What Licentius failed to see was that *figmenta* are "half true and half false," the very knowledge that enabled the mature Augustine to deal with pagan poetic fiction and even to reinterpret Vergil's *Aeneid* with Christian insight (see Bennett, 63–65, 68–69). The spiritual value of poetry found outside of the Bible and patristic commentaries was still widely accepted, particularly when Christian, as seen in Augustine's own acknowledgment at that time of the poetry of Paulinus of Nola. Although Augustine never renounced his Cassiciacum plan of a well-balanced program of liberal arts as a propedeutic to biblical studies, he virtually abandoned it in *De doctrina christiana* in place of a program founded on the study of the Christian classic, the Bible itself.[5] By understanding the aesthetics of the Bible, the exegete was to better understand the purpose of scriptural eloquence.

Biblical aesthetics displays furthermore a clear pedagogical orientation. The author introduces book 1, entitled *De Rebus investigandis in Scriptura,* with the fundamental observation that "there are two things necessary to the treatment of Scriptures: a way of discovering those things which are to be understood, and a way of teaching what we have learned."[6] For Augustine, learning and teaching become reciprocal activities: the learners teach to others what they discover in Scripture, but also in useful secular literature—and teachers learn continually from insights into Christian truth and the responses of those whom they instruct.[7] *De doctrina christiana* provides the methods for these activities as a practical expression of the concept of the learner as teacher—a concept that will dominate Christian education in the West for over nine centuries until the two activities eventually diverge in the work of Thomas Aquinas.[8]

However, this orientation toward the very practical needs of educating the monks, priests, and *conversi* who were to spearhead Augustine's reform of Christian learning did not overturn the validity of another Augustinian concept, namely Christ as "the teacher within us."[9] This notion of the interior teacher underlies *De magistro,* Augustine's dialogue with his son and pupil, Adeodatus, which distinguishes between kinds of teaching.[10] Christ as the *magister interior* is the real teacher who divinely illuminates the truth.[11] The *magister exterior* is but the conventional teacher whose words remind learners of what to contemplate and stimulates them into consulting willingly the teacher within.[12]

A process of self-instruction precedes this inner consultation. We gain access to the interior teacher through introspection, and in the case of *De magistro,* by questions leading from partial to full knowledge of a particular truth. As Gerard O'Daly aptly notes: "We are no passive recipients of these truths. We also teach ourselves. Cognition is an active process,"[13] and one that depends on the learner's ability and initiative, not on the words of an exterior teacher. Augustine addresses this point when he says of the learner:

> If he is guided . . . by the words of the questioner, still he does not accomplish the grasp of the whole by means of verbal instruction, but by means of questions put in such a way that he who is questioned is able to teach himself through his inner power according to the

measure of his ability. . . . Thus, it was suitable for me to formulate my questions in such a way that your powers might be brought under the direction of the inner teacher.[14]

Words in the epistemological scheme of *De magistro* act as intermediaries.[15] As outward signs, they are agents reminding us to search inwardly for truth and illumination.[16] This concept of admonishing signs used by an exterior teacher to move the learner toward self-instruction and the interior teacher is uncontested in the *Retractiones*.[17] And when the immediate needs of preaching and pastoral care require Augustine to uphold the conventional practice of teaching and use of words in *De doctrina christiana,* he will do so by extending the sign theory of *De magistro* to meet the needs of the learner in interpreting Scripture. Thus, students of Scripture learn by self-instruction. Yet when learners act as teachers, facilitators, and motivators, they must know both their subjects and how to employ words to convey it to others. *De doctrina* equips the learner with the practical guidelines needed for interpreting the signs in Scripture and communicating what is understood.[18]

Indeed, the concept of the learner as teacher in *De doctrina* complements the idea of the exterior and interior teacher in *De magistro,* whereby the Christian community remains first and foremost an active community of learners, disseminating what is learned and ultimately learning for themselves in consultation with Christ, the teacher within.

SCRIPTURAL EXEGESIS AS AEDIFICATIO

In book 1 of *De doctrina christiana,* Augustine directs the reader to an important exegetical guideline: the precept of charity as a determining factor in understanding the Bible, especially the Old Testament. Not only must the reader as exegete view the things told in Scripture in the light of charity, he must use them in fostering charity in himself and others. And he must know how to use the things of the world.[19]

Augustine evokes the image of pilgrimage to a spiritual homeland to show the proper use of *res* (1.2.2).[20] What exists in this world should be used as a vehicle and not be enjoyed for its own sake, but rather its usefulness in conveying the traveler to his destination (1.4.4). The evocation of a homeward journey from a foreign land recalls the transition from the corporal and temporal to the eternal and spiritual. Furthermore, our journey ought to be a cleansing, a *purgatio animi*, which makes us receptive to Christ as "our native land . . . also the Way to that native land" and thereby truth and wisdom (1.10.10; 1.11.11). We are to journey as pilgrims toward the proper object of our enjoyment and love—the Trinity (1.5.5).

Once the qualities of the divine persons as triune God are enumerated, however, Augustine modifies the exposition we might expect. After professing *deus pater* (1.5.5, 9.9), and then *Christus* (1.10.10, 14.13), Augustine speaks not of the Holy Spirit—but of the Church instead (1.15.14, 18.17).[21] An important motivating agent of Christian instruction—*timor* as salutary fear—precedes the theme of "the Church." If the Resurrection and Ascension are to inspire faith with hope, then Christ's coming as "the Judge of the living and the dead" is to strike "great fear into the negligent . . . that they devote themselves to earnest effort and long for Him by leading a saintly life" (1.15). Augustine points out that Christ disciplines and cleanses "His Body"—the Church—"with certain afflictions." Purged in this fashion, its members continue their journey, traversing the road not spatially, but "with affections of the heart." These affections reveal themselves in the transformation of their lives, and in the belief in Christ's forgiveness of sin through his crucifixion.

Once the narrative has proceeded from the Trinity to Christ and his Church, Augustine turns to the last things at the fulfillment of time. He affirms the bliss that awaits believers who die unto the world—and the "punishment beyond imagination" in store for the despairing who do not. Sharpening the eschatological tone of these passages (1.19.18–21.19), salutary fear urges the reader to approach the *res* in Scripture ever mindful of the Call to Judgment and culmination of salvation history.[22]

Created in the divine image and endowed with rational souls, humans, too, share in the divine order: "A great thing is man, made in the image and likeness of God."[23] As *res* in the above category, humans signify by their deeds either acceptance or rejection of that in their nature that is divine.[24] Augustine foresaw that the learner must be taught how to use Christian self-love for the greatest spiritual benefit: "Thus man should be instructed concerning the way of loving, that is, concerning the way of loving himself profitably" (1.25.26). Under the heading of *Praeceptum generale*, the most beneficial use is shown to be the expression of charity: "a love of God and a love of our neighbor."[25]

Just as true Christian self-love derives from love of God, so too does love of one's neighbor: "For when love of God is placed first and the character of that love is seen to be described so that all other loves must flow into it, it may seem that nothing has been said about the love of yourself. But when it is said, 'Thou shalt love thy neighbor as thyself' at the same time, it is clear that love for yourself is not omitted" (1.26.27).[26] Augustine further underscores this derivation by alluding to the authority of Christ's testimony in the Gospel as well as that of Paul (1.30.31). Charity also includes the exercise of mercy. After referring to Christ's exhortation to emulate the mercy shown by the Good Samaritan (Luke 10:27–37), Augustine defines the concept of neighbor in terms that depict the showing of mercy (1.30.31). This definition further encompasses the love of one's enemy (1.29.30). The growth of charity is, then, an underlying theme that provides the exegete with a continual point of reference:

> Whoever, therefore, thinks that he understands the divine Scriptures or any part of them so that it does not build the double love of God and of our neighbor does not understand it at all. Whoever finds a lesson there useful to the building of charity [*aedificandae caritati sit utilis*], even though he has not said what the author may be shown to have intended in that place, has not been deceived, nor is he lying in any way. (1.36.40)

When choosing to understand a passage in the sense of charity and by so doing failing to express the biblical author's immediate intention, the exegete abandons the given path for the sake of a detour that leads eventually to the same destination, though not always without difficulty (1.36.41). An essential goal of scriptural study and indeed of a Christian life remains according to Augustine, the "building of charity." Referring to the greatest of virtues (1 Cor. 13:8, 13), Augustine closes book 1 with an affirmation of charity in Pauline terms: "Therefore, when anyone knows the end of the commandments to be charity 'from a pure heart, and a good conscience, and an unfeigned faith,' and has related all of his understanding of the divine Scriptures to these three, he may approach the treatment of these books with security" (1.40.44).

Purification and Wisdom

Deogratias, a deacon at Carthage, wrote to Augustine to request a manual for the instruction of pagan catechumens. The bishop of Hippo

Concepts of Learning and Teaching

responded with *De catechizandis rudibus*. The beginning of this short work takes up the theme of charity through a reference to 1 Timothy 1:5, the same Pauline scriptural passage to which Augustine refers in *De doctrina christiana* (1.26.27). Once attention is called to the building of charity as a fundamental goal of Christian education, Augustine particularly notes the importance of the learner's salutary fear of God.[27] At this point, Augustine does not hesitate to remind the teacher to transfer the catechumen's awe of God into an ardent desire for scriptural study (*De cat.rud.* 6.10). The most saving terror (*saluberrimus terror*) and fear and reverence (*timor*) are to be used and cultivated by the teacher for the spiritual benefit of those in his charge.[28]

The pedagogical use of *timor* as the salutary fear of God appears prominently in *De doctrina*, where Augustine views the building of charity within the framework of an exegetical learning process. In this process, the learner embarks on a purifying ascent to wisdom, where each level (*gradus*) is also a step upward in a spiritual pilgrimage.[29] The first of seven steps is a reverent fear of God:

> Before all it is necessary that we be turned by the fear of God toward a recognition of His will, so that we may know what He commands that we desire and what He commands that we avoid. Of necessity this fear will lead us to thought of our mortality and of our future death and will affix all our proud motions, as if they were fleshly members fastened with nails, to the wood of the cross. (2.7.9)

The effects of *timor Dei* as well as of the fear of death serve to promote meekness and to suppress pride. This progression leads to the second step, piety, which predisposes the learner to scriptural study by fostering an acceptance of scriptural authority. Even when a biblical passage is not immediately understandable, it is not to be discounted, but rather scrutinized all the more diligently. Augustine is adamant in upholding the authority of the Bible against any willful interpretation that is but a reaction to the uncomfortable condemnation of personal vices or arises from the rejection of a scriptural text due to its obscurity (2.7.9). From the levels of the fear of God and piety, the learner proceeds to that of *scientiae gradus,* or knowledge:

> In this every student of the Divine Scriptures must exercise himself, having found nothing else in them

except, first, that God is to be loved for Himself, and his neighbor for the sake of God; second that he is to love God with all his heart . . . and third, that he should love his neighbor as himself, that is, so that all love for our neighbor should, like all love for ourselves, be referred to God. (2.7.10)

In scriptural study the exegete discovers how one becomes encumbered by the love of temporal things. This recognition heightens through the fear of divine Judgment and piety, which strengthens the belief in scriptural authority. As a consequence, the learner as exegete is forced to lament his condition.

Lamentation, in turn, elicits a plea for divine help against despair and leads to the fourth ascending step, *fortitudo.* At this level, the learner is said to "hunger and thirst for justice." His emotional, spiritual and physical state, his *affectus,* guides and urges him onward in his ascent: "And by means of this affection of the spirit [*hoc enim affectu*] he will extract himself from all mortal joy in transitory things, and as he turns aside from this joy, he will turn toward the love of eternal things, specifically toward that immutable unity which is the Trinity" (2.7.10).[30]

By the fifth step the learner becomes skilled in the counsel of mercy. Now purged of the appetite for inferior things, the mind perfects itself in the practice of charity (2.7.11). But it is only when the learner arrives at the love of his enemy (*ad inimici dilectionem*) that he may ascend to the sixth step and begin to see God. Though the inner sight (*oculus cordis*) is cleansed from the temporal and corporeal, the learner must perceive divine truth mainly by faith. Augustine again evokes the imagery of pilgrimage: "And now although the light of the Trinity begins to appear more certainly . . . it is still said to appear 'through a glass in a dark manner' for 'we walk more by faith than by sight' when we make our pilgrimage in this world" (2.7.11).[31] No longer diverted by efforts to please his fellow human beings or avoid life's adversities, the pilgrim begins the final ascent: "Such a son ascends to wisdom, which is the seventh and last step, where he enjoys peace and tranquillity. 'For the fear of the Lord is the beginning of wisdom.' From fear to wisdom the way extends through these steps" (2.7.11).[32]

After recounting the seven-step ascent and the causal relation of *timor* to wisdom, Augustine abruptly returns to the third level, the study of the Bible, and recommends to the exegete the canon of scriptural literature (2.8.12, 13). Augustine reaffirms the important effect of *timor* as well as *pietas* on the learner's disposition: "In all of these books those fearing God [timentes Dei] and made meek in piety [*pietate mansueti*] seek the will of God" (2.9.14). The learners are clearly designated by their *affectus*, the spiritual and emotional state they display: those who revere and fear God as they grow in wisdom; and those who become meek through piety, seeking the divine will in sacred literature and recognizing scriptural authority.

In *De doctrina christiana*, the building of charity involves each learner in a twofold process of purification and ascent to wisdom. Regarding this process in the tradition of Christian *aedificatio*, Reinhart Herzog has shown the influence of Greek Christian literature upon biblical aesthetics.[33] Origen, Saint Basil, and especially John Chrysostom, Augustine's contemporary in the East, all perceived the use of catharsis for spiritual purification as a prerequisite to Christian learning. And the influence of Aristotelian literary tradition in Late Antiquity was not confined to the Eastern Empire; it also encompassed the Latin West.[34] Herzog points out that the use of catharsis as a purifying agent complemented stylistic, compositional devices such as "paraphrastic intensity"[35] and allegory within the Christian learning process.

Yet catharsis in a Christian poetics would need to modify the use of fear and pity—the emotions characteristic of Attic tragedy.[36] For if a Christian learner would ascend through purification to wisdom, there could be no purging the fear of God, and no diminishing of charity. Each *affectus* must be an agent to purge impediments to judgment as the learner strives to imitate Christ.[37] Thus, affected by the supreme act of charity, Christ's passion, the learner judges more acutely whether his own actions are also expressions of charity. Augustine not only upholds the use of fear and pity, he sustains both through anticipation of the imminent Call to Judgment.[38] Even the Pauline virtue of hope (*spes*) serves to maintain the tension inherent in the Second Coming; hope for salvation is in part an ongoing response to the fear of damnation, in which the fear of God as Judge compels humans to grow in faith and perfect themselves in charity.[39]

In sum, Augustine's *De doctrina christiana* and *De catechizandis rudibus* reveal the influence of the Aristotelian tradition of "affect teaching"—the use of the *affectus* to move the learner to the proper use of reason in judgment. Within the Christian tradition of this practice, the reverent fear of God (*timor Dei*) can act as a means of catharsis in predisposing the Christian learner to judge correctly in choosing the path to salvation, namely, that of scriptural study, the building of charity, and the ascent to purification and wisdom.

Although *timor Dei* is a prerequisite in the Christian learning process, an additional means of purification appears in Augustine's advice to the exegete on how best to discover the *sensus spiritualis* in Scripture. Before describing the seven-step process of *purificatio* and *ascensio*, Augustine speaks of the beneficial effect of deciphering obscure scriptural passages: "But many and varied obscurities and ambiguities deceive those who read casually. . . . I do not doubt that this situation was provided by God to conquer pride by work and to combat disdain in our minds, to which those things which are easily discovered seem frequently to become worthless" (2.6.7).

Yet, *labor* as a means of purifying the exegete is not required of everyone. Those who display the necessary humility to accept scriptural authority or lack the ability to deal with biblical obscurity may rely on readily understandable passages. Augustine describes the manner in which the Holy Spirit has modified Scripture to accommodate those who hunger for truth, providing them with open passages (*locis apertioribus*) and to deter by obscurity those who seek with pride and disdain. Augustine takes care to state that almost nothing can be uncovered in obscure passages—such as the allegory of the Church as a beautiful woman in the *Song of Songs*—that cannot be found clearly expressed in others. Consequently, although skill in allegorical interpretation may be useful, even necessary in understanding some scriptural passages, it is by no means a prerequisite of general Christian edification.

The essential criterion of Augustine's instruction on the proper use of knowledge is its value in understanding Scripture and teaching the Gospel (2.18.28, 40.60). Even truths expounded by the philosophers (*maxime Platonici*) are not to be feared, but reclaimed as from unjust possessors for Christian use. Although the conversion and appropriation of pagan teachings can be valid, all are overshadowed by the Bible as the ultimate manual of wisdom: "The knowledge collected from the books of the pagans, although some of it is useful, is also little as compared with that derived from the Holy Scriptures. For whatever a man has learned elsewhere is censured there if it is harmful; if it is useful, it is found there" (2.42.63). By censuring learning that can inflate the reader with pride, the Bible measures nonscriptural knowledge according to its spiritual utility in strengthening faith and charity.

With Christian goals for the use of knowledge clearly established, Augustine still takes the precaution of providing the exegete with advice to heed when approaching Scripture. The exhortation toward the close of book 2 tells the learner: "Always bear in mind the apostolic saying,

'Knowledge puffs up; but charity edifies' [1 Cor. 8:1]." Just as knowledge for its own sake leads to pride, knowledge used for biblical exegesis must aim to build charity. Augustine reinforces this Pauline admonition with the paschal image of the hyssop, the deep-rooted herb used by the Israelites in Egypt to mark their doorposts with the blood of the lamb (Exod. 12:22). The hyssop symbolizes the correct disposition of the student of Scripture: "This is a meek and humble herb, and yet nothing is stronger or more penetrating than its roots. Thus 'rooted and founded in charity,' we 'may be able to comprehend' . . . which things make up the Cross of our Lord." The hyssop also represents purification: "And then the Psalmist adds as a consequence that he may show hyssop to signify a cleansing from pride, 'and the bones that have been humbled shall rejoice'" (2.41.62). Fortified with the attributes of the hyssop, the learner may better prepare for scriptural study and know (*cognoscere*) the nature of Christ's sacrifice on the Cross:

> In the Sign of the Cross the whole action of the Christian is described: to perform good deeds in Christ, to cling to Him with perseverance, to hope for celestial things, to refrain from profaning the sacraments. *Having been cleansed by this action*, we shall be able 'to know also the charity of Christ, which surpasseth all knowledge' . . . so that we 'may be filled unto all the fullness of God.' (2.41.62, emphasis mine)

Again we see the influence of the *affectus* within the Christian learning process. Not only do the effects of *signum crucis* spiritually strengthen the learner and promote charity, they also purify the learner and, in doing so, make possible the ascent to wisdom.

Modus proferendi

The medieval tradition of preaching in the West is founded on Augustine's *De doctrina christiana*.[40] What did this tradition imply in the early fifth century? As Augustine recalls (1.1) at the beginning of the fourth and concluding book, he reiterates the two necessary activities involved in the treatment of the Scriptures: *modus inveniendi* and *modus proferendi*. He alerts the reader that books 1–3 together with book 4 form a compositional and pedagogical unity. The study of the Bible and the teaching/preaching of what was learned went hand in hand as one educational process. This was not a process, however, in which the clergy alone participated.

In the late fourth and early fifth centuries educated laypersons played a prominent literary role in the Church. This was a Christian laity that had received its education in the Roman system of the Late Empire, as had Augustine himself. The works of Prudentius and later of Sedulius evince the literary activity of Christian laymen who wrote out of religious fervor and the wish to bear witness to their faith. The borders of teaching and preaching were flexible, even though the exposition of Scripture from the pulpit was restricted to the clergy, in particular to the bishops.

De doctrina christiana was designed to be more than a clerical handbook.[41] As a cultural program it offered guidelines to those contemporaries of Augustine who were equipped with the pagan educational skills available in the Late Empire that could provide access to scriptural exegesis. Not only was Augustine's concept of such a program of learning and teaching Scripture much wider than is inferred by the modern term "preaching," the range of literary expression encompassed by this program was also more extensive.[42] The sermon was one of many forms of Christian eloquence serving to teach the Gospel and biblical exegesis; others were letters of correspondence, theological treatises, books in prose, and poetry. Both *modi*—that of discovering and interpreting the scriptural message as well as that of conveying what was learned—were represented within a broad spectrum of written and spoken literary expression. The *modus proferendi* in *De doctrina christiana* did not rely on the elaborate rules of declamation and Late Roman rhetorical style as a basis for eloquence. Augustine departs from the academic overemphasis of rules that is prevalent in the Late Empire in favor of learning by imitation:

> Therefore, since infants are not taught to speak except by learning the expressions of speakers, why can men not be made eloquent, not by teaching them the rules of eloquence, but by having them read and hear the expressions of the eloquent and imitate them in so far as they are able to follow them? Have we not seen examples of this being done? For we know many men ignorant of the rules of eloquence who are more eloquent than many who have learned them; but we know of no one who is eloquent without having read or heard the disputations and sayings of the eloquent. (4.3.5)

Augustine's advocacy of *imitatio* reemphasizes established pedagogical tradition. One source in this line of continuity is the oratory of Isocrates. An Athenian rhetorician and educator of the fourth century before Christ, Isocrates built upon the already existing tradition of Homeric education and its principles of "example" and "imitation."[43] As a critic of the formalized rhetoric of his time Isocrates introduced only the minimum of rules necessary for the learner to imitate literary texts.[44] These texts were chosen for their importance as ideals of style and as models of wise as well as unwise behavior. Influence on classical education continued into the Late Republic of Cicero's time and through the Empire into the age of Augustine.

The Bible, as the essential literary model chosen by Augustine, was to supersede classical texts and provide Christians with a source of wisdom and eloquence that would enable them to defend and expound their faith (4.2.3). By emphasizing the preeminence of the Bible as the prime source material for the educated Christian, the conversion of classical rhetoric for the service of the Church, and a virtue uncharacteristic of antiquity, *humilitas,* Augustine transcended his own classical education. Henceforth classical education and rhetorical skills are useful only if applicable to the study of the Bible, "the highest kind of Christian learning."[45]

Conceived neither as a guide for understanding pagan literature nor as a manual for the conversion of pagans, *De doctrina christiana* aims to educate scripturally an established Christian congregation. By means of this training, Christian teachers could more effectively reach an already converted audience of varied educational backgrounds. Augustine advises the teacher to suit the rhetoric and level of instruction to the needs of the audience and its level of education: "What profits correctness in a speech which is not followed by the listeners when there is no reason for speaking if what is said is not understood by those on whose account we speak?" (4.10.24). If necessary, the teacher is to depart from the correct word usage and grammatical form for the sake of clarity (4.13.29).

As a seasoned orator and product of the Late Roman educational system, Augustine knew the value of eloquence. Under his supervision, "conventional Ciceronian rhetoric" entered into the service of Christian education. The twelfth chapter of the fourth book clearly refers to Cicero:

> Therefore a certain eloquent man said, and said truly, that he who is eloquent should speak in such a way that he teaches, delights, and moves. Then he

added, 'To teach is a necessary, to please is a sweetness, to persuade is a victory' [Cicero, *De orat.* 21.69]
... Just as the listener is to be delighted if he is to be retained as a listener, so also he is to be persuaded if he is to be retained. (4.12.27)

Persuasion in Christian rhetoric is not the classical rhetoric of Cicero, where the orator seeks victory chiefly in the political or legal arena by shaping opinion according to the dictates of an arbitrary case, using arguments of probability if need be.[46] The Christian rhetorician in Augustine's program addresses an already converted audience and seeks to move the listener to keep the tenets of faith in accord with established doctrine. Yet the need for conversion as ongoing process of spiritual reform—a turning back of the Christian from error toward salvation—would remain.[47] To meet this need, Augustine recommends persuasion as a means to victory in the arena of faith, should the listener doubt, lack zeal or become too lethargic to apply what has been learned. Only with the grace to understand and consent, does the listener require little or no persuasion and is moved to act by faith (4.12.27).

Despite differing aims for persuasion, Augustine and Cicero share in a common tradition—the Aristotelian—in which image and ethical imitation are closely allied to legal rhetoric.[48] As the "oldest of the three branches" of rhetoric in respect to technique, forensic persuasion had a marked influence on the deliberative and epideictic: "The principles of persuasion which Aristotle extends to all rhetorical discourse, in other words, derive from legal procedure, and more specifically from the practice of presenting proof in court."[49] The image, in league with metaphor, instructs by demonstrating the proof *pro ommaton,* "before the eyes" of the spectators.[50] While instruction evokes delight, the image persuades the eyewitness toward a prescribed action by the vividness—the *enargeia* or in Latin *evidentia*—of the particular account.[51] Discerning the false image from the true plays a role not only in judicial procedure, but also in the Christian learning process.[52] Augustine envisions Christian education to be a progression from cognition to judgment and, finally, to action in realizing the image of God in each learner. In addition, Augustine adjoins the psychological concept of will as *intentio voluntatis* to the legal concept of intention; the learner who strives to reform according to the the divine image, the *imago Dei* within, will be judged according to his or her intentions.[53]

Thus, it is through the Christian notion of the Last Judgment that

Augustine augments the classical idea of image and intention.[54] The Christian's preparation for facing the Divine Judge becomes the ultimate measure of success of the Christian learning process: "But the image which is being renewed day by day in the spirit of the mind and in the knowledge of God, not outwardly but inwardly, will be perfected by the vision itself which will then be after the judgment face to face, but it is making progress towards it now through a mirror in an obscure manner [*per speculum in aenigmate*]" (*De trinitate* 14.19.25).[55]

Christian learning not only aspires to wisdom (*sapientia*)—knowledge of eternal, immutable truths—but also to knowledge required in leading our daily lives (*scientia*). This knowledge of changeable things is needed for the development of "practical virtues" in preparation for Judgment.[56] To acquire *scientia*, the learner must distinguish true from false images; while the former can lead to *imitatio Christi* and humility, the latter may deceive the learner into *imitatio Dei*, the imitation of God's power—the sin of pride.[57]

Referring once again to "the author of Roman eloquence himself" and the tripartite formula: "to teach, delight, and persuade," Augustine instructs the Christian teacher and orator to pray—an expression of *humilitas*—and to act so that the audience might hear with understanding, willingly, and obediently (4.17.23).[58] The manner in which the teacher seeks to elicit the proper learning disposition is provided by the use of the *affectus*.[59] As a means of persuasion inherent in legal oratory and Attic tragedy, affectivity aims to move the audience—especially through the emotions of fear and pity—toward right judgment and conduct.[60] Yet while Augustine approves the use of the emotions in Christian rhetoric, he places on their use an essential condition.[61] The Christian must apply the emotions "rightly" under the control of reason.[62]

Christian affectivity (*Affektenlehre*), which instructs the learner by confrontation with the *affectus* of a particular narrative character,[63] assumes distinct rhetorical form by means of three additional Ciceronian categories of style from the legal arena: "He therefore will be eloquent who can speak of small things in a subdued manner, of moderate things in a temperate manner, and of grand things in a grand manner" (*De orat.* 29.101). Augustine is quick to add, when the Christian orator addresses the spiritual welfare of the listener, especially from the pulpit, *de loco superiore*, all things are considered to be important: "Among our orators, however, everything we say, . . . must be referred, not to the temporal welfare of man, but to his eternal welfare and to the avoidance of eternal punishment" (4.18.35). In other words, the *tria genera* that Cicero prescribes in a forensic context need not correspond to degrees of importance for subject matter in a Christian context.[64] The Christian orator, in teaching what is useful for salvation, is to use the three categories of style according to the particular spiritual purpose of the oration and the manner in which it is to affect the audience:

> Nevertheless, although our teacher should speak of great things, he should not always speak about them in the grand manner, but in a subdued manner when he teaches something, in a moderate manner when he condemns or praises something. But when something is to be done and he is speaking to those who ought to do it but do not wish to do it, then those great things should be spoken in the grand manner in a way appropriate to the persuasion of their minds. And sometimes concerning one and the same important thing, he speaks in a subdued manner if he teaches, in a moderate manner if he is praising it, and in a grand manner if he is moving an adverse mind to conversion. (4.19.38)

Augustine emphasizes these categories as a *modus proferendi* through stylistic examples from the Apostle Paul (4.20.39), Saint Ambrose, and Saint Cyprian (4.21.45–50). The pedagogical force of imitation also appears in his use of ecclesiastical literary models to exemplify the categories of style; students may learn the *tria genera* "by assiduous reading, or hearing, accompanied by practice" (4.21.50). Augustine further draws from experience to add his own example of the use of style to the preceding ones. Commenting on the effects of the grand style, Augustine confides:

> But I did not think that I had done anything when I heard them applauding, but when I saw them weeping. They indicated by applause that they were being taught or pleased, but tears indicated that they were persuaded. ... There are many other experiences through which we have learned what effect the grand style of a wise speaker may have on men. They do not show it through applause but rather through their groans, sometimes even through tears, and finally through a change of their way of life [*postremo vitae mutatione*]. (4.24.53)

Although the plain style, too, can effect a change of spirit by directing the listener toward wisdom, imparting knowledge and fostering belief (4.24.54),[65] it does not necessarily move the listener to do what should be done. "To bend hardness of this kind," the teacher uses the grand style when the listener "will confess that the speech is true and agreeable, but will not do what it says should be done" (4.26.58). Persuading the audience to judge rightly, therefore, is not a matter of arousing tears at the expense of reason. On the contrary, it is by appealing to reason that argument persuades the listener to judge its validity. The grand style can then offer further persuasion that the listener may follow the judgment willingly.[66]

Augustine envisions the moderate style as playing an auxiliary role (4.25.55) to delight the hearer by eloquent praise of God and the saints,[67] and by eloquent admonition: "When praises and vituperations are eloquently spoken, although they belong to the moderate style, they so affect some that they are not only delighted by the eloquence of praising or blaming, but also desire to live in a praiseworthy way and to avoid living in a way that should be blamed" (4.24.54).

Augustine, however, does not fail to warn the Christian orator against the use of eloquence in the moderate style to please the listener as an end in itself (4.35.55). Although *delectatio* remains problematic for Augustine, it retains a place within Christian eloquence. For an audience already disposed toward learning through understanding, willingness, and obedience (4.12.28), persuasion is not necessary. But when this is not the case, the orator may employ eloquence "in a manner leading to persuasion." The use of *delectatio* in the moderate style, therefore, is designed to assist the grand and subdued styles. Augustine takes further care to instruct the Christian teacher in what manner styles may vary with one another to evoke the desired effect. The *tria genera dicendi* can be combined as follows:

> Thus even in the grand style the beginning of the discourse should always, or almost always, be moderate. . . . Therefore in the grand style the two others have a place, and the same is true of the subdued style. The temperate style sometimes but not always needs the subdued style if, as I have said, a question arises to be solved, or, when some things which could be expressed with ornament are left plain and spoken in the subdued manner so that certain extravagances, so to speak, of ornament may seem more eminent. But the temperate style does not need the grand style, for it is used for purposes of delight rather than for persuasion. (4.23.52)

Augustine is also careful to stress that the message in Christian teaching far outweighs the medium: "In his speech itself [the teacher] should prefer to please more with the things said than with the words used to speak them; nor should he think that anything may be said better than that which is said truthfully; nor should the teacher serve the words, but the words the teacher" (4.28.61).

Augustine wishes to leave no doubt in the mind of his reader concerning the relationship of *sapientia* to *eloquentia*. If a teacher cannot command both eloquence and wisdom, it is better that he speak wisely without eloquence, than foolishly with it (4.28.61). Returning to a fundamental theme of Christian education, the implementation of what is taught, Augustine affirms that the very example of a good life is itself eloquence. He lends special emphasis to this statement by positioning it as a heading and introduction to chapter 29. While referring to anyone who cannot express Christian virtues in words, Augustine advises: "Let him so order his life that he not only prepares a reward for himself, but also so that he offers an example to others, and his way of living may be, as it were, an eloquent speech" (4.29). The utility of teaching and learning through examples offered for imitation appears clearly in the foreground of Christian education. At the close of *De doctrina christiana*, Augustine comments on teachers of good character who have rhetorical ability, yet require instructional material. He advises them to memorize the wise and eloquently written words of others; for by putting such words into practice: "They make their own those things which they themselves could not compose when they live in accordance with them" (4.29.62).

As mentioned in the seven-step ascent to wisdom, *timor Dei* acts as a cathartic agent to move the learner toward *aedificatio*—the building of charity. Another tool in this process of Christian education is *labor*. The toil of the exegete in discovering the figurative meaning of Scripture—though the immediate focus is directed toward charity—has a purifying effect by fostering humility and combatting pride. The discrepancy between the literal and figurative levels of the text which the learner seeks to resolve elicits a narrative and pedagogical tension. And while the eventual resolution of a difficult figurative passage may yield delight, it can also bring an awareness of the possible limits of human language and understanding.[68] The "gap" between what is revealed and what is hidden evokes in the learner a sense of terror for the *mysterium tremendum*.[69] Even after resolution, a degree of tension must remain as the exegete cannot know with complete certainty whether he has discovered the divine intention or merely substituted his own for a particular passage.[70] Yet the terror and delight that the learner experiences can move him to transcend his own limits and ascend toward the knowledge of the sublime.[71]

In deciding whether a passage is to be interpreted literally or figuratively, *caritas* acts as the determining factor. Augustine advises the learner to rely on the following method: "Whatever appears in the divine Word that does not literally pertain to virtuous behavior or to the truth of faith you must take to be figurative. Virtuous behavior pertains to the love of God and of one's neighbor; the truth of faith pertains to a knowledge of God and of one's neighbor" (3.10.14). When a passage cannot be taken literally, the learner must interpret it figuratively so that its secrets may be extracted like kernels from the husk for the nourishment of charity (3.12.18). Augustine informs the exegete that figurative scriptural texts contain the modes of expression designated by the Greek word *tropos*: "And not only examples of all of these tropes are found in reading the sacred books, but also the names of some of them, like *allegoria, aenigma, parabola*" (3.29.40). Yet while a formal knowledge of them is useful, Augustine hastens to add that most tropes "find a place in the speech of those who have never heard the lectures of grammarians and are content with the usage of common speech." Figurative modes of expression offer examples of *caritas* or its opposite, *cupiditas* (3.10.16). And the effects of cupidity as carnal passion, for instance, appear in the Old Testament in the *affectus* and negative example of Solomon (3.21).

Whether viewed figuratively or literally as the passage requires, Scripture presents positive or negative models of conduct for the Christian learner either to imitate or reject according to clear criteria: "Scripture teaches nothing but charity, nor condemns anything except cupidity, and in this way shapes the minds of men" (3.10.15). While the teacher is to forewarn the learner of the forms of error that arise from cupidity, the learner and exegete should follow those scriptural models of behavior that serve charity. The three rhetorical categories of style provide additional means of eliciting the desired pedagogical effect upon the learner: teaching by reasoned argument in the plain style, delighting by praise of God and right conduct in the moderate style, and persuading by affectivity in the grand style. And by combining and varying the categories, the teacher evokes a narrative and pedagogical tension that moves the learner to resolve it by judging wisely and following the judgment with appropriate action.

In this process, the listener's delight does have a role to play in Christian education, delight in hearing eloquent language, in discovering the figurative meaning of a passage, and in recognizing the error in the conduct of a biblical character and the subsequent effects. This process of *aedificatio* envisioned by Augustine aims at implementing the lessons learned. The Christian learner—purified by *timor Dei* and moved by the effects of *caritas* exemplified in Scripture—is to prepare for the Last Judgment while time remains. To this end, *De doctrina christiana* offers more than guidelines for preaching; it goes beyond the *modus proferendi* to encompass an entire educational program of Christian culture.

PASTORAL CARE ACCORDING TO GREGORY THE GREAT

In his treatise *Regula pastoralis,* Gregory presents pedagogical elements articulated in Augustine's program of Christian culture to a clerical audience, particularly to those most responsible for pastoral care within the Church, his fellow bishops. In the wake of the Lombard invasion and the ensuing disorder within the Italian bishoprics, Gregory was struck by the laxity of the clergy, especially of the episcopacy, in providing moral example for those in its spiritual charge, and in administering its ecclesiastical office.[72] His treatise attempted to remedy this dilemma by offering instruction in what Gregory deemed the highest episcopal art—pastoral care.[73] Gregory's pastoral advice for Christian living, instruction, and right judgment in governing one's actions, enjoyed a long-term reception in both the early medieval monastery and episcopate.[74]

The thrust of his advice appears in practical guidelines for Christian education. The reader learns in part one of the four-part treatise the importance of exemplary living as a model for imitation. Gregory urges that the life of a pastor and teacher exemplify what is taught: "et bene vivens, qualiter docens" (*Reg. past.* 1.1). His repeated reference to the catalogue of episcopal virtues from 1 Timothy 3:1 lends precision to the guidelines that the final two chapters then contrastively reinforce.[75] Gregory observes that by living in an exemplary manner (*ad exemplum vivendi*), the bishop is to have the strength to cultivate the spiritual lives of his listeners and move them to spiritual change.[76] The traits that preclude the holding of episcopal office, however, display a negative model of conduct characterized by cupidity and the misuse of knowledge.

The second part, *De vita pastoris,* outlines the pastoral responsibilities of the bishop. Through the duties of teaching and preaching, the bishop assumes the office of herald—awakening those in his care so they may prepare for the coming of Christ as Judge.[77] The source of the herald's message is Scripture. And following Augustine, the teacher must continue to be a learner, whereby learning and teaching comprise reciprocal activities aimed at the study of the Bible and the dissemination of its message. The bishop must not only memorize the Psalter—the minimal requirement for episcopal office established by the second canon of the Council of Nicea (325);[78] he is to study Scripture regularly.[79]

While parts 1 and 2 show how a pastor is to live in accord with his own teaching and actively preach what he learns from the study of Scripture, part 3 shows how he is to preach.[80] Analyzing the prologue of part 3 from the perspective of rhetorical scholarship, James J. Murphy notes that Gregory does not develop a rhetorical theory to explain the practical skill of making "simultaneous appeals to masses of presumably different individuals."[81]

Although convincing a diverse audience of one message is a "truly rhetorical precept,"[82] it does not concern Gregory. Having depicted what qualities the pastor ought to embody, Gregory now advises him how to teach.[83] First, however, a reference to Gregory Nazianzen follows. The fourth-century preacher informs us that one and the same exhortation does not suit all listeners, since an equally strong moral character does not bind everyone.[84] Consequently, the *exhortatio* varies due to the varied *morum qualitas,* the quality of character and conduct of the listeners, who are to be warned and advised, stirred and encouraged to act. The teacher applies the proper exhortation much as a physician the proper medicine in attaining the desired healing effect. Subsequent examples illustrate different effects, and indicate the importance of appropriate means of eliciting the beneficial effects.[85] The teacher must shape his discourse to suit the spiritual and temporal condition of the listeners he is to instruct. Yet in addressing the individual members of separate groups within the community, the teacher is never to abandon the art of common edification: "a communis aedificationis arte nunquam recedat" (*Reg. past.* 3, prologue). When the teacher's discourse moves and instructs a particular group, the entire congregation learns and benefits. This is reinforced by the image of the *cithara.* The teacher appears as *artifex,* an artist playing upon the minds and feelings of his listeners, who are like strings plucked by the same plectrum. And though all are not plucked with the same force, they produce a harmonious melody.[86]

The prologue concludes by restating the theme of *ars communis aedificationis* as the building of charity. The teacher exhorts the hearts and minds of his listeners in a varied manner, yet builds charity according to one doctrine, the Scriptures. Through the common call to charity, the teacher is able to make a "simultaneous appeal" to the entire community and focus his remarks on a specific group within it.

The power of the *affectus* within scriptural teachings for a particular group also serves the *aedificatio communis*. *Regula pastoralis,* in chapter 2 of part 3, develops the theme of diversity in preaching. Analyzing Gregory's purpose from a pedagogical standpoint, we note that he provides the teacher with thirty-six "exemplary arguments" useful in fulfilling a dual pedagogical purpose: *docere et admonere.*[87]

The varied examples depicted by the thirty-six pairs of opposing characteristics all bear the designation *admonitio*. In writing book 3 from the teacher's point of view for the edification of fellow bishops, Gregory offers them examples of effective strategy for instructing and warning their listeners of a particular error or possible danger in a course of action or manner of conduct. Pedagogical concepts from Augustine's *De doctrina christiana* are also present in Gregory's examples. When the first major *admonitio* advises the rich and the poor, the use of the *affectus* initiates a spiritual process of compunction to introduce the theme.[88] The poor (*inopes*) are granted the consolation that their ordeal in the "furnace of poverty" can be an act of purification for their election to the chosen of God.[89] The rich (*divites*) however, are to renounce arrogance, and place their hope in God rather than wealth.[90] The teacher, then, must console the poor by placing their suffering within the positive context of trial and eventual spiritual triumph, and sway the recalcitrant rich through *timor.*[91] The teacher may also seek to move the haughty rich man (*superbus dives*) to contrition by subdued eloquence, much as David's harp could calm Saul's fury.[92] Gregory presents both David and Saul as biblical models of conduct.[93] Saul represents *hujus saeculi potentes,* the arrogance of the ruthless bearing power. David symbolizes the humility required of the good teacher and ruler: a fitting symbol for the bishop as rector and for all who hold power.[94]

The subsequent chapters of book 3 reveal other examples of affect teaching which also employ biblical models of conduct. In the fourth *admonitio,* Gregory depicts the strategy of teaching by *affectus.*[95] The teacher is to instruct those in his charge by showing the consequences of a certain *affectus* upon a biblical character, which in turn may move the learner to imitate or reject the given model. The fifth *admonitio* concerns prelates and those subject to them (*subditi*) whereby the biblical characters of Saul and David again portray opposing manners of conduct and

Concepts of Learning and Teaching 25

their consequences.[96] The second admonition of chapter ten concerns the kindly disposed (*benevoli*), and the envious.[97] Gregory begins by advising when to intervene for the spiritual welfare of the former.[98] The bishop is to offer the *benevoli* a corrective example and make them aware of their error whenever they pervert their acts of charity through the ulterior motive of self-gain, desiring the goods and properties of others. Indeed, the social and political instability of late sixth-century Italy may well have heightened the urgency of this particular *admonitio*.[99] Gregory urges the episcopal teacher further to remind the kindly disposed that the praiseworthy deeds of others are to be loved and imitated.[100]

If necessary, the teacher must employ an appropriate *affectus* and compel the indolent *benevoli* to follow the good deeds of their neighbors.[101] After demonstrating *docere et admonere* for the *benevoli*, Gregory turns to the envious. The importance of this section is conveyed by its length—two-thirds of the entire chapter. The teacher reminds the envious (*invidi*) of their spiritual affliction that they may consider their condition carefully.[102] The *invidi* violate the precept of charity by not loving their neighbor as themselves. The analogy of the Christian community as many members in one body intimates how one neighbor is to perceive the other: just as each member of the body in performing its individual task serves the other members and the entire body, so, too, each Christian serves his or her neighbor and the entire Christian community.[103] In addition, each member has an exemplary role to play that must be worthy of imitation.[104] The teacher strives, then, to lead the envious out of the isolation of self-love (*cupiditas*), toward a community orientation and *caritas*. Even when the work of others cannot be imitated, just as one corporal member cannot imitate the work of others in gathering specific sense knowledge, all members merit love in contributing to the well-being of the whole.[105]

After presenting a positive model of communal conduct based on the imitation of charitable acts, Gregory introduces the biblical model of Cain and Abel. He first, however, cites scriptural authority to confirm the diabolical origin of envy.[106] The admonition that follows alerts the envious *ex negativo* to their perilous condition and the risk of damnation. By relating envy of one's brother to fratricide, Gregory applies the negative model of conduct to full effect.[107]

The *admonitio* of chapter 10 concludes with the use of affect teaching to move the learner toward the correction of error. Gregory reaffirms the plight of the envious by repeating the theme of the *invidi* being consumed by their own affliction.[108] Scriptural authority then intensifies the *affectus* through the image of death and damnation, namely, envy as the rottenness of the bones, destroying even the outwardly strong.[109] This image of envy provides the final sting of remorse, *compunctio*, in compelling the learner—as a witness to the depicted event—to judge his own case correctly and act upon his judgment while time remains. Gregory's approach to teaching remained a standard method well into the twelfth century and beyond to the early thirteenth. The simplification and reduction of rhetorical rules in favor of learning by imitation we find in Augustine's *De doctrina christiana* also appears in *Regula pastoralis*. Gregory teaches his bishops with the same persuasive techniques that they themselves would use to teach their congregations: the presentation of positive and negative biblical models of conduct designed for imitation or rejection; the use of affect teaching to move the learner to act through compunction in implementing the given lesson; and of the *affectus* as a signal to the audience whether or not a manner of conduct merits imitation; also by increasing the effect through the adaptation of biblical texts (*paraphrasis*), and by using contrasting models of conduct together with affect teaching in a complementary manner. Gregory not only answers the question of "what to preach" but also "how to preach."[110]

Part 3, moreover, when we view it within the context of the entire work, offers more than just a "collection of sermonettes"[111] or a "treatise on moral pathology."[112] Together with Augustine, Gregory goes beyond an *ars praedicandi*. While *Regula pastoralis* does not present a complete program of Christian culture as does Augustine's *De doctrina christiana*, Gregory's work continues a tradition of Christian education founded on the Bible as the source for the learning and teaching of charitable conduct. And like Augustine, Gregory advocates concepts of learning and teaching that sharpen the learner's twofold sense of judgment, whereby the learner must judge wisely whether a particular course of action merits imitation or rejection;[113] and by acting accordingly, prepare to account for his or her own actions at the Last Judgment. Thus, the strategy of persuasion aims both at the educational and the salvific orientation of the learner.

TRADITIONS OF LEARNING AND TEACHING ACCORDING TO HRABANUS MAURUS

A vital center for the dissemination of concepts of learning and teaching in the ninth century was the monastery school at Fulda.[114] Its most influential and active figure, Hrabanus Maurus,[115] completed *De clericorum institutione* three years before his election to abbot in 819. It was his major work,[116] written as a manual for priests at the request of his students and Haistulf, archbishop of Mainz. The three-book manual begins by instructing that priests as teachers must be able to discern between the sacred and the profane, teach God's people divine precepts, and judge wisely: "ut judicent inter justum et injustum."[117] Hrabanus wishes his priests to be discerning and exercise right judgment for these are the attributes they must impart to the Christian learner. After dealing with ecclesiastical offices, vestments, and the sacraments in the first book, and the observance of the canonical hours, fasting, and other Church practices in the second, the author concentrates in the third book on the complementary activities of exegesis, teaching, and preaching.[118] The teacher, however, must first be a learner. Following Augustine, Hrabanus, together with his teacher Alcuin,[119] does not exclude the study of pagan literature and the classical liberal arts as long as they are helpful in illuminating the meaning of Scripture.[120]

Augustine's influence is also present in other areas. Hrabanus incorporates numerous sections, at times verbatim, from *De doctrina christiana.*[121] In *De clericorum institutione,* familiar Augustinian themes appear extensively. Chapter 4 (*De gradibus sapientiae et caritatis*) describes the levels that correspond to the seven step process of purification and ascent in book 2 of *De doctrina.* In words borrowed directly from Augustine, Hrabanus highlights the role of the *affectus* in moving the learner by compunction; the choice of verbs (*incutiat, percutiat*) is especially vivid within the imagery of crucifixion.[122] Although the recognition of our own mortality leads to fear, *timor Dei* makes us receptive to Christian arguments and as such is the beginning of the ascent to wisdom.[123] Thus Hrabanus describes the duties of the teacher as one who teaches by way of arguments that appeal to reason.[124] Another duty is moving the learner to apply what is learned. The teacher seeks to accomplish this end through affect teaching that not only makes the learner receptive to Christian reasoning, but motivates the learner to act accordingly.[125]

The reader of Hrabanus's work discovers several other Augustinian themes: the fostering of love of God and neighbor as the goal of scriptural studies and the key to scriptural understanding;[126] the use of labor in uncovering the meaning of obscure scriptural passages as a means of *purificatio,* cleansing the exegete of pride;[127] and the Augustinian approach to the interpretation of signs.[128] Further chapters reflect the Augustinian attitude toward wisdom and eloquence.[129] Hrabanus even adopts the passage quoted in *De doctrina christiana* from Cicero (*De inven.* 1.1.1.), in which eloquence without wisdom is deemed useful to none.[130] This acknowledgment of the need for wisdom by teachers of rhetoric is of even greater import for the Christian speaker who views Scripture as the source of wisdom.[131] Exegesis and understanding, teaching and preaching are again perceived as integral parts of one activity. Scripture not only provides useful testimony and arguments for persuasion, but also a source of wise and eloquent speech.[132] Since wisdom with eloquence is preferable to wisdom alone, the teacher should strive in scriptural studies to acquire both through *imitatio*. When instructing others, moreover, the eloquent speaker may vividly employ affect teaching so that the learner can witness the consequences of a given model of conduct, and judge whether it merits imitation. Hrabanus takes care, however, to instruct the teacher that eloquence is not to be used for gaining praise, but for clarity of expression.[133]

The tradition of legal rhetoric—with its aim of persuading a jury to endorse a particular judgment—exerts a further influence on Hrabanus's work. The author introduces the Ciceronian categories that figure prominently in forensic rhetoric: *docere, delectare, and flectare*.[134] Hrabanus also refers to the three levels of style.[135] Yet the illustrations he provides are scriptural examples from Saint Paul: "Exempla in Apostolo, de praedictis generibus tribus."[136] Hrabanus further demonstrates how to sharpen persuasion by suitably combining the levels of style.[137] But when the teacher lacks rhetorical skill, the author follows Augustine by affirming that even a good life can itself be an eloquent and persuasive example to others.[138]

After adopting strategies of persuasion from *De doctrina christiana*, Hrabanus complements these strategies by an important excerpt from Gregory's *Regula pastoralis*. Hrabanus repeats the prologue (*Reg. past.* 3, prologue) almost in its entirety and supplies the first fifteen admonitions in condensed form. While the reference to Gregory recalls the common need for the edification of the Christian community, the use of admonitions recalls the means, namely, the use of affect teaching together with models of conduct. Hrabanus affirms the value of the remaining admonitions for learning and teaching how to judge wisely by citing the source of patristic authority: "Reliqua vide apud Gregorium loco quo supradictum est."[139]

The strategies from *De doctrina christiana* that appear in the influential works of Gregory the Great and Hrabanus Maurus attest to the vitality of concepts of learning and teaching from Augustine's program of Christian culture, and to their value for the religious instruction of the Christian community and the propagation of its sustaining values. The central tenet held in common by the three authors is the advocacy of

Concepts of Learning and Teaching

scriptural studies for the building of charity and the use of the Bible as the chief literary model and textbook for the *aedificatio communis*. The works of these three authors apply similar pedagogical techniques and strategies of persuasion. Biblical models of behavior promote charity by *imitatio* and forewarn against cupidity *ex negativo*. Affect teaching complements these models to intensify compunction and move the learner to implement the lesson. Hrabanus offers a more balanced transmission of learning and teaching concepts than does Gregory, by including the ascent to wisdom and charity, the study of tropes and the *artes* for the purpose of interpreting biblical signs, and the Ciceronian categories of style. Hrabanus also follows Augustine by underscoring the importance of the complementary activities of learning and teaching, whereby the learner as exegete teaches what has been discovered. In this Augustinian tradition, God remains the ultimate source of instruction as *magister interior*, the teacher within us. Nevertheless, Augustine recognizes in *De doctrina christiana* the common need of the Christian community for pastoral care and Christian education. To meet this need, Augustine offers guidelines so that Christians may instruct themselves through scriptural study. Each learner in turn acts as *magister exterior*, as a guide and facilitator to remind others of scriptural truths and motivate them—using persuasion when necessary—to learn for themselves.

Furthermore, though the works of the authors may differ in emphasis, all reveal the influence of legal rhetoric on early Christian education, a tradition that aims to persuade the Christian learner to judge wisely and choose the course of action that best prepares for the Last Judgment. The purpose of Chapter 2 is to show how strategies of persuasion in Christian education shaped the vernacular literature of the early German Middle Ages.

NOTES

1. Peter Brown, *The Body and Society* (New York: Columbia University Press, 1988), 6.
2. Henri Irénée Marrou, *The Resurrection and Saint Augustine's Theology of Human Values*, trans. Mother Maria Consolata (Villanova: Villanova University Press, 1966). Marrou's observation on Augustine's "theology of human values" is also applicable to the learning of moral tenets and correct conduct. Marrou states: "What are the true human values? From Augustine's viewpoint the answer is easy, but its practical consequences are limitless. As always with the Fathers, and as in all true theology, theory is oriented to praxis, speculation flowers in spirituality" (35). See also Hans Robert Jauss, *Alternität und Modernität der mittelalterlichen Literatur* (Munich: Fink, 1977), 20.
3. Pierre Riché, *Education and Culture in the Barbarian West*, trans. John J. Contreni (Columbia: University of South Carolina Press, 1976), 9.
4. Camille Bennett, "The Conversion of Vergil," *Revue des Études Augustiniennes* 34 (1988): 47–69.
5. Peter Brown, *Augustine of Hippo* (Berkeley and Los Angeles: University of California Press, 1969), 263; George Howie, *Educational Theory and Practice in Saint Augustine* (New York: Teachers College Press, 1969), 236–39; Gerhart B. Ladner, *The Idea of Reform: Its Impact on Christian Thought and Action in the Age of the Fathers* (Cambridge: Harvard University Press, 1959), 373–77.
6. Augustine, *De doctrina christiana*, trans. D. W. Robertson (Indianapolis, Ind.: Liberal Arts Press, 1958), 1.1: "Duae sunt res quibus nititur omnis tractatio Scripturarum modus inveniendi quae intelligenda sunt, et modus proferendi quae intellecta." All translations of *De doctrina christiana*, unless otherwise cited, are from this edition.
7. See Howie, *Educational Theory and Practice in Saint Augustine*, 221; also Cornelius Mayer, "Res per Signa," *Revue des Études Augustiniennes* 20 (1974): 104.
8. See Christoph Schönborn, "Die Autorität des Lehrers nach Thomas Aquin," in *Christian Authority, Essays in Honour of Henry Chadwick*, ed. G. R. Evans (Oxford: Clarendon Press, 1988), 101–26. In Aquinas's commentaries on teaching and learning in *De magistro* (1257–58), and on question 11 of *De veritate*, Schönborn notes that Aquinas reacts against the distortion that "equates Avicenna's intellectus agens separatus with Augustine's magister interior." Moreover, Thomas does not criticize Augustine; Thomas's "light of understanding," with God as its originator, does not differ significantly from Augustine's magister interior. Thomas does, however, view the powers of language positively, whereby the teacher's words are able to communicate intellectual intentions (intentiones intelligibiles) to the learner. Thomas also argues that a learner has the advantage of receiving material in "an ordered form" when instruction is given by a teacher. See Howie, *Educational Theory and Practice in Saint*

Augustine, 206–7. On Thomas Aquinas's resolution of the conflict between the Augustinian and Aristotelian traditions in the thirteenth century, see Wolfgang Fischer and Dieter-Jürgen Löwisch, *Pädagogisches Denken von den Anfängen bis zur Gegenwart* (Darmstadt: Wissenschaftliche Buchgesellschaft, 1989), 49–60.

9. Ladner, *The Idea of Reform*, 376–77.

10. Gerard O'Daly, *Augustine's Philosophy of Mind* (Berkeley and Los Angeles: University of California Press, 1987), 171–78; Howie, *Educational Theory and Practice in Saint Augustine*, 203–5.

11. For Augustine's symbolism of word and light in the learning process and in primordial creation, see David Chidester, "The Symbolism of Learning in St. Augustine," *Harvard Theological Review* 76, no. 1 (January 1983): 84–90.

12. Howie, *Educational Theory and Practice in Saint Augustine*, 125.

13. O'Daly, *Augustine's Philosophy of Mind*, 176.

14. *De magistro* 12.40, trans. George G. Leckie, in *Concerning the Teacher* (New York: Appleton-Century-Crofts, 1938), 50.

15. What at first appears to be a devaluation of words for instructional purposes is merely a description of their function as intermediaries. Augustine notes that "for the present I have warned you not to attribute more to words than is proper." Refering to God as our only master and teacher in heaven, Augustine avers the proper use of words: "But what in heaven means He Himself will advertise to us by means of men, through signs and outwardly, so that we may by turning inwardly toward Him be made wise" (*De mag.* 12.46).

16. See Mayer, "Res per Signa," 102–3, especially in regard *to foris intus* and *utilitas verborum*, whereby signs are "Warner und Mahner"; "Ego uero didici admonitione ueborum tuorum nihil aliud uerbis quam admoneri hominem, ut discat" (*De mag.* 46 [CCSL 29, 203, 34–35ff.]).

17. Chapter 11, *De magistro liber unus*.

18. In regard to the prologue of De doctrina christiana, Ulrich Duchrow deduces ex negativo: Augustine "[habe] seine metaphysisch verfestigte Sprachtheorie vergessen." See *his Sprachverständnis und biblisches Hören bei Augustin* (Tübingen: J. C. B. Mohr, 1965), 210. C. Mayer refutes this assertion by showing the admonishing use of signs *in De doctrina* in perceiving praecepta; See his "Res per Signa," 109–10.

19. Although I follow Augustine's historical usage of the pronoun "he" in referring to the "learner" or "exegete," the reader should note that it encompasses persons of either gender except when "she" is explicitly applicable. The ranks of highly educated women in Late Antiquity cannot be excluded from participation in the educational process of the Church.

20. Hennig Brinkmann, *Mittelalterliche Hermeneutik* (Darmstadt: Wissenschaftliche Buchgesellschaft, 1980), 24–25.

21. In this observation I refer to the article of Hermann-Josef Sieben, "Die Res der Bibel in Doctrina Christiana," *Revue des Études Augustiniennes* 21, nos. 1–2 (1975): 74–75.

22. See Sieben for an argument against neoplatonistic transcendence as the

basis for understanding *Res* in the above passages in favor of salvation history (75).

23. *De doct. chr.* 1.22.20: "Magna enim quaedam res est homo, factus ad imaginem et similitudinem Dei."

24. Regarding "the process of reform of the image of God in man," see Ladner, *The Idea of Reform*, 185-203.

25. *De doct. chr.* 1.26.27: "Diliges, 'inquit,' Dominum Deum tuum ex toto corde tuo, et ex tota mente tua, et diliges proximum tuum tanquam teipsum. In his duobus praecepta tota Lex pendet et Prophetae [Matt. 22:37-40]. Finis itaque praecepti est dilectio [I Tim. 1:5], et ea gemina, id est Dei et proximi [1.26.27]." For all citations from the Latin text I use the edition from Joseph Martin, ed., *CCSL* 32.(Turnhout: Brepols, 1962), 1-167.

26. Christian self-love with its source in the love of God contrasts vividly with prideful self-love as the cause of man's fall. For a consideration of this negative self-love in view of Augustine and Gregory the Great see the valuable study of Carole Straw, *Gregory the Great, Perfection in Imperfection* (Berkeley and Los Angeles: University of California Press, 1988), 112-23.

27. The *Conditio* states: "De ipsa etiam severitate Dei, qua corda mortalium saluberrimo terrore quatiuntur, charitas aedificanda est; ut ab eo quem timet, amari se gaudens, eum redamare audeat, ejusque in se dilectioni, etiamsi impune posset, tamen displicere vereatur" (*De cat. rud.* 5.9). The text I cite is provided by I. B. Bauer, ed., *CCSL* 46 (Turnhout: Brepols, 1969), 115-78.

28. Gerald O'Daly notes that "Augustine distinguishes *(De civitate Dei* 14.9) between two senses of 'fear': (a) the ordinary language usage, meaning being frightened by an evil that can happen'; (b) is the fear 'holding fast in the good that cannot be lost.' It is an aspect of love (caritas), and, as the Psalmist indicates (Augustine inevitably interprets the verse eschatologically), it lasts eternally" (52). See also Augustine on "holy fear" in *De civitate Dei* 14.9.

29. Augustine uses a seven-step ascent pattern with varying categories in various works to describe "spiritual progress." See O'Daly for the seven gradus as comparable with "the seven stages of moral and intellectual ascent of *vera rel.* 49 and *doctr. chr.* 2.9-11" (13-15). For another perspective of ascent, in this case in regard to "the return to origins" in the *Confessions,* see Robert McMahon, *Augustine's Prayerful Ascent* (Athens: University of Georgia Press, 1989), 1-155.

30. O'Daly notes that "Augustine can distinguish two kinds (*genera*) of mutability of the soul. . . . In the former group the examples given are: aging, sickness, pain, fatigue, distress and pleasure. In the latter group are included: the affections such as desire, joy, fear, anger—but also diligence and learning" (Augustine's *Philosophy of Mind,* 34). Also see O'Daly for an analysis of the body-soul relationship in Augustine's view of the affections (46-54).

31. *De doct. chr.* 2.7.11: "in aenigmate adhuc tamen et per speculum videri dicitur [I Cor. 13:12], quia magis per fidem quam per speciem ambulatur, cum in hac vita peregrinam [II Cor. 5:6-7]." For a discussion of Augustine's view of life as peregrinatio, see Robert J. O'Connell, S.J., *Soundings in St. Augustine's*

Imagination (New York: Fordham University Press, 1994), 69–94.

32. *De doct. chr.* 2.7.11: "Talis filius ascendit ad sapientiam, quae ultima et septima est, qua pacatus tranquillusque perfruitur. Initium enim sapientiae timor Domini (Ps. 110:10, et Eccli. 1:16). Ab illo enim usgue ad ipsam per hos gradus tenditur, et venitur."

33. Reinhart Herzog, "Exegesse—Erbauung—Delectatio," in *Formen und Funktionen der Allegorie,* ed. W. Haug (Stuttgart 1979), 62.

34. See also the important study by Kathy Eden, *Poetic and Legal Fiction in the Aristotelian Tradition* (Princeton: Princeton University Press, 1986), 7–175.

35. Reinhart Herzog, *Die Bibelepik der lateinischen Spätantike* (Munich: Fink, 1975), 3–154. In regard to paraphrasis, the poetic adaptation and amplification of biblical texts, see Michael J. Roberts, "The Hexameter Phraphrase in Late Antiquity: Origins and Application to Biblical Texts" (Ph.D. diss., University of Illinois at Urbana-Champaign, 1978). See also Carl P. E. Springer, "Sedulius' Paschale Carmen: A Literary Reexamination" (Ph.D. diss., University of Wisconsin-Madison, 1984), 12–51.

36. Eden notes: "The transmission of fear and pity into Christian poetic theory and practice indirectly through Christian ethics, rather than directly through the domination of Aristotle's authority on literary matters, points to an even more profound continuity in the Aristotelian tradition" (*Poetic and Legal Fiction,* 156).

37. On "imitation and image," see ibid., 132–41.

38. *De doct. chr.* 1.15.

39. For a discussion of the role of the Pauline thought in Augustinian aesthetics, see Reinhart Herzog, "Augustins Gespräch mit Gott," in *Das Gespräch, Poetik und Hermeneutik XI* (Munich: Wilhelm Fink Verlag, 1984): "Die paulinische Sytèmatik der augustinischen Ästhetik [caritas, fides, spes] wird in De doctrina christiana wesentlich verfeinert und um einen Inhaltsbegriff, die aedificatio, erweitert" (241).

40. See James J. Murphy, *Rhetoric in the Middle Ages* (Berkeley and Los Angeles: University of California Press, 1974): "But striking fact is that in the next twelve hundred years after Christ and Paul there is only one major perceptive treatise on preaching Saint Augustine's *De doctrina christiana,*" (284–85); also George A. Kennedy, *Classical Rhetoric and its Christian and Secular Tradition* (Chapel Hill: University of North Carolina Press, 1980): "De Doctrina Christiana is Augustine's major contribution to the history and theory of rhetoric" (153).

41. Marrou observes that *De doctrina christiana* is not a simple clerical manual, moreover, that there is nothing specifically ecclesiastical about Augustine's program of Christian culture: "Le de Doctrina christiana n'est donc pas un simple manuel de institutione clericorum; il n'y a rien de spécifiquement ecclésiastique dans ce programme de culture" (381).

42. Marrou further notes that Christian eloquence encompassed more than the art of preaching; it is incorrect to view the fourth book of *De doctrina christiana* as a simple homiletic treatise. Yet, even though the sermon does not

constitute all of Christian eloquence, one should recognize that it holds a place of honor. He recalls that in antiquity the modern distinction between written literature and spoken eloquence was also not as clear as it is today: "J'ai rappele d'autre part que dans l'antiquité la distinction moderne entre litterature écrite et éloquence parlée n'était pas aussi nette qu'aujourd hui" (*Saint Augustin*, 506).

43. George A. Kennedy, *Greek Rhetoric under Christian Emperors* (Princeton: Princeton University Press, 1983): "The orations of Isocrates, actually elaborate literary pamphlets, are the classical models for literary rhetoric" (18). For Werner Jaeger's discussion of the role of example in education, see his *Paideia: The Education of the Greek*, vol. 1 (Oxford: Basil Blackwell, 1954), 24–32, and "Homer as Educator," 35–56. Also Jaeger, *Paideia: The Ideals of Greek Culture*, vol. 3, trans. by Gilbert Highet (New York: Oxford University Press). Here Jaeger notes how Isocrates in *To Nicoles* acknowledges the effectiveness of poetic form as an educational tool: "Books are like food; most of us enjoy what tastes sweet more than what does us good. It is best to imitate Homer and the early tragedians—for they saw through human nature, and made their wise words palatable by mixing them with myths and legends" (103–4); and Jaeger, *Early Christianity and Greek Paideia* (Cambridge: Harvard University Press, 1965): "The formative mold of early Greek paideia was Homer, and as time went on that role was extended to Greek poetry at large. In the end, the word meant Greek literature as a whole" (91).

44. Stanley F. Bonner, *Education in Ancient Rome* (Berkeley and Los Angeles: University of California Press, 1977): Discussing the rhetoric of Quintilian, Bonner recalls the Isocratean preference for a minimum of rules in imitating good rhetorical practice: "Traditional doctrine, much influenced by the Isocratean school, required that the statement of facts should have three qualities—it should be lucid, brief and plausible" (292).

45. "The book of mysteries was also an encyclopedia which contained all knowledge useful to man, sacred and profane. Saint Augustine accepted this Alexandrian concept and worked out its consequences for Christian education. Bible study is the highest kind of Christian learning. Since the content of Scripture is encyclopaedic, it calls for encyclopaedic knowledge in the student; hence all the resources of late-antique culture are brought to bear upon Bible reading . . . he [Augustine] could only insist on the best training that schools of rhetoric could supply: Scripture requires the same erudite treatment as the pagans give to Virgil. . . . The sciences and liberal arts are necessary in so far as they contribute to an understanding of Scripture." Beryl Smalley, *The Study of the Bible in the Middle Ages* (Notre Dame, Ind.: University of Notre Dame Press, 1964), 26.

46. For probability, see Eden, *Poetic and Legal Fiction*, 36–37; regarding Cicero, see ibid., 115–17; judgment in legal rhetoric can also exert a "religious sanction," Cicero, *De inventione*, 30.48.

47. Geoffrey Galt Harpham, *The Ascetic Imperative in Culture and Criticism*, 91–106. Thomas Merton describes the distinction between conversatio morus and and conversio morum and the former's relation to imitatio and praecepta in *The*

Monastic Journey, ed. Brother Patrick Hart (Garden City, N.Y.: Doubleday, 1978).

48. George A. Kennedy, *New Testament Interpretation through Rhetorical Criticism* (Chapel Hill: University of North Carolina Press, 1984), 12.

49. Regarding the correspondence of legal and poetic procedures in the Aristotelan tradition, see the important work of Kathy Eden, *Poetic and Legal Fiction*, 9–10. See also Kennedy, *New Testament Interpretation*, 19.

50. See *Rhetoric* 3.10.4 and 3.11.1, in *The Rhetoric and Poetics of Aristotle*, trans. W. Rhys Roberts and Ingram Bywater, ed. Friedrich Solmsen (New York: Modern Library, 1984). See also Eden, *Poetic and Legal Fiction*, 71.

51. Eden, *Poetic and Legal Fiction*, 71–75. See also O'Daly, *Augustine's Philosophy of Mind*, 95. O'Daly notes evidentia as the translation of the Stoic *erargeia* in Cicero's *Academica Priora* 17.

52. For a discussion of ideas as standards (regulae) in distinguishing true from false images, see O'Daly, *Augustine's Philosophy of Mind*, 97. Clearly, one can also distinguish between the "pure image" of God in Christ and the "imperfect image" in humankind. See Johann Mader, *Aurelius Augustinus* (St. Pölten-Vienna: Niederösterreichisches Presshaus, 1991), 370.

53. After discussing Augustine's debt to Aristotelian and Stoic psychology, Eden notes: "Not only, then, is the psychological image a necessary instrument of cognition, judgment, and action, but man in his status as image—the image of God—is in turn judged by his own intentions. And it is precisely through his good intentions, accordingly to Augustine, that man reforms the divine image within himself" (*Poetic and Legal Fiction*, 130–31).

54. I owe this observation to Evans, 129.

55. Augustine, *The Trinity*, trans. Stephen McKenna, C.S.S.R., in *The Fathers of the Church*, ed. Roy Joseph Deferrari (Washington, D.C.: Catholic University of America Press, 1963), 447. Augustine refers to I Corinthians 13:12.

56. O'Daly, speaking of sense perceptions of images and regulae, refers to *Trin.* 12.16f.

57. See Eden, *Poetic and Legal Fiction*, 113, 135–36.

58. On the duties of the orator in Cicero's *The Orator* and Augustine's fourth book of *On Christian Doctrine*, see Kennedy, *New Testament Interpretation*, 25.

59. O'Daly cites *De civitate Dei* (9.4) in referring to the affectus: "These motions of the soul, which the Greeks call pathe, while some of our own writers, such as Cicero, call them perturbations, some affections [affectiones vel affectus], and some, like him [sc. Apuleius], translating more accurately from the Greek, call passions" (*Augustine's Philosophy of Mind*, 46–47).

60. Kennedy, *New Interpretation through Rhetorical Criticism*, esp. 86–96.

61. O'Daly: "Christians may fear eternal punishment, desire eternal life, fear to commit sin, feel pain over sins committed, feel gladness at good works, and they may also feel all these emotions on account of others. The emotions felt by Paul and Christ are scrupulously documented. Augustine asks: But since these affections, when they are exhibited in an appropriate way, follow right reason, who would dare to assert they they are diseases or evil passions (*De civ.* 14.9)?"

(*Augustine's Philosophy of Mind*, 50). On the Augustinian distinction between argument and pathos—reason and volition, see Debora K. Shuger, *Sacred Rhetoric* (Princeton, New Jersey: Princeton University Press, 1988), 46.

62. On the relation of emotions to reason see O'Daly, *Augustine's Philosophy of Mind*, 49. Also referring outside the rhetorical context to the role of the emotions in *De civitate Dei*, Shuger observes: "Affectivity, instead of being an irrational perturbation, thus moves into the center of spiritual experience. The emotions springing from a rightly directed will—love of God and neighbor, the desire for eternal life, penitential sorrow—are inseparable from holiness [*De civ.* 9.5, 14.9]. The angels and the blessed, even Christ himself, feel joy, sorrow, love, and compassion. Affectivity thus suffuses Christian existence" (*Sacred Rhetoric* [Princeton, N.J.: Princeton University Press, 1988], 46–47); further on the inseparability of volition and affectivity, see 48-49. On charity and cupidity as motions of the soul and volition, see *De doct. chr.* 3.10.16.

63. For an introduction to the pedagogical, literary tradition of "affect teaching," see Erwin Rotermund, "Der Affekt als Literarischer Gegenstand: Zur Theorie und Darstellung der Passiones im 17. Jahrhundert," in *Die Nicht Mehr Schönen Künste, Poetik und Hermeneutik III*, ed. H. R. Jauss (Munich: Wilhelm Fink Verlag, 1968), 239–69.

64. See Shuger, *Sacred Rhetoric*, 44. See also Peter Prestel, *Die Rezeption der ciceronischen Rhetorik durch Augustinus in >>de doctrina Christiana<<* (Frankfurt am Main: Peter Lang, 1992), 252–74. Prestel highlights Augustine's pragmatic integration of the genera (258).

65. Eberhard Lämmert, *Reimsprecherkunst im Spätmittelalter* (Stuttgart: Metzler, 1970): "Da die Predigt keine Differenzierung in der Würde ihrer Themen kennt, tritt an die Stelle dieser Scheidung die Differenzierung der Stilarten nach der erstrebten Wirkung auf die Zuhörer: Wissensvermittlung—Anspornung durch Lob und Tadel—Erschütterung" (252). See also Erich Auerbach, *Literatursprache und Publikum in der lateinischen Spätantike und im Mittelalter* (Bern: Francke, 1958), 5–33. Augustine's combination of the plain and grand styles in the sermo humilis and its influence on medieval thought are analyzed in this important study.

66. Shuger, *Sacred Rhetoric*, 47. On the tension in the grand style that arises between the use of passion in the forensic mode of invective and reproof and its role in Christian spirituality, ibid., 49.

67. Shuger notes: "The middle style loses the aura of sophistic aestheticism; instead, it delights the hearer and by praising God and the saints draws its audience to love what is truly good" (ibid., 43).

68. Lynn Poland, "The Bible and the Rhetorical Sublime," *in The Bible as Rhetoric, Studies in Biblical Persuasion and Credibility*, ed. Martin Warner (New York: Routledge, 1990), 29–47, esp. 39–41. Poland speaks of Augustine's view of allegory, but her comments are applicable to figurative language in general.

69. Poland notes: "What we learn from Augustine, I suggest, is that the 'mysterium tremendum' of scripture is located in the labour of interpretation to

reconcile the two poles of our tension, to match fulfilment with 'gap.' But we also learn that the specifically religious power, the terror of interpretation, lies in experiencing the possibility that these tensions are not reconcilable. Augustine's belief that God's intention is inscribed in the grammar of creation is an article of faith. Textual obscurity creates a crisis of faith; confronted with the failures of human rhetoric, Augustine experiences affectively the question of what, if anything, lies behind the letter. The pleasures of discovery depend upon this prior negative moment of interpretation. The veil, or the gap, in the text functions to introduce doubt. I speak of this process as 'rhetorical,' because there is something gratuitous about the hide and seek of allegory. It is a crisis in 'stages' to give the truth Augustine already believes affective power" (*The Bible as Rhetoric*, 38–39.

70. On the derivation of the Latin term intentio from the Greek tonos in Aristotelian and Stoic psychology, see Eden, *Poetic and Legal Fiction*. In order to judge properly the phantasiai it encounters, the soul in its capacity as will must possess the proper tension: tonos or intentio (99–100, 121, 130).

71. Poland, in *The Bible as Rhetoric*, relates the rhetoric of sublimity to the grand style: "Throughout the medieval period and the Renaissance, we find Augustine's understanding of allegory linked to rhetoric by the notion of the grand, or sublime, style, the oratio gravis. Medieval theorists tended to translate gravitas as difficultas, however: the grand style is therefore characterized by difficulta ornata, difficult ornament" (39).

72. Riché, *Education and Culture in the Barbarian West*, 172–73.

73. *Reg. past.* 1.1 (PL 77.3).

74. Leclercq, O.S.B., *The Love of Learning and the Desire for God* (New York: Fordham University Press, 1961), 177: "In monasticism, they were content to imitate the models of genius that the Fathers of the Church had been, particularly Saint Augustine, and to follow their suggestions, especially those Saint Gregory had made in his Pastoral Rule, and, to an even greater degree, those of Saint Augustine in Book IV of his great work on Christian education, the De doctrina christiana." Further, Murphy observes: "It became enormously popular almost at once, receiving a wide circulation in his lifetime; the Church officials of 813 and 836 ordered bishops to study it. King Alfred translated it into English in the early tenth century. Rabanus Maurus and other writers as late as the fourteenth century cited it" (292). On the Carolingian reception of Gregory the Great in the monastery at Reichenau, see Rosamond Mckitterick, *The Carolingians and the Written Word* (Cambridge: Cambridge University Press, 1989), 180. See also the Praefatio to the Migne edition *of Regula Pastoralis*, where according to Archbishop Hincmar of Rheims, a candidate to be installed and consecrated as bishop in the middle of the ninth century stood before the altar: "una cum libro sacrorum Canonum Regulam Pastoralem beati Gregorii in manu acciperet, cum hac obtestatione: ut ita servaret in vivendo, docendo et judicando, sicut ibidem descriptum est," Hincmar of Reims, *Praef. Opuscula et Epistolae* (PL 126, 292).

75. Gregory frequently uses contrasting models of conduct. Chapters 10

and 11, the final two chapters of part 1, for instance, are titled, respectively, *Qualis quisque ad regimen venire debeat,* and *Qualis quisque ad regimen venire non debeat.*

76. Gregory uses water and drought imagery to depict the instructor's task of reviving man's spirit (*Reg. past.* 1.10.10): "Qui sic studet vivere, ut proximorum quoque corda arentia doctrinae valeat fluentis irrigare."

77. The role as a precursor to the Last Judgment figures prominently in the herald theme (*Reg. past.* 2.4.17): "Praeconis quippe officium suscipit, quisquis ad sacerdotium accedit, ut ante judicis qui terribiliter sequitur, ipse scilicet clamando gradiatur."

78. Riché, *Education and Culture in the Barbarian West,* 173.

79. *Reg. past.* 1.11 (PL 77.34).

80. Gregory combines three activities in the title of part 3 of his treatise, namely, leading an exemplary life, teaching, and admonishing those in one's care (*Reg. past.* 3): "Qualiter rector bene vivens debeat docere et admonere subditos."

81. Murphy, *Rhetoric in the Middle Ages*: "Gregory's appreciation of internal diversity within an audience is at first glance a hopeful sign.... But he very quickly demonstrates that he has no intention of providing a new rhetorical theory for preachers. Part three, it develops, deals with subject matter, not rhetorical form" (294).

82. Murphy, *Rhetoric in the Middle Ages,* 293.

83. Gregory states the purpose of part 3—to show how to teach—in the introductory sentence (*Reg. past.* 3, prologue): "Quia igitur qualis esse debeat pastor ostendimus, nunc qualiter doceat demonstremus."

84. *Reg. past.* 3, prologue: "Ut enim longe ante nos reverendae memoriae Gregorius Nazianzenus edocuit, non una eademque cunctis exhortatio congruit, quia nec cunctos par morum qualitas astringit."

85. Ibid.

86. Ibid.

87. Murphy maintains that the thirty-six pairs form a random and unsystematic list only meant to be a "sample" of possible character types. He observes further that the list is "a guide for detecting types of sins, based on the character of the potential Sinner, rather than audience analysis for the sake of public exhortation" (295–96). Murphy's disappointment stems from Gregory's method, which neglects rhetorical form and rules for the presentation of a discourse.

88. On the double aspect of compunction of fears and compunction of desire, see Leclercq, *The Love of Learning*: "Compunction becomes pain of the spirit, a suffering resulting simultaneously from two causes: the existence of sin and our own tendency toward sin—compunctio paenitentiae, timoris, formidinis—and the existence of our desire for God and even our very possession of God. Saint Gregory, more than others, accentuated this last aspect: an obscure possession, awareness of which does not last and consequently gives rise to regret at seeing it disappear and to a desire to find it again. The 'com-

punction of the heart,' 'of the soul'—compunctio cordis, animi—always tends to become a 'compunction of love,' 'of delectation' and 'of contemplation'—compunctio amoris, dilectionis, contemplationis." (38–39).

89. The scriptural teaching is: "Eligi te in camino paupertatis" (Isaiah 48:10).

90. Gregory highlights his message to the rich through the Pauline command (I Tim. 6:17): "Divitibus hujus saeculi praecipe non superbe sapere, neque sperare in incerto divitiarum suarum."

91. *Reg. past.* 3.2 (PL 77, 36).

92. I Samuel 16:23.

93. *Reg. past.* 3.2 (PL 77, 36).

94. Straw observes: "Gregory appears as the consummate professional in his terse, formulaic manual for the clergy, Pastoral Rule, an astute handbook useful not only to ecclesiastical rectors but to anyone bearing power" (6, 88–89).

95. *Reg. past.* 3.3 (PL 77, 37).

96. Intimating bad rulers and good subjects respectively (*Reg. past.* 3.4, 39): "Quid enim per Saul, nisi mali rectores; quid per David innuitur, nisi boni sublati designatur."

97. In describing Chapter 10, admonitio II: Quomodo admonendi benevoli et invidi as an "exemplary argument," Murphy presents only the final admonitio addressed to the envious. However, an examination of the chapter as a whole reveals a wider range of teaching and learning concepts.

98. *Reg.past.* 3.10.45: "Admonendi namque sunt benevoli, ut sic alienis bonis congaudeant, quatenus habere propria concupiscant."

99. Riché, 172–73. In regard to the Frankish kingdom, see Albert Hauck, *Kirchengeschichte Deutschlands*, 5 vols. (Berlin: Academie, 1958), 1: 200–202. Hauck examines the disorder in the Frankish Church of the sixth century and the abuse of episcopal power. On the often disruptive theological climate of late antiquity, see Straw: "The theological disputes of late antiquity had a sharp and bitter edge. Partisan camps marred the Church's tranquillity with their contentious zeal and unsavory tactics" (147).

100. By means of a litotes construction, the word *merces* is used in a positive sense to emphasize the spiritual profit derived from imitatio. Merely praising the good deeds of others is not enough (*Reg. past.* 3.10.45): "Valde quippe peccamus, si aliena bene gesta non diligimus. Sed nil mercedis agimus, si ea quae diligimus, in quantum possumus non imitamur. Dicendum itaque est benevolis, quia si imitari bona minime festinant quae laudantes approbant, sic eis virtutum sanctitas sicut stultis spectatoribus ludicrarum artium vanitas placet."

101. *Reg. past.* 3.10 (PL 77, 45).

102. Ibid., 46.

103. Ibid.

104. Ibid.: "In ipsa igitur corporis positione accipimus, quod in actione servemus. Nimis itaque turpe est non imitari quod sumus."

105. Ibid., 46.

106. Gregory refers to Wisdom 2:24: "Invidia autem diaboli mors intravit in

orbem terrarum."

107. *Reg. past.* 3.10.46: "Admonendi sunt invidi ut cognoscant quantis lapsibus succrescentis ruinae subjaceant, quia dum livorem a corde non projiciunt, ad apertas operum nequitias devoluntur. Nisi enim Cain invidisset acceptam fratris hostiam, minime pervenisset ad exstinguendam vitam." In order to strengthen the appeal of the admonitio, Gregory again appeals to scriptural authority: "Iratusque est Cain vehementer, et concidit vultus ejus" (Gen. 4:4). He reinforces the lesson with the commentary, in *Reg. past.* 3.10.46: "Livor itaque sacrificii, fratricidii seminarum fuit."

108. *Reg. past.* 3.10 (PL 77, 46).

109. Gregory refers to (Prov. 14:30): "Vita carnium sanitas cordis, putredo ossium invidia."

110. Murphy, *Rhetoric in the Middle Ages*, 296–97.

111. Ibid., 296.

112. Ibid., 297.

113. Learning to discern wisely the spiritual implications of an action aims at self-evaluation and individual reform, without advocating that the Christian learner pronounce judgment on others. See John 8:1–15.

114. Hauck: "In Deutschland erstreckte sich der Einfluss der Fuldischen Schule weithin: in Weissenburg und Reichenau, in St. Gallen and Ellwangen, auf den bischöflichen Stühlen von Halberstadt und Regensburg begegnet man spater Männern, die ihre Bildung in Fulda erhalten hatten" (2:631).

115. Hauck: "Hraban ist der fruchtbarste und tätigste unter den theologischen Schriftstellern der deutschen Kirche nach Karl d. Gr. Alle anderen sind mehr oder weniger unvollkommene Parallelen zu ihm. Sie haben die gleichen Interessen, befolgen die gleiche Methode, vertreten dieselben Anschauungen: es hätte jeder von ihnen jedes beliebige Werk des andern ebenfalls schreiben können" (2:659).

116. Hrabanus refers to judging as distinguishing between (inter) just and unjust actions, not to passing judgment on others. *De cler. inst.* 1 (PL 107, 297). Also see *De cler. inst.* 3 (PL 107, 377–78).

117. *De cler. inst. Praefatio* (PL 107, 296): "Tertius vero liber edocet quomodo omnia quae in divinis libris scripta sunt, investiganda sunt atque discenda, nec non et ea quae in gentilium studiis et artibus ecclesiastico viro scrutari utilia sunt."

118. Hauck: "Aber Hraban zeigt sich darin als der echte Schüler Alkuins, dass er einen Zwiespalt zwischen der theologischen Bildung und der auf dem Studium der antiken Literatur ruhenden allgemeinen Bildung nicht zugibt; ähnlich wie sein Lehrer zieht er aus der Verwerfung des Heidnischen nicht die Folgerung, dass die heidnische Literatur verwerflich sei; auch sie enthält Wahrheiten, welche wie die geoffenbarten von Gott stammen" (2:653). Arguably, Hrabanus as a "genuine" student of Alcuin would perhaps have referred to Virgiliis mendacia as does his mentor in Epistle 69 (PL 100, 440–41). Yet the issue is not the mendacious nature of pagan literature per se, but rather the usefulness of such

literature in contributing to an understanding of Scripture. See also Max Manitius, *Geschichte der Lateinischen Literatur des Mittelalters* (Munich: C. H. Beck, 1911), 296–97. In regard to Alcuin, see Manitius, 276.

119. *De cler. inst.* 3.18-25 (PL 107, 395–404); and the adaptation of Egyptian wisdom by Moses, *De cler. inst.* 3.26 (PL 107, 404–5).

120. Murphy, *Rhetoric in the Middle Ages*, 85.

121. *De cler. inst.* 3.4 (PL 107, 380): "Timor autem iste cogitationem de nostra mortalitate et de futura morte necesse est incutiat, et quasi clavatis carnibus, omnes superbiae motus ligno crucis affigat."

122. On the role of timor Dei as stated at the beginning and conclusion of Chapter 4, see *De cler. inst.* 3.4 (PL 107, 380–82).

123. *De cler. inst.* 3.28 (PL 107, 406): "documentis adhibitis ratiocinandum est."

124. *De cler. inst.* 3.18 (PL 107, 406): "Qui vero audiunt *movendi sunt potius quam docendi*, ut in eo quod jam sciunt, agendo non torpeant, et rebus quas veras esse fatentur, assensum accommodent, majoribus dicendi viribus opus est; ubi *obsecrationes* et *increpationes, concitationes* et *exercitationes*, et quaecunque alia valent *ad commovendos animos*, sunt necessaria" (emphasis mine). Also compare *De doct. chr.* 4.4.6.

125. Hrabanus also adopts the theme of gemina caritas Dei et proximi from Augustine's description of the seven step ascent to wisdom: *De doct. chr.* 2.7.10, as well as from 1.22.21. The scriptural references are Lev. 19:17, 18; Deut. 6:5; and Matt. 22:37-39. See *De cler. inst.* 3.4 (PL 107, 381); compare *De doct. chr.* 1.36.40.

126. *De cler. inst.* 3.3 (PL 107, 380). This corresponds to *De doct. chr.* 2.4.6, 7, and comprises more than half of Hrabanus's third chapter.

127. Augustine's interpretation of signa from *De doct. chr.* 2.3 appears in *De cler. inst.* 3.9, 10 with the image of the hyssop and in chapters 11–15. Hrabanus recommends that the learner consult Augustine for more information on signs: *De cler. inst.* 3.15 (PL 107, 392).

128. Compare *De cler. inst.* 28, 29, and 30 with *De doct. chr.* 4.5.8, 4.6.9, 4.8.22, 4.9.23, and 4.10.24.

129. *De cler. inst.* 3.28 (PL 107, 407): "(Fassi sunt enim) sapientiam sine eloquentia parum prodesse civitatibus; eloquentiam vero sine sapientia nimium obesse plerumque, prodesse nunquam." Also see Augustine, *De doct. chr.* 4.5.7.

130. Hrabanus reaffirms this with Augustine's own words (De cler. inst. 3.28 (PL 107, 407): "Sapienter autem dicit homo tanto magis vel minus, quanto in Scripturis sanctis majus minusve proficit. Non dico [Hrabanus and Augustine!] in eis multum legendis memoriaeque mandandis, sed bene intelligendis, et diligenter earum sensibus indagandis.

131. *De cler. inst.* 3.28 (PL 107, 407).

132. See *De cler. inst.* 3.29 and 3.30 together with *De doct. chr.* 4.2.22, 9.23, and 10.24. On clarity of expression, see *De cler. inst.* 3.31 and *De doct. chr.*

4.8.22.
133. *De cler. inst.* 3.31 (PL 107, 408). Also see *De doct. chr.* 4.12.27.
134. Chapter 32 bears the title: De triplici genere locutionis, quod Romani doctor ita distinxit; and chapter 33: Quando submisso genere, et quando temperato, quandoque grandi utendum sit. Compare *De doct. chr.* 4.18.35.
135. *De cler. inst.* 3.34 (PL 107, 410).
136. See *De cler. inst.* 35 and 36 (PL 107, 412–43).
137. *De cler. inst.* 3.36 (PL 107, 412). Also compare *De doct. chr.* 4.27, 28, and 29.
138. *De cler. inst.* 3.37 (PL 107, 413): De discretione dogmatum juxta qualitatem auditorum.
139. *De cler. inst.* 3.37 (PL 107, 415).

2

THE LESSON OF THE *MUSPILLI*

De doctrina christiana is not an *ars poetica*, nor did early medieval authors of poetry write according to "Augustinian poetics."[1] The transmission of major tenets of Augustine's program of Christian culture served a different purpose.[2] Augustine's program centered on the study of the Bible; it was a programmatic compendium of older, acknowledged exegetical and pedagogical techniques designed to serve as a guide for learning about the Bible and teaching its message to others. These exegetical and instructional methods clearly predate *De doctrina christiana:* for example, the codified use of Christian allegory emanated from the Alexandrian school;[3] the Aristotelian use of catharsis to affect the reader and learner was practiced by John Chrysostom; and the pedagogical use of *imitatio* was already advocated by Isocrates. Likewise the Aristotelian tradition of legal rhetoric—discerning the false image from the true—as a prelude to ethical imitation, guided Cicero in shaping the opinion of Roman judges before it aided Augustine in persuading Christians to prepare for the Divine Judge. The programmatic compilation and explanation of these traditional concepts in Augustine's *De doctrina christiana* facilitated their transmission and dissemination into the medieval period.

At the beginning of this period, Gregory the Great's *Regula pastoralis* highlighted a salient part of Augustine's program—the tradition of Christian learning based on the Scriptures as a repository for models of charitable and uncharitable conduct; Gregory's work also emphasized the task of Christian education in preparing the learner for Last Judgment.[4] In German-speaking lands, Hrabanus Maurus's *De clericorum institutione* played a major role in fostering these concepts.[5] This chapter shows how traditional strategies of persuasion and Christian educational concepts shaped early German literature and medieval learning.

RELIGIOUS POETRY AS AN EDUCATIONAL MEDIUM

In Christian education of the German Middle Ages, the Call to Judgment was the topic of new literary forms that defy classification with modern categories of genre.[6] Nevertheless, major manuscript collections with varied literary forms constitute a unity, one "Gattung."[7] This literature comprises chiefly biblical poetry as a unified program of Christian practical teachings on the history of salvation.[8] Thus, this extensive literary corpus forms a collective genre of religious instructional poetry.

One witnesses the influence of this tradition of edification in the *Bibelepik* of Late Antiquity. Biblical poetry preceding *De doctrina christiana* transmitted concepts of learning and teaching later formalized by Augustine. An example of such a poetic work is the *Evangelium* in verse of the fourth-century Spanish presbyter, Juvencus. Writing in the early decades of the fourth century in opposition to the lies, *mendacia*, of classical pagan epics, Juvencus offered his own biblical epic as a Christian alternative: "mihi carmen erit Christi vitalia gesta" (*Proömium* 15).[9] This poetic affirmation of the *Evangelium* was at once a meritorious act. By virtue of his poetic work in the service of his faith, Juvencus hoped to merit eternal praise and escape damnation.[10] It is no wonder, then, that the poet viewed the use of the earthly trappings of language, *ornamenta terrestria linguae*, not as mere decoration, but as means of poetically expressing divine law and presenting it for the edification of both author and reader.[11] Juvencus's poetic representation of biblical texts was thus conceived as a spiritual service to the Word and Christian education.[12]

In the middle of the fifth century, the theme of *aedificatio* continues in the works of the Late Latin poet Caelius Sedulius, who affirms the educational value of Christian poetry in the dedication to his *Paschale Carmen*.[13] Sedulius admonishes his readers and reminds them of the spiritual truth so that they might be invited to the bounty of the spiritual harvest: "ut alios exhortationibus veritatis ad frugem bonem messis invitans" (*Dedication*, 138–39). He also writes that his work may fortify him in times of weakness and shield him against the enemy. When the goals of spiritual and worldly literature are compared at the beginning of the epistle *ad Macedonium*, Sedulius echoes the Augustinian theme: "nec doctor verbis serveat, sed verba doctori."[14]

Both traditions of biblical studies and of biblical poetry pass from Late Antiquity into the early Middle Ages. The former tradition was concerned with teaching exegetical method, interpreting biblical texts, and teaching what one had learned from them. The latter sought to sweeten the learning process at first by the metrical representation of the Bible, then more and more by the poetic expression of biblical themes through *paraphrasis;* this was paraphrase not as a rhetorical school exercise, but rather the poetic embellishment of a biblical text as a means to heighten its impact on the reader and listener. Although the Bible continued to lie at the heart of both traditions, biblical poetry was involved in a process of emancipation from the biblical text.[15] After the metrical version of the Bible by Juvencus (A.D. 330), a further step in this process occurs in the poetry of Prudentius at the close of the fourth century. Prudentius's work was well represented in medieval catalogues.[16] His *Psychomachia* departed from the biblical text and depicted the battle between Christian virtues and pagan vices in poetry. Just as the patriarch Abraham fought against ungodly tribes to deliver his kinsman Lot from bondage, so, too, should the Christian seek to free himself from the inner bondage of enslaving vices.[17] A growing interest among Christian readers in the poetic expression of biblical themes becomes evident in Sedulius's *Paschale Carmen* (c. 425–450). This hexameter poem does not adhere to the composition of New Testament biblical texts, but presents major miracles through extensive rhetorical ornamentation, *amplificatio,* for the sake of "paraphrastic intensity" to heighten not only the spiritual, but also the poetic effect upon the listener.[18] Sedulius's *Paschale Carmen* also marks a shift in the perception of biblical poetry, a *Literarisierung.*[19] This growing acceptance of *Bibeldichtung* from the latter half of the fifth century provided a juncture for both biblical studies and biblical poetry and fostered religious poetry as an educational medium.

In conjunction with the tradition of biblical studies, authors and readers of vernacular religious poetry, especially biblical epics, were likely to have known of the prominent Latin biblical epics.[20] Thus a familiarity with the tradition of biblical poetry belonged to the common heritage of the cultured Christian author and reader.[21]

In addition to the traditions of biblical studies and Latin biblical poetry, authors of vernacular religious poetry both in German and Old English regions were influenced by the Germanic literary tradition.[22] And yet this was not a mere *Germanisierung* of Christian material to make it more palatable for missionary efforts.[23] On the contrary, the poetic works that were written down were not *sermo rusticus* (*sermo piscatrius*); they were primarily designed for the instruction and enjoyment of the elite.[24] In Bede's acccount of the story of Caedmon, a monastic audience hears the *hymnus* composed by Caedmon with astonishment not because of its similarities with the beauty of biblical verse, but due to its composition in the highly cultivated style and verse of traditional aristocratic Germanic poetry.[25] The "miracle of Caedmon," which evoked such wonderment among the monks familiar with this tradition, was the skilled use of complicated, traditional verse forms by an untrained practitioner of the art.[26]

Caedmon's hymn as *laus Domini* was also a meritorious work beneficial to the poet's spiritual welfare. As a model for the praise of God, it provided a model for imitation as well as spiritual food for meditation, *ruminatio*.[27] These activities served the *aedificatio communis*, though not the general community but a chiefly monastic one, cultivated and, in part, aristocratic by heritage.[28]

Biblical poetry also served an artistic goal, and the poetic ambitions of the author.[29] This literature not only provided a Christian alternative to pagan poetry, it also fulfilled the needs of a Christian audience and its authors for poetic expression of the history of salvation. The poetic medium proved to be a useful means to make tropological lessons more palatable for the learner, while not diminishing their effectiveness.

THE STRATEGY OF PERSUASION

This chapter will now look at the tradition of Christian *aedificatio* in the Old High German poem, the *Muspilli,* to determine in what form concepts of learning and teaching continued from the early Christian era to the Middle Ages, and how these concepts contributed to a strategy of persuasion, both to move the recalcitrant and to inform the strivings of the diligent. An examination of the poem will highlight this strategy and its means of preparing the learner for Judgment.

The *Muspilli* is preserved in the margins and available space of the Regensburg Saint Emmeram codex containing the Latin instructional text—the Pseudo-Augustinian sermon, *Sermo de Symbolo contra judaeos, paganos et arianos.*[30] Walter Haug and Wolfgang Mohr were the first to attempt a complete interpretation of the *Muspilli* based on the form in which it appeared in the codex, and not on a speculative reconstruction of a possible "Urtext."[31] Scholars have viewed the poem either as a break with tradition, a new beginning without a future, or as a transitional work between Old and early Middle High German.[32] For the purpose of this study, I will examine the *Muspilli* first as an instructional

The Lesson of the Muspilli

text, and then as a transcribed poem in relation to the *Sermo de Symbolo,* the major text of the codex. The codex itself was dedicated by Bishop Adalramm of Salzburg to the young Louis the German, to whom it was presented between 825 and 836. The orthography of the poem and the hand in which is was written point, however, to the late ninth century. The year of Louis's death, 876, is probably the earliest date of inscription.[33] When the *Muspilli* was transcribed in the codex, Old High German literature had already survived in written form for almost a century. The official use of German vernacular literature was tied to Charlemagne's *Admonitio generalis,* a capitulary that set standards for the reform of the Frankish Church and religious education.[34] Learners with no or little command of Latin were to receive elementary instruction in the faith in their own tongue, a practice which often required authoritative vernacular translations of Latin catechetical texts.

And yet, not all vernacular instructional texts were solely translations. The major epics *Heliand,* the Old Saxon *Genesis,* and Otfrid von Weissenburg's *Evangelienbuch* constituted new literary beginnings. Otfrid's work, in particular, was a literary historical expression of the growing status of the Frankish language as a vehicle of the cultural politics of Louis the German.[35] This literary development of the vernacular, however, was to diminish during the Ottonian period through the official support for Latin to represent the universal claims of the Western Empire.

In contrast to the major vernacular epics, the *Muspilli* is a relatively short work. Its genre is that of the Christian Judgment narrative.[36] The extant poem—whose initial and final verses were lost with the covers of the codex—begins the narrative by depicting the soul's departure from the body.[37] Angelic and Satanic forces appear and vie for the soul's possession. The learner immediately encounters a vision of fear and uncertainty: "In anxious concern the soul must endure, till the decision is rendered as to which of the warring bands it shall fall as the spoil."[38] The evocation of fear in a situation of potential salvation or damnation also appears in other Judgment narratives: the dreamer's vision at the beginning of the *Dream of the Rood,* Venerable Bede's poem *De die iudici,* and the vision in *Christ III* (867–1664).[39]

The outcome of the forces' struggle confirms the judgment that awaits the soul; its fate hangs in the balance as the prize of battle. This imagery does not constitute a germanization, but derives instead from biblical battle metaphors as found in the Old Testament tale of the Maccabees and later in the biblical poetry of Sedulius.[40] The contest between heavenly and Satanic forces as well as the resulting tension in the narrative remain unresolved. We hear of the two possible resolutions in rapid succession. If the satanic forces win the battle, the judgment will be fearful:

> If Satan's band win the battle for the soul, they
>   shall lead it thither without delay where only
> suffering awaits it, in fire and darkness. (8-10)[41]

Yet should the heavenly contingent be victorious, it will carry the soul immediately to heaven:

> But if they, who come from heaven, fetch the soul,
>   and it comes in the possession of the angels,
> then they shall accompany it swiftly up to the
>   kingdom of heaven:
> where there is life without death,
>   light without darkness,
> a dwelling without cares,
> [and] no one suffers from sickness anymore.
> [For] should one receive a dwelling in paradise
>   —a home in heaven—then help shall come
> to him in fullness. (11–17)[42]

After the anonymous poet enumerates the joys of heaven and the terrors of hell, the narrative flow breaks off to introduce the lesson.

> Thus everyone's heart must lead to doing God's
>   will with joyful accord,
> [and] fearfully to avoid the coals of hell,
> [and] the agony of hellfire.
> [For] there awaits the ancient Satan with
>   burning flames.
> [So] you ought to ponder this [lesson] and
>   consider [it] with care,
> if you know yourself to be in sin. (18–24)[43]

The signal lines 18 through the middle of 23, which alert the learner of the necessity of wholeheartedly doing God's will, do not combine with the preceding description of heaven, but with the subsequent description of the pain of hellfire, *pehhes pina.* The image of Satan keeping the glowing flames in readiness heightens this necessity. The verses that immediately follow are preceptive: whoever knows himself to be in the state of sin should think of what has been said and take care (23–24). The poet quickly amplifies the impossibility of atoning in hell for sins committed on earth:[44]

> Woe to him who must pay the penalty of his
> sins in darkness
> and burn in hellfire: [for] it is truly a dreadful thing,
> when one cries out to God and help comes no more.
> The unfortunate soul shall hope for mercy, yet it
> [the soul] no longer rests in the loving memory
> of the heavenly God, for here in this life it did not
> prove itself worthy by [good] deeds. (25–30)[45]

Although its cries to God bring no help, the damned soul continues to hope in vain for mercy. God no longer remembers the soul since its work on earth did not merit remembrance. We can view these verses as exemplary.[46] The poet presents us with a negative model of conduct, set off by the use of end rhyme as a signal to take heed.[47] The soul, blind to the futility of its condition, must suffer the eternal fire that burns without light. Once the learner has witnessed the soul's afflicted spiritual state and subsequent conduct, he is immediately taught the cause: deeds performed in this life that were not meritorious of salvation. By recognizing both the soul's *affectus*[48] and *actio* then the error responsible for it, the learner may be moved to avoid the same grounds for condemnation. And with the specific nature of the damning works unrevealed, the audience remains in uncertainty and the narrative tension unresolved. The poet elicits fear as an instructional tool to intensify the audience's disposition to learn what must be avoided. Yet, at the moment when the unresolved tension is at its height, the second major section of the poem introduces the theme of God as Judge and impending divine Judgment.

Religious ritual in the Carolingian culture of the *Muspilli* poet highlighted the depiction of God as Judge, the *iudex* called upon to grant justice as well as mercy. Jacques Le Goff has shown this represenation to lie within a binary system of heaven and hell. "Carolingian liturgy introduced not the hope of Purgatory but the growing fear of Hell, coupled with the more tenuous hope of Heaven."[49] It is within this context that the listener learns of the Call to Judgment:

> When the mighty king determines the day of judgment, every clan must appear: for none can dare be absent on the appointed day, [in the mistaken belief that] not everyone is obligated to face judgment. [For] there before the judge one must account for all that one has done in this life. (31–36)[50]

What is revealed does not resolve the tension of earlier verses (25–30) by specifying the error and cause for damnation. The poet leaves the specific condemning acts unnamed. The only certainty granted the learner is that of the inevitability of Judgment. As in the Late Antiquity tradition of *salutissimus timor,* the poet evokes fear to intensify the ongoing narrative tension.

The description of Judgment in the *Muspilli* differs in part from biblical eschatological tradition by the introduction of Germanic legal terminology.[51] The legal term *daz m(a)hal kipannit* has no exact biblical equivalent.[52] In calling for the court to assemble, the mighty king, *der mahtigo khuninc,* exercises a major right and privilege of Frankish kingship, *Banngewalt* (OHG *pan*).[53] No one dares to disregard the call, *den pan furisizzan,* and no one will escape Judgment. Everyone must give an account, *az rahhu stantan,* of all earthly deeds before the Lord.[54] The preponderant emphasis placed on the fear of hell in the Carolingian period allows for a contextual interpretation of *rahha*.[55] This Germanic legal term, as found in the poetic context of the Judgment narrative *Muspilli,* encompasses a range of meaning from accountability for an act to revenge and punishment.[56] The contextuality of the word amplifies the fear of accountability before the Lord and of impending punishment. As would be expected, the influence of legal rhetoric on Christian education appears in the aim to persuade learners to judge wisely in leading their lives—and prepare to account for them at Judgment. Having taught the inescapable demands of the call to Judgment, the poet relates the battle of Elias with the Antichrist. A reference to authority begins the narration:

> I have heard how the men learned in secular
>   law have said, [that]
> the Antichrist shall wage battle with Elias. (37–38)[57]

The Lesson of the Muspilli

The first-person narrator informs the listeners that the depiction to be given rests on the authority of learned men of law, *uueroltrehtuuison*.[58] The antithetical models of Elias and the Antichrist that follow belong to established Church tradition. The narrator presents contrastively the typological struggle between the exponents of good and evil and the consequences for both:[59]

> The warriors are filled with such power, [for] the matter is so great. Elias battles for the life eternal, [and since] he wishes to enforce the rule of the just, He who rules heaven, then, shall help him. Yet the Antichrist stands by the side of the old enemy, by Satan, who must leave him to his fate: thus the Antichrist shall fall wounded on the field of battle and in this struggle be without victory. (40–47)[60]

Elias fights for salvation and eternal life. In seeking to strengthen the rule of the just at the convening of the final tribunal, he is aided by the ruler of heaven. In contrast, the Antichrist relies on Satan. The association with the devil and the reliance on his help leads ultimately to defeat and eternal death. That the fear of punishment is magnified and made more specific by fear of association should not be surprising. Even the mightiest representative and ally of Satan cannot escape judgment and must fall. Thus, the antithetical models juxtapose the struggle for salvation—and justice—of one who awaits divine aid with that of one whose fate rests on the deceptive alliance with Satan. Indeed, these exemplary verses provide a simplified rhetorical argument to persuade the audience to repeat or avoid given acts according to their usefulness for salvation.[61] Persuasion aims at *conversio*, at moving learners away from falsehood and *superbia* toward truth and *caritas*.

After the statement that the wounded Antichrist will fall vanquished to the ground, the listeners discover that Elias, too, may be injured in battle: "Indeed, many servants of God believe, that in this struggle Elias will be wounded" (48–49).[62] Elias's blood calls attention to the possible wounds to be suffered by those who strive for eternal life and the rule of the just in the struggle against evil.

To emphasize the consequences of serving God or Satan and to heighten the *affectus*, the *Muspilli* depicts a victorious Elias and a defeated Antichrist. This selective use of patristic eschatological tradition alerts us to the importance of these exemplary verses and their contrasting models for the teaching strategy of the poem. By examining the two major Elias traditions in apocalyptic literature the source of the Elias victory becomes evident.[63] The dominant one depicts Elias and Enoch as martyred witnesses, while the less frequent one portrays Elias as the victor. The battle of Elias with the Antichrist in the *Muspilli*, where Elias vanquishes his adversary, deviates from the standard theological viewpoint of the Carolingian period, whereby Elias and his companion—commonly held to be Enoch—suffer martyrdom by the Antichrist.[64] In the Greek tradition, the *Elias Apocalypse* tells of martyrdom, yet also of the later victory of Elias and Enoch. Scholars have already called attention to parallels between the *Elias Apocalypse* and *Muspilli*.[65] This line of research also extends to the patristic tradition of the Latin West, whereby the commentary of Cassiodorus on Psalm 51 in *Expositio in Psalterium* provides an important parallel to Elias's victory in the *Muspilli*.[66] Thus, the Elias depiction in the *Muspilli* remains within recognized patristic tradition.

Furthermore, the use of the least common account accentuates the contrast; Elias is the immediate victor rather than the martyred witness. The clarity of contrast between imminent victory for the servant of God and defeat for the servant of Satan magnifies the force of persuasion. And from a pedagogical viewpoint, the depiction not only of the warriors and their antithetical values, but also of the consequences of their affiliations may serve to foster the internalization of knowledge by relating it to personal experiences and expectations, namely, to one's own struggle to merit salvation. Thus, the very magnitude of the contest and outcome, sanctioned by the authority of those learned in law, is a signal for the reader and listener to take heed and consider the consequences of the account for their own lives:

> The enemy is armed, so shall the battle between
>   them begin.
> The warriors are filled with such power (39–40)[67]

While the ensuing lines (40–47) may delight due to the poetic manner of their depiction, they also aim to predispose the learner to *convertere*, a change of spirit and a subsequent change of conduct.[68] And while persuading the learner to consider the course of action that brings salvation, and then act, the Elias account continues to further the narration of

The Lesson of the Muspilli

the poem. The appearance of Elias and the ensuing battle—both events belonging to apocalyptic tradition—signal the approach of the *mahal*. Elias is not only a precursor of imminent judgment, but also its instrument in striking down the damned Antichrist.

In amplified verse, the learner hears an account of the approaching *Muspilli*, the destruction of the world by fire. One is faced with the prospect of standing alone with little or no time to reflect on one's life, and little opportunity to change it:[69]

> When Elias' blood shall drip upon the earth, [and] the mountains begin to burn, not a tree on earth shall stand, [and] the waters shall dry out, the moor shall devour itself, the sky disolve in flames, the moon shall fall [from the sky], [and] the whole world shall burn.
>
> No stone on earth shall remain in anyone's possession, for then the Day of Judgment shall arrive in the land. It shall come with the fire, to plague humankind. [And] one relation shall no longer be able to help another at the *Muspilli*. [For] when the whole earth burns, [and] fire and air shall sweep away all things, where then is the land which one subdued with the help of one's relations? The land shall be burned, [and] the soul shall stand replete with sorrow, [and] not knowing what is to be done: it shall go to hell. (50–62)[70]

And yet, apart from the obvious imagery of perdition, how else does the poet seek to persuade the reader and listener? The biblical prelude to judgment day is clearly the destruction of the world by fire, the imagery which permeates the above verses. Through the paraphrastic intensity in depicting apocalyptic themes, the *Muspilli* poet aims to predispose the learner to emulate the acts of Elias: to fight for eternal life and strengthen the rule of the just (41–42). For the poet, it is this course of action that includes the possibility of help from the ruler of heaven (43). In other words, one learns that at the *Muspilli*, one will be alone and helpless—save for the divine intervention one has merited. No kin, *mac* (57), will be able to help. This is emphasized by the alliteration: *ni mac . . . mak—Muspilli*. Even the mark, *marha* (60), where one member of a family may support the cause of another before court, no longer remains.[71] Thus, the poet admonishes us that all means of mutual aid practiced at an earthly court of justice will vanish. The purpose of the passage (50–

62) is to move the learner toward a spiritual transformation—to convert from the practice of damning to saving acts. This is at once the twofold process of purification and ascent to wisdom that lies well within the tradition of Christian edification.[72] Once again, the effects of saving *[saluberrimus]* terror may hasten a purifying ascent to wisdom. And while the poet accentuates the expression of loss for the mark: "uuar ist denne diu marha" ("Where then is the land" [60]), through alliteration: *marha -man . . . mit . . . magon,* the response appears in rhymed verse— the new Christian verse form in Old High German as a signal for the learner:[73] "With the mark [the land] destroyed, so, too, is the chance for atonement; [and] no longer knowing the way to penance, the fearful soul shall go to hell."[74] Thus, striking in the use of a new verse form, the above passage constitutes the highpoint of the amplified destruction imagery—and of its *affectus* on the learner. And yet, by discovering the condemned soul's plight, the learner may become more receptive to the tropological message: "Thus, it is useful, when one appears before [an earthly] court (*ze demo mahale*), to have judged everything justly. [For] then one need not worry, when one appears before this court [*zu deru suonu*]" (63–65).[75] Here, the poet gives advice for *convertere,* for changing one's ways in the administration of justice on earth while opportunity still remains. *Mahal* refers above to the earthly court of justice, in contrast with its initial use as a term for the Last Judgment (34).[76] The contextual application of *mahal* strengthens the connection between conduct at court in this life and its consequences at the court of the Last Judgment for eternity. Thus, when passing judgment, one must do so justly, for one is also accountable to God for each judgment. In other words, it is only by heeding this lesson that the learner—as a judge in this life—may appear with impunity before the ultimate tribunal. The use of the term *suona* (65) not only provides an alternative expression for the Last Judgment, it also prepares the learner for the arrival of the one who will judge, "der dar suonnan scal" (85).

Yet the poet employs another theme to persuade the learner of the need for spiritual accountability at an earthly court of justice. Fear of being overheard reinforces the lesson by exemplary verses *ex negativo.* The *uuenago man,* the weak and pitiable man who impedes justice by bribery, does not know he is being watched in secret by the devil.[77] The *tiuual* quietly notes the evil the offender has committed and discloses it when the guilty party appears before the final tribunal. The learner is shown the error in the offender's conduct and becomes privy to what the offender does not know along with its consequences at the Last Judg-

The Lesson of the Muspilli 55

ment. The models of correct and incorrect conduct and their outcome offer simplified rhetorical arguments. The learner is presented with two sets of *affectus* and *actio*. The first set (63–65) depicts the man who gives just decisions at the court in this world and accordingly need not be troubled when he himself is judged in the next. In contrast, the second set (66–67) teaches that the *uuenago man* must fear the day of Judgment and the *ius talionis* for his deeds, in particular for the acceptance of bribes.[78] Not only is the learner persuaded to *conversio*, but also dissuaded from potential offenses. Both purposes are served by the paraphrastic amplification of the theme of the watcher, the *uuartil* (66), and by the adaption, the paraphrasis, of the theme of the devil as accuser, Apocalypse 12:10. Similar means of persuasion and dissuasion are found in the Pseudo-Augustinian *Sermo de Symbolo, contra judaeos, paganos et arianos*, the Latin codex in which the *Muspilli* itself is preserved.

In section 3 of this codex, *Renuntiare satanae*, the listener first learns of the devil as exactor, contextually as both overseer of those who incur debt through sin as well as the exactor of payment.[79] Chapter 4, *Relapsus a baptismo*, begins with the admonition that Christians be vigilant in keeping their baptismal vows lest the devil accuse them of being one of his number.[80] Just as the devil in the *Muspilli* reveals the crimes of the recalcitrant offender at the Last Judgment, so does the devil in *Sermo de Symbolo* act as accuser before Christ the Judge. During the profession of vows the adversary is secretly at hand. And when anyone remiss leaves this life:

> The adversary shall exalt in view of the severest judge of all, invoking the tribunal and pleading such a case before a judge so great: he shall exclaim, "Judge, render your verdict, justly and most fairly—[as] justice and judgment in preparation for your throne. Judge to be mine, whoever does not wish to be yours: [for] he is mine, [and] together with me he must be condemned."[81]

These amplifying passages also develop the theme of bribe taking. The palace of the Divine Judge will be incorruptible; and he will approve of no one who has been corrupted regardless of one's rank or power. "Dreaded shall be the Day of Judgment, [for] present shall be the most equitable judge, [He] who shall receive the personage of no one powerful [and proud], [and He] whose palace no one shall corrupt with gold and silver."[82] It is in this context that the author evokes the fear of God to move the learner to vigilance and, if required, to conversion. For on the day of Judgment all must answer for their deeds. The devil will plead for the possession of those who wear his mark—*suos pannos* (the devil's rags!)—before the sternest of judges. And, by the *ius talionis,* the incorruptible judge will condemn all who have renounced their baptismal vows and whose judgments reveal bribery.[83]

The magnitude of the crime and sin of bribe taking is evident throughout the Carolingian period.[84] Alcuin's instructional work, *De virtutibus et vitiis liber ad Widonem Comitem,* addresses the problem of incorrect judicial practices, in particular of bribery. In a series of three chapters, Alcuin forewarns practitioners of injustice of their eternal condemnation. Chapter 19, *De Fraude cavenda,* warns that "to acquire money you bare false witness, you lie, [and] you plunder people. You swear, [and] you perjure yourself, which the law forbids. When you do all these things, why do you not fear that you may wholly burn forever?"[85]

In chapter 20, *De judicibus,* judges hear that fear of God is a prerequisite for administering justice. They also learn that it may yet prevent their condemnation for having pardoned the wicked and judged friend and foe with partiality.[86] In condemning the taking of bribes, the author explicitly contrasts such conduct with judgments based on *timor Dei* that merit reward: "Qui Deum timentes juste judicant, aeterna a Domino accepturi sunt praemia" (They who fearing God judge justly, are they who shall receive from God everlasting reward).

Alcuin, after offering positive models of judicial conduct, does not refrain from providing the reader with negative models in the last chapter of the series. Chapter 21, *De falsis testibus,* contains a catalog of four ways to subvert justice—and incur damnation:

> Justice can be overturned in judgments in four ways: through fear, avarice, hatred, and love. Through fear, as long as anyone begins to dread judging or saying the truth out of fear of anyone's power; through avarice, as long as a judge is corrupted by a bribe for any service; through hatred, so long as any one wishes to inflict injury on another for reason of hostility; through love, as long as one more ably defends friends or neighbors in opposition to justice. In these four ways the equity of a judgment is often subverted, and blamelessness is harmed. They who crush the poor

will lament more than they who suffer the injustice.
They who are suppressed, namely, quickly end their
temporary misery; but they who suppress them through
injustice will be condemned to unending flames. (translation mine)[87]

These ways comprise the misdirected fear of the power of influential men, *potentes*, rather than fear of God; the corruption of a judge by bribery out of love for money; the injury of an enemy out of malice; and the subversion of justice out of partiality to friends and relations. All lead to punishment by eternal fire in accord with the *ius talionis*.[88]

The admonition against bribery also appears in book 4 of the *Dialogues* of Gregory the Great, a work that exerted continuous influence on early medieval Christian edification.[89] In *Dialogorum Liber IV*, Pope Gregory answers the question whether burial within the walls of a church is beneficial to the souls of the dead. He replies that it cannot help those who die in the state of mortal sin. Gregory then employs negative models of conduct using exemplary stories to facilitate instruction.[90] In chapter 52, *De Valeriani patricii sepultura*, Gregory begins by affirming the reliability of the witness, who personally related to him the story of Valerianus, the corrupt patrician of Brixa. The reader learns that the local bishop has received a bribe, *accepto pretio*, from Valerianus, an unrighteous man, for a burial vault within the church.[91] In the very same night, the holy martyr Faustus and patron saint of the local church appears to the sexton with a warning for the bishop: "should he fail to cast the stinking flesh from the church within thirteen days, he himself will die."[92] Unfortunately, the sexton fears to confide his vision. And when the putrid corpse of Valerianus has not been removed from the church by the foretold day, the bribed bishop dies suddenly after retiring in good health for the night.

After teaching the causal relationship between *affectus* and *actio*, Gregory strengthens the lesson preceptively by directing the learner to shun what the model demonstrates. In doing so, he does not hesitate to employ *timor Dei* as fear of Judgment, and the *ius talionis*, to strengthen the exemplary argument and its force of persuasion.

> Therefore, Peter, consider that were they to have themselves buried in a holy place, grave sins may weigh them down; [so] it remains, namely, that they be judged on their presumption, seeing that the sacred places may

not set them free, but the fault of temerity [their arrogance] may call [them] to account.⁹³

Gregory concludes the fourth book of his *Dialogues* with the admonition to perform acts of charity in the time that remains before the day of Judgment.⁹⁴

In the second quarter of the ninth century—the time of the *Sermo de Symbolo* codex and its transcription of the *Muspilli*—similar concepts of learning and teaching as well as the prohibition against bribery and judicial corruption appear in an important work of Benedictine reform. The monk Walahfrid Strabo, writing in 825, completed his Latin hexameter version of the recorded visions of Wetti, his former teacher at the island monastery of Reichenau.⁹⁵ These visions offer not only both positive and negative models of conduct, but also recall the outwardly positive, yet *de facto* negative models in Gregory's *Dialogues*. Several exemplary visions, in particular, illustrate this variation. The first tells of an eyeless clergyman who, equipped with instruments of torture, informs Wetti that torments await him the very next day when he is to receive his just reward. With punishment foretold according to the *ius talionis*, demons come to take possession of the hapless monk when an angel dispells them and Wetti suddenly awakens. Surrounded by his fellow monks, Wetti makes use of this edifying reprieve to read in Gregory's *Dialogues* of the soul's fate after death—the major theme of *Dialogorum Liber IV.*⁹⁶

The next series of visions lead Wetti to a mountain of purgation, where he sees Waldo, the former abbot of Reichenau, being purged by the elements for his transgressions; the bishop Adalhelm suffering purgation for lack of charity by neglecting his promise to pray for Waldo; and finally the emperor Charlemagne himself being purged for his carnal sins.⁹⁷ The inverse depiction of formerly positive models of conduct emphasizes the consequences of discrepancy between external bearing and inner moral qualities.⁹⁸ Walahfrid Strabo applies the *affectus* of those undergoing purgation, and simplified rhetorical argumentation in exemplary form, to move and persuade his reader to refrain from imitating deeds that require expiatory punishment.⁹⁹ Thus, the portrayal of outwardly positive models from the Reichenau's history that are flawed from within by hidden vice challenges learners to reexamine established models of conduct and ultimately themselves in accord with the austere demands of Benedictine reform.¹⁰⁰ After viewing the mountain of purgation and those being purged there who will eventually gain heaven, the angelic guide directs Wetti to a place of punishment for the damned.

Wetti learns that the tormented he sees are damned for the misuse of office in the acquisition of material wealth.[101] They are *muneribus capti*.[102]

The author further reinforces the lesson through the juxtaposition of negative models such as those of the damned Counts Udalrich and Ruadrich, with a series of positive models.[103] Among these the reader encounters the uncle of Louis the Pious, Count Gerold, who, having donated his property to the monastery Reichenau, offers an example of correct monastic conduct. In contrast with those damned for bribery and desire for earthly possessions, Gerold sought the rewards of eternal life: "*munera perpetuae capiens ingentia vitae.*"[104] Walahfrid underscores the correctness of the model by recalling the martyrdom of Gerold in defense of his faith against the pagan "Awaren" of Hungary.[105]

The concepts of learning and teaching in the examined Latin texts with judgment themes and in the Old High German *Muspilli* reveal a common origin in the tradition of Christian edification which extends from *De doctrina christiana* into the early Middle Ages. The verses in the *Muspilli* dealing explicitly with bribery and misuse of judicial office also employ a form of teaching that Norman Perrin sees as characteristic of the early Church.[106] Referring to Ernst Käsemann's "Sätze heiligen Rechts im Neuen Testament," Perrin notes the existence in the early Church of

> an eschatological judgment pronouncement tradition having its roots in Christian prophecy and its *Sitz im Leben* in the Eucharist. The characteristic form of this tradition is that of a two-part pronouncement with the same verb in each part, in the first part referring to the activity of man and in the second to the eschatological activity of God.[107]

Fulfilling this definition, the *Muspilli* poet states that it is good for each one who appears at an earthly tribunal: *denner ze demo mahale quimit* (63), to act justly. If one does this, one need not be afraid when appearing before the tribunal of the Last Judgment: *denne er ze deru suonu quimit* (65).

The use of this type of judgment pronouncement is especially effective in the *Muspilli* because it "legalizes" the lesson being taught.[108] The manner in which one exercises judgment before an earthly court has the force of a binding legal contract that determines the degree of reward or punishment one may expect before the heavenly tribunal—a quid pro quo as a reminder that one's ethical standard of conduct as a judge in this life dictates the treatment one may expect from the Divine Judge. This type of pronouncement is also prominent in the *Sermo de Symbolo*, at the beginning of the first chapter, *Christianae vigiliae*.[109] A reference to Matthew 25:26–27, a section from the *Parabola talentorum* (Matt. 25:14–30), tells how the servants in the parable receive their rewards according to the degree of profit they turn by investing the coins their master has entrusted to them. The unworthy and slothful servant, *nequam et piger*, does not merit reward for he did not increase the wealth of his master. The *Sermo de Symbolo* presents a "legalized" concept of reward and punishment based on the practice of charity; the amount of charitable acts performed determines the degree of reward or punishment.[110] Because only Matthew 25:26–27 appear, the poet may have been addressing an audience already familiar with Scripture. Furthermore, scripturally knowledgeable listeners and readers would know that the section immediately following Matthew 25:26–27, is *Postremi iudicii descriptio* (Matt. 25:31–46). The *Sermo de Symbolo*, as the title of the first chapter: *Christianae vigiliae* affirms, lies well within an eschatological framework. The immediacy of observing Christian beliefs, of vigilance in upholding them as well as of *conversio* if need be, heightens through the mood of impending judgment.[111] The renunciation of Satan and the avoidance of bribery as a violation of charity (false testimony against enemies) require the Christian learner to reaffirm and act upon what is already known: the obligation to guard against the temptations of the devil, perform acts of charity, and implement the lesson while time remains before the arrival of Judgment Day.

Both the *Muspilli* and the codex known as the *Sermo de Symbolo* in which it is transcribed, are instruments of persuasion in the interest of reform; both texts address the problem of misuse of office, in particular of bribe-taking. Abuses in the exercise of judicial authority are well documented for the period from Charlemagne to Louis the German.[112] These abuses appear in the conflict between the Carolingian policy of establishing centralized rule with uniformly administered jurisdiction, and the particularistic interests of the local aristocracy.[113] The traditional acceptance of gifts by the local counts, who exercised the office of judge as the hallmark of their authority, now constituted bribe-taking by imperial officials and clashed with the goals of Carolingian reform and the enforcement of the *norma rectitudinis*.[114] In combating the misuse of judicial office, whether committed by aristocratic laymen, monks or clergy, both the *Muspilli* and the *Sermo de Symbolo* apply the force of

The Lesson of the Muspilli 61

moral sanction within a binary system; the offender and potential offenders learn the consequences of their acts in terms of reward and punishment, salvation and damnation. Yet, while both works reinforce this polarity by *saluberrimus terror* of the impending Last Judgment and by the *affectus* and *actio* before and after death of those who are judged, it is ultimately the learner who must choose the destination. For as a pilgrim in this world the learner traverses an interim time and space between life and death, reward and punishment. And no matter how persuasively the lesson and poetic medium may convey a sense of immediate salvation or damnation, one returns eventually to the everyday demands and inescapable decisions of life—and accordingly, the need to reflect on the lesson in the context of one's own life and experience.

Having reinforced the lesson with a preceptive verse against bribetaking, the author of the *Muspilli* again confronts the learner with the Second Coming of Christ—the Parousia.

> When the heavenly trumpet resounds, and the Judge,
> who shall pass judgment on the living and the dead, sets forth,
> the greatest of the heavenly hosts shall rise up with Him.
> It is so bold [courageous], that none can withstand it.
> He shall then proceed to the place of judgment, which shall be
>   marked off: [for] there is to be the court, as foretold.
> Then angels shall move throughout the mark, [and] awaken the
>   people, and call them to judgment. (73–80)[115]

The account of Judgment day in the final section of the *Muspilli* begins with the approach of *Christus iudex,* who immediately proceeds with an invincible army to the site of judgment, *ze deru mahalsteti.*[116] The process of purification and ascent directs the learner towards *conversio*: the renouncement of acts deserving condemnation, the doing of penance and the application of what has been learned.

The narrative increases in intensity as angels awaken the nations and the dead arise to account for their conduct and be judged according to their deeds: "There everyone shall rise up from the dust to become free of the weight of the grave, [and] to regain possession of the body, so that one may account for oneself and be judged according to deeds done" (81–84).[117] After the poet reminds us that nobody can avoid accountability, we hear of the group that need not worry in the presence of the judge: "[And] then he, who shall preside there and judge the living and the dead, shall take his seat, [and] about him shall stand a host of angels, and holy men: [for] the place of the tribunal is great" (85–88).[118] The positive depiction in the preceding verses sharpens the contrast with the verses that immediately follow and serves to intensify the saving terror of the learner: "So many are coming to the hearing—who arise from the sleep of death—to that place where no one can hide anything" (89–90).[119] Not even the slightest transgression can be concealed before the judge. The poet focuses on the theme of inescapable accountability by referring to murder as the greatest transgression against charity and the antithesis of brotherly love. Paratactic amplification highlights the lesson and promotes the learner's spiritual purification through *timor Dei.* "The hand shall speak, the head shall confess, each of the members down to the smallest finger [shall confess] what deeds of murder one has committed among men" (91–93).[120] Although the term *mord* can contextually encompass a range of meanings as "schwere Missetat," the primary meaning of murder predominates.[121] Johannes Singer observes that lines 89 and 93 refer to the murderer, while lines 91–92 refer to the victim. In accord with Germanic judicial custom, the corpse of the murder victim or part of the corpse—the hand or head—could be brought before court as an accusation of murder.[122] Thus, the murder victim could effectively accuse the murderer.[123] Singer's study answers the objection that the testimony of the devil against the bribe taker at the Last Judgment (63–72) makes the above verses superfluous, which would then indicate a text interpolation.[124] Viewed within the Christian pedagogical tradition of the early Middle Ages, the poet adapts Germanic legal custom to purify learners in their ascent to wisdom and prepare them for conversion to right action. The anticipated damnation of the murderer by the testimony of the victim highlights the causality between *affectus* and *actio.* Because of dishonest acts in this world, the bribe taker will hear the devil's prosecuting testimony, and the hand and head of the murdered will speak out against their murderer.

The *Muspilli* poet can now begin the concluding lesson:

> At this court not even the best deception is of use to anyone in denying anything, [or] in concealing any deed at all: it [all] shall become manifest before the King, [that is,] unless one can make recompense [for one's sins] by giving alms and having done penance for [one's] crimes through fasting. (94–98)[125]

The lesson is unequivocal. Since no one is clever enough to conceal a single deed from the king, *rex* and *iudex,* by deceit, the only recourse is to penance: performing acts of charity by the giving of alms, and acts of contrition and purification by fasting. The remaining extant verses aim to reinforce the lesson and intensify the learner's disposition to implement it. The poet reminds the learner by association of the earlier judgment (63–65) and its "legalized" lesson. This associative connection of the judgment pronouncement of lines 63–65 and 99–99a provides the learner with a striking frame of reference. On the one hand, if a person judges justly at an earthly court, there is no cause to worry when coming to the Last Judgment, "denne er ze deru suonu quimit" (65). On the other, lines 99–99a relate that it is the person who has done penance that need not worry when coming to judgment.[126] Not only the arrangement of the lines and the identical expression: *ze deru suonu quimit* (65 and 99a) catches the learner's attention, but also the thematic shift from the exercise of judgment to the exercise of penance in preparation for the Last Judgment. Both verse groups (63-65 and 99–99a) present a simplified rhetorical argument in exemplary form. Thus, by depicting *affectus* and *actio,* the poet seeks to direct the learner to right action and penance as a response to the misuse of power, specifically of judicial office. Furthermore, the learner is to be vigilant in guarding against potential offenses.

The final verses constitute the ultimate expression of *purificatio* and *ascensio*: "The revered cross shall be carried before, whereon holy Christ was nailed. For He will look at the wounds, which he received as man, [and] which he sustained for the love of humankind" (100–103).[127] The Cross and especially the *stigmata* recall the suffering, the very penetration of the crucifixion nails, that Christ endured out of love, *duruh desse mancunnes minna.* The Cross further evokes the image of Christ triumphant as *rex* and *iudex*.[128] With the representation of Christ's supreme act of charity, the learner can attain the highpoint of the *ascensio* process—*imitatio Christi* in implementing the lessons of the poem.

The *Muspilli* gives evidence of major concepts of learning and teaching that were transmitted from Late Antiquity into the German Middle Ages through Augustine's *De doctrina christiana,* the *Regula pastoralis* and *Dialogi* of Gregory the Great, and Hrabanus Maurus's *De clericorum institutione*—a ninth-century work and contemporary of the Saint Emmeram codex that contains the poem. The use of positive and negative models of conduct, the depiction of causality between *affectus* and *actio* in moving and persuading the learner, provide simplified rhetorical arguments in exemplary form. These arguments, as has already been mentioned, reveal the influence of legal rhetoric. And although they aim to persuade, they clearly aim to educate. For why must one take care to judge wisely? And how must one lead one's life so that one is pleasing both to God and the world? By addressing these issues, the *Muspilli* poet fosters the *aedificatio communis*—and, in particular, the edification of those with power in society to translate charity into correct judicial practice. Thus, the teaching strategy focuses on the call to Judgment to effect not only *conversio*—penance and reform, but vigilance in maintaining correct moral conduct in the exercise of Carolingian justice. Indeed, the pronouncement of judgment in the poem's eschatological context sanctions the lessons. These the poet reinforces by paraphrastic intensity in the selective depiction of eschatological tradition, and by amplifying themes to heighten the *affectus* and its impact on the learner. Thus, the evocation of *timor Dei* and *saluberrimus terror* forms an essential part of the teaching strategy in the *Muspilli,* where the simplified twofold process of purification and ascent to wisdom culminates in *catharsis* and *compunctio.*

Chapter 3 will continue to trace the above concepts of learning and teaching by examining an eleventh-century vernacular work, Noker's *Memento Mori,* whose teaching strategy—though focused on the call to Judgment—contrasts sharply with that of the *Muspilli.*

NOTES

1. Bernard F. Huppé, *Doctrine and Poetry: Augustine's Influence on Old English Poetry* (Albany: State University of New York, 1959), 99. Huppé does attempt to distinguish between *De doctrina christiana* and a poetic manual: "The Christian poet, though he would not have found in the *De doctrina* any specific practical assistance, he would have found in it clear theoretical expression of what he should attempt and what he should avoid" (13). Yet, Huppé overemphasizes the hermeneutical side of Augustine's work—the use of allegory as an intellectual exercise in separating the kernel from the shell to derive the *sententia*: "The Christian understanding of the Bible and of pagan literature made almost inevitable the development of a theory that serious poetry should be allusive, enigmatic, paraphrastic" (30). In doing so, Huppé underrates the equally important homiletic-edifying dimension of Augustine's work, which Herzog describes as the "homiletischerbauliche Disziplin." See Herzog, *Bibelepik*, 176–77, esp. n. 52.

2. Herzog, *Bibelepik*, 176–77. Herzog comments on Augustine's use of hermeneutics and homiletic-edification in the exegetically oriented aesthetics of *De doctrina christiana*: "Was oben Bibelästhetik genannt wurde, beschränkt sich bei Hieronymus auf das exegetische Postulat. Die Vollendung dieser Tendenz findet sich in Augustins De doctrina christiana. . . . Die ingeniöse, in ihren philosophischen Voraussetzungen oft untersuchte Konstruktion der Bibel als eines (hermeneutisch gesehen) Supertexts, der über die sekundäre Konsistenz der direkt symbolischen res-res-Verweisung zwischen Schrift und Wirklichkeit verfügt, zerschlägt nach der von Augustin gezogenen Konsequenz die antike Ästhetik endgültig: Rhetorik, ja schon Grammatik spalten sich nun in eine hermeneutische und eine homiletischerbauliche Disziplin. Und beide werden von Augustin zu einer exegetischen Produktionsästhetik herangezogen."

3. Freitag, *Die Theorie der allegorischen Schriftdeutung*, 17–19.

4. Straw, *Gregory the Great*, 202–11.

5. Jacque Le Goff, *The Birth of Purgatory* (Chicago: University of Chicago Press, 1981), 103–4.

6. Hugo Kuhn, *Dichtung und Welt im Mittelalter* (Stuttgart: Metzler, 1959), 54–55.

7. Friedrich Ohly, *Schriften zur Mittelalterlichen Bedeutungsforschung* (Darmstadt: Wissenschaftliche Buchgesellschaft, 1977), 16.

8. Dieter Kartschoke, *Bibeldichtung: Studien zur Geschichte der epischen Bibelparaphrase von Juvencus bis Otfrid von Weißenburg* (Munich: Fink, 1975), 225.

9. Herzog, *Bibelepik*, xlv–xlvi.

10. One of the most quoted verses of Juvencus throughout the Middle Ages attents to this hope. The context of the passage is the destruction of the world by fire before Judgment and the coming of Christ as Judge. The poet tells us

that the flames of the world will sweep away his work, yet his work may save him from the fire. (*Proömium* 21-24): "Nec metus, ut mundi rapiant incendia secum hoc opus; hoc etenim forsan me subtrahet igni, tunc cum flammivoma discendet nube coruscans Iudex, altithroni genitoris gloria, Christus."

11. Herzog, *Bibelepik,* xlvii.
12. Herzog, *Bibelepik,* xlviii: as "geistlicher Dienst am Wort, als Heilsmittel, also als Erbauung."
13. Kartschoke, *Bibeldichtung,* 64-68.
14. Ibid., 65. See also *De doct chr.* 4.28.61.
15. Herzog, *Bibelepik,* lvii.
16. Stanley B. Greenfield and Daniel G. Calder, *A New Critical History of Old English Literature* (New York: New York University Press, 1986), 7-12. See also G. R. Wieland, ed., *The Latin Glosses on Arator and Prudentius in Cambridge University Library MS Gg. 5. 35.* (Toronto: Pontifical Institute of Mediaeval Studies, 1983); and Ernst Robert Curtius, *Europäische Literatur und Lateinisches Mittelalter* (Bern: Francke, 1948), 59-61.
17. Prudentius, *Psychomachia:*

> haec ad figuram praenotata est linea,
> quam nostra recto vita resculpat pede:
> vigilandum in armis pectorum fidelium,
> omnemque nostri portionem corporis,
> quae capta foedae serviat libidini,
> domi coactis liberandam viribus.

This picture has been drawn beforehand to be a model for our life to trace out again with true measure, showing that we must watch in the armour of faithful hearts, and that every part of our body which is in captivity and enslaved by foul desire, must be set free by assembling forces at home. (*Praefatio* v. 50-55)

18. Carl P. E. Springer, "Sedulius' Paschale Carmen, A Literary Reexamination" (Ph.D. diss., University of Wisconsin-Madison 1984), 1-341. Springer views the poem as an epic form, rather than as "the school exercise of paraphrasis" (328). Also see Carl P. E. Springer, *The Gospel as Epic in Late Antiquity, the Paschale Carmen of Sedulius* (Leiden: E. J. Brill, 1988).
19. Herzog, *Bibelepik,* lii.
20. Kartschoke, *Bibeldichtung,* 123. Kartschoke argues that early medieval authors of biblical poetry are likely to have had knowledge of texts ranging from Juvencus to Arator. Further, such poetry was not a literary imitation of school authors, or a mere transcription into the vernacular, but a new beginning of Christian literary aspirations in the given cultural context: "Aber wo immer künftig Bibeldichtung entsteht, ist sie anderseits nicht literarische Nachahmung dieser Schulauthoren, Umsetzung etwa in die Volkssprachen, sondern Neubeginn im Sinne einer christlich-literarischen Ambition unter den jeweiligen kulturellen Bedingungen. Und sie ist—soweit wir darüber unterrichtet sind—kirchliche

Dichtung: sie entsteht im Umkreis von Kirche und Kloster, findet hier ihr Publikum und wirkt darüber kaum darüber hinaus" (123).

21. Kartschoke, *Bibeldichtung*, 338.

22. Ibid., 218.

23. Ibid., 186–90.

24. Ibid., 136–39.

25. Huppé, *Doctrine and Poetry,* 122. See also Kartschoke, *Bibeldichtung,* 136.

26. C. L. Wrenn, "The Poetry of Caedmon," *Proceedings of the British Academy* 32 (1946): 286. "Though in general only the poetry of aristocratic origin has been preserved in writing by the Anglo-Saxons, there must have been a native peasant poetry with which Caedmon's companions were familiar, which he was ashamed he could not recite or compose. The miracle, then, I would propose, which instantly struck the monks and was so piously recorded by Bede was not that a herdsman attached to the monastery recited a poem of his own composition merely: but rather that one obviously quite untrained in the aristocratic heroic tradition of the Anglo-Saxon poetic manner, its highly technical diction, style, and metre, suddenly showed that in a night, as it were, he had acquired the mastery over his long and specialized discipline." See Greenfield and Calder, *A New Critical History of Old English Literature,* 227–31. The authors note that Caedmon's *Hymn* poses "four interrelated problems," in particular, "a second problem is the nature of the miracle Bede saw in Caedmon's vision and performance: Was it the gift of traditional poetic language, 'aristocratic' and heroic, to an illiterate for the expression of Christian ideas? Insight into Scripture, along with the gift of language? The gift of memory? The fact that God chose someone 'unsullied by the trivial qualities of pre-Christian verse and a complete novice in composition' to herald 'a clean break with the heathen past symbolized by all previous poetry.'" Greenfield and Calder cite Huppé, *Doctrine and Poetry,* 99–130; Donald K. Fritz, "Caedmon: A Monastic Exegete," *American Benedictine Review* 25 (1974): 351–63; and P. R. Orton, "Caedmon and Christian Poetry," *Neuphilologische Mitteilungen* 84 (1983): 163–70.

27. Max Wehrli, "Sacra Poesis: Bibelepik als europäische Tradition," *Die Wissenschaft von deutscher Sprache und Dichtung, Festschrift. Friedrich Maurer,* (Stuttgart, 1963), 59; Herzog, *Bibelepik,* xxxix; Kartschoke, *Bibeldichtung,* 186.

28. Greenfield and Calder, *A New Critical History of Old English Literature,* 230. Also see George K. Anderson, *The Literature of the Anglo-Saxons,* rev. ed. (Princeton: Princeton University Press, 1966), 116.

29. Kartschoke, *Bibeldichtung,* 186, 192, 227.

30. The codex is designated: CLM 14098 (St. Emm. B6), fols. 61–121.

31. Walter Haug and Wolfgang Mohr, *Zweimal 'Muspilli': Das 'Muspilli' oder über das Glück literaturwissenschaftlicher Verzweiflung* (Tübingen: Niemeyer, 1977). For the postulation of an "Urtext," see Cola Minis, *Handschrift, Form und Sprache des Muspilli,* Philologische Studien und Quellen, 35 (Berlin: Schmidt, 1966), 1–112.

32. Georg Baesecke's attempt to construct a line from Charlemagne, Alcuin, and Hrabanus Maurus to the monastery of Fulda as the literary center of Old High German literature has proved untenable. Werner Schroder has convincingly shown that Old High German literature is best characterized as a series of new beginnings and interruptions. Within this framework, Walter Haug views the *Muspilli* as a "Montage," a break with tradition. The mixture of traditional elements such as alliteration, *Stabreim*, and new elements, end-rhyme, forms an original work of art to be analyzed in relation to the moment of its appearance in recorded literary history. The theme of literary continuity and discontinuity recalls Hugo Kuhn's "Nötigung zu neuer Struktur," the pressing need for new structure in early medieval literature. Haug concludes that *Muspilli* remained a new beginning without a future. A differing opinion is held by Wolfgang Mohr, who postulated that the *Muspilli* is a transitional work between Old and early Middle High German literature. Both classified the poem as a mixture of new and traditional elements. See Werner Schröder, Grenzen und Möglichkeiten einer althochdeutschen Literaturgeschichte, in *Bericht über die Verhandlungen der sächischen Akademie der Wissenschaften zu Leipzig*, Philologisch-historische Klasse 105/2 (Leipzig: 1959), 91. See also Walter Haug, Zweimal '*Muspilli*,' 34, 58, 69, 23.

33. Walter Haug and Wolfgang Mohr, Zweimal '*Muspilli*,' 26; Georg Baesecke, "Muspilli II," in: *Zeitschrift für Deutsches Altertum und Deutsche Literatur* 82 (1948/50): 201.

34. Josef Fleckenstein, *Die Bildungsreform Karls des Grossen als Verwirklichung der Norma Rectitudinis* (Bigge-Ruhr, 1953), 10–11.

35. Haug, Zweimal '*Muspilli*', 74–76.

36. Richard C. Payne, "Convention and Originality in the Vision Framework of The Dream of the Rood," *Modern Philology* 73 (1975–76): 329–41. Payne has shown that this genre applys to the Old English *Dream of the Rood*, and *Christ III*—a poem bearing textual similarities to *Muspilli* and probably known to the *Muspilli* author. See also Christopher L. Chase, "'Christ III,' 'The Dream of the Rood,' and Early Christian Passion Piety," *Viator* 11 (1980): 21–22.

37. Minis, *Handschrift, Form und Sprache des Muspilli*, 11–12.

38. "Sorgen mac diu sela, unzi diu suona arget / za uuederemo herie si gihalot uuerde" (6–7). The Old High German text of the *Muspilli* is from the edition by Horst Dieter Schlosser, *Althochdeutsche Literatur* (Frankfurt am Main: Fischer, 1980), 200–205. The letter "s" in majuscule emphasizes the term *Sorgen* (worry, anxiety). See Minis, *Handschrift, Form und Sprache des Muspilli*, 9. All English translations of the *Muspilli* are mine. I have also consulted the German translation by Schlosser.

39. *The Dream of the Rood*, in *The Anglo-Saxon Poetic Records* 2, *The Vercelli Book*, ed. G. P. Krapp (New York: Columbia University Press, 1932); also by Bruce Dickens and A. S. C. Ross, eds., *The Dream of the Rood*, 4th ed. (London: Methuen,1954); and Michael J. Swanton ed., *The Dream of the Rood*

(Manchester: Manchester University Press,1970); Bede's poem *De die iudicii* in *Corpus Christianorum Series Latina,* ed. J. Fraipont, *Bedae Venerabilis Opera:* Pars IV. *Opera Rhythmica.* 122. (Turnhout: Typographi Brepols, 1955), 439–44; and *Christ III,* ed. in *The Anglo-Saxon Poetic Records* 3, *The Exeter Book,* eds. G. P. Krapp and E. V. K. Dobbie (New York: University of Columbia Press, 1936). See also Payne, *Convention and Originiality,* 332; Greenfield and Calder, 19, 193–94; Lapidge, "Some Remnants of Bede's lost Liber Epigrammatum," *English Historical Review* 90 (1975), 798–820; and Kartschoke, *Bibeldichtung,* 239.

40. Kartschoke, *Bibeldichtung,* 190–92.

41.
uuanta ipu sia daz Satanazses kisindi k(i)uuinnit,
daz leitit sia sar dar iru leid uuirdit, in fuir enti (in) finstri:
daz ist re(h)t(o) uirinlih ding. (8–10)

42.
Upi sia auar kihalont die, die dar fona himile quemant,
enti si dero engilo eigan uuirdit,
die pringent (sia s)ar uf in himilo rihi:
dar (i)st lip ano to(d), lio(h)t ano finst(r)i,
selida ano sorgun: da(r nist) neoman siuh.
denne der man in par(dis)u pu kiuuinnit,
hus in himile, (dar) quimit imo hilfa kinuok. (11–17)

43.
pid(iu) ist (durft) mihhil
al(l)ero manno uuelihemo, daz in es sin muot kispane,
daz er kotes uuillun kerno tuo
enti hel(l)a fuir harto uuise, pehhes pina: dar piutit der Satanaz altist
heizzan lauc. so mac hrnckan za diu,
sorgen drato,
der sih suntigen uueiz. (18–24)

Hermann Schneider sees verse 18 ("Therefore it is necessary . . .") as a "Tonwechsel," a change in the mood of the poem. See Hermann Schneider, *Kleinere Schriften* (1962), 162–94; also *Zeitschrift für Deutsches Altertum,* 73 (1936), 1–32. Cola Minis deems lines 18–24 to be a "Moral-predigt," a moralizing sermon and an interpolation characterized by the change in rhyme structure. See Minis, *Handschrift, Form und Sprache des Muspilli,* 40. Minis notes that until verse 18, the first half of the long lines have the correct rising rhythm and the second half the correct falling rhythm. See also Friedrich Maurer, *Die religiösen Dichtungen des 11. und 12. Jahrhunderts,* 3 vols. (Tübingen: Niemeyer, 1964), 1:9–24. Exceptions are the incorrect falling rhythm in lines 3 and 5 and the missing alliteration in line 13. See Minis, *Handschrift, Form und Sprache des Muspilli,* 42. The apparent inconsistency perceived by Minis is significant when the effort to reconstruct the "original" text is abandoned in favor of the given text as documented in the codex. See Haug, *Zweimal 'Muspilli,'* 38–39. Wolfgang Mohr accurately observes that verse 18 is a signal to both the reader and listener. See Mohr, *Zweimal 'Muspilli,'* 20.

44. Heinrich Lausberg, *Handbuch der Literarischen Rhetorik* (Munich: Hueber, 1960), 145 §258: "Die amplificatio ist eine affektische (s. § 257m 203) Erscheinung." It is important to note that Lausberg deals with classical rhetorical elements. Thus, caution is warranted when examining these elements in the context of medieval texts.

45.
    uue demo in uinstri scal sino uirina stuen,
    prinnan in p(e)hhe: daz ist rehto paluuic dink,
    daz der man haret ze gote enti imo hilfa ni quimit.
    uuanit sih kinada diu uuena(ga) sela:
    ni ist in kihuctin himiliskin gote,
    uunanta hiar in uuerolti after ni uuerkota. (25–30)

46. Two working definitions derived from Chapter 1 will aid in examining these concepts and their application in the *Muspilli* and all subsequent works. 1) *Exemplary (lehrhaft)* is defined as instruction within the tradition of *imitatio* by the use of positive or negative models of conduct. These models depict the *affectus*, the spiritual, emotional and physical state of the character as the consequence of the given *actio*, the course of action taken by the character. Simplified rhetorical argument in exemplary form aims to persuade the reader and listener as learner to imitate or not to imitate the given model. The purpose of this type of argument is to lead the learner either to *conversio*, to moral change, or to affirmation of his present conduct and course of action. See Claude Bremond, Jacques Le Goff, and Jean-Claude Schmitt, *Typologie des Sources du Moyen Age Occidental: L'Exemplum* (Turnhout: Brepols, 1982), 36–38. Exemplary instruction with negative models teaches the learner by the depiction of *affectus* and *actio* to recognize error and to refrain from imitation. The negative use appears in such expressions as "to make an example of someone" and its German counterpart: "ein Exempel statuieren." 2) I define preceptive (*didaktisch*) as an explicit command that directs the learner to implement a given rule of conduct, either to follow or refrain from a particular course of action. Preceptive and exemplary components may complement each other within the teaching strategy of the poem.

47. Mohr, *Zweimal 'Muspilli,'* 18.

48. Hans-Jörg Spitz, *Die Metaphorik des Geistigen Schriftsinns* (Munich: Fink, 1972), 214.

49. Le Goff, *Purgatory,* 123. See also Eileen Gardiner, ed., *Visions of Heaven and Hell Before Dante* (New York: Italica Press, 1989).

50.
    So denne der mahtigo khuninc daz m(a)hal kipannit,
    dara scal queman chunno kilihaz:

denne ni kitar parno nohhein den pan furisizzan,
ni al(l)ero manno uuelih ze demo m(a)hale sculi.
Dar scal er uora demo rihhe az ra(h)hu stantan,
pi daz er in uuerolti kiuuerko(t) hapeta. (31-36)

51. The introduction of Germanic legal terminology has long been established. See Gustav Grau, *Quellen und Verwandtschaften der älteren germanischen Darstellungen des Jüngsten Gerichtes* (Halle: Niemeyer, 1908), 254-56; Mohr, *Zweimal 'Muspilli,'* 22; and Heinz Finger, *Untersuchungen zum 'Muspilli,'* (Göppingen: Kümmerle, 1977), 93-105.

52. Finger, *Untersuchungen zum 'Muspilli,'* 90-91.

53. Hans Planitz, *Deutsche Rechtsgeschichte*, 3d ed. (Graz: Böhlau, 1971), 82.

54. Finger, *Untersuchungen zum 'Muspilli,'* 95-99.

55. The use of the fear of hell in Old English literature to forewarn the hearer to prepare for Judgment and build character poses the question of how uniquely Carolingian is it. See, for example, homilies 10 and 15 in D. G. Scragg, ed., *The Vercelli Homilies and Related Texts* (New York: Oxford University Press, 1992), 196-213, 253-61. Scragg notes that the composition of the homilies "ranges from the later ninth to the later tenth centuries [and] must remain open" (xxxix). The *Vercelli Homilies* are probably of a later date that the *Muspilli*.

56. Rudolf Schützeichel, *Althochdeutsches Wörterbuch* (Tübingen: Niemeyer, 1974), 142. Schutzeichel offers two variations of the word: 1. ran (h) a can mean "Rechenschaft;" 2. also "Rache, Strafe, Vergeltung."

57. "Daz hortih rahhon dia uueroltrehtuuison, daz sculi der antichristo mit Eliase pagan." (37-38)

58. The interpretation by Herbert Kolb of the *hapax legomenon*: dia weroltrehtwison (37) as "die Weltrechtkundigen," *Zeitschrift für deutsche Wortforschung* 18, (1962), 88-95, is rejected in favor of "die Gelehrten" in the translation of Horst Dieter Schlosser, *Althochdeutsche Literatur,* 201; "gelehrte Männer" by Heinz Finger, *Untersuchungen zum 'Muspilli,'* 22. Finger convincingly demonstates (56-58) that Kolb's word analysis based on the so-called *Quadripartitus*, a twelfth-century Latin translation from France of the ninth-century Old English words: *witan* and *woruldricht* cannot be applied to the *Muspilli*. Schützeichel translates *weralt* as *Zeit, Zeitalter, Weltalter, Ewigkeit, Weltall, Welt, Erde* (228); *reht* as *reht, Gerechtigkeit, Rechtssache, Gebot, Pflicht, rechter Glaube, Wahrheit, das Gerechte,* 149-50. Haug translates : "die das Weltgesetz kennen," *Zweimal 'Muspilli,'* 41.

59. Minis, *Handschrift, Form und Sprache des Muspilli,* 57.

60.
    khenfun s(int) so kreftic, diu kosa ist so mihhil:
    Elias stritit pi den (eu)uigon lip,
    uuili den rehtkernon daz rihhi kistarkan
    pidiu scal imo helfan der himiles kiuualtit.

der antichristo stet pi demo altfiante,
stet pi demo satanase, der inan uarsenkan (s)cal:
pidiu scal er in deru (uuics)teti uuunt piualla(n)
enti in demo sinde siga(lo)s uuerdan. (40–47)

61. Le Goff, "L'Exemplum," 82.
62. Doh uuanit des (uilo) gotmanno,
daz Elias in demo uuige aruuartit (uuerde).
(so daz) Eliases plout in erda kitriufit. (48–50)
In regard to Elias becoming wounded in battle, see Minis, *Handschrift, Form und Sprache des Muspilli*, 59.
63. Finger, *Untersuchungen zum 'Muspilli,'* 32–45.
64. Tertullian, *De Anima (PL* 2, 735). The renowned commentary of Beatus Lièbana represents the mainstream of early medieval exegetical thought on Saint John's Apocalypse 11: 3–14, *Duo testes Dei.* See Beatus Lièbana, *Apocalipsin libri duodecim,* ed. H. A. Sanders, vol. 7, Papers and Monographs of the American Academy in Rome (1930). The mainstream of theological interpretation of Apoc. 11: 3–14 is summarized by Finger, *Untersuchungen zum 'Muspilli,'* 46–48.
65. G. Steindorff, ed., *Die Apocalypse des Elias. Texte und Untersuchungen zur Geschichte der altchristlichen Literatur*, vol. 2 (Leipzig: n.p., 1899). See also Schneider, *Kleinere Schriften,* 1–32. Hermann Schneider first noted the parallels in 1936. Four decades after Schneider's study, Hans-Peter Kursawa demonstrated a parallel between a passage from the patristic writings of Theodoret of Cyrus and the depiction of Elias's victory over the Antichrist in the *Muspilli.* See Hans-Peter Kursawa, "Antichrist, Weltende und Jüngstes Gericht in mittelalterlicher deutschen Dichtung" (Ph.D. diss., University of Köln, (Cologne: n.p., 1976), 193.
66. Cassiodorus, *Expositio in Psalterium (PL* 70, 11-1056). See Finger, *Untersuchungen zum 'Muspilli,'* 29. Finger concludes that: "Bei der im 'Muspilli' berichteten Version des Elias-kampfes handelt es sich um den Seitenzweig eines Seitenzweiges der Uberlieferung" (45).
67. der uuarch ist kiuuafanit, denne uu(i)rdit (u)ntar in uu(ic) arhapan. / khenfun stin(t) so kreftic, diu kosa ist 50 mihhil. (39–40)
See also Finger, *Untersuchungen zum 'Muspilli,'*72. Finger notes: "Der Antichrist wird im 'Muspilli' gerade in dem Augenblick als 'uuarch' bezeichnet, wo er als zum Zweikampf gerüstet erscheint. Zum gerichtlichen Zweikampf aber kann kein 'wargus' erscheinen. Der Kampf des Elias gegen den Antichristen kann daher kein gerichtlicher Zweikampf sein."
68. See Le Goff, "L'Exemplum," 27–28. Le Goff states, "In the Middle Ages, the exemplum is presented by a teacher, or more often, by a preacher whose aim is to convert, that is to say, to transform the listener himself" (46, translation mine).

69. Haug, *Zweimal 'Muspilli,'* 43.
70. (s)o inprinnan(t) die perga, poun ni kistentit
(e)nihc in erdu, aha artrukn(e)nt,
muor uar(s)uuilhit sih, suilizot lougiu der himil,
mano uallit, prinnit mittilagart;

For three renderings of line 55 compare:
1) Schlosser, *Althochdeutsche Literatur,* 203: "sten ni kistentit eiken (in) erdu uerit denne tuatago in lant."
2) Haug, *Zweimal 'Muspilli,'* 43: "(d)enni kistentit eik in erdu uerit denne (s)tuatago in lant."
3) Minis, *Handschrift, Form und Sprache des Muspilli,* 71:

denni kisten ti teikin erdu, uerit denne tuatago in lant
uerit mit diu uuiru u(i)r(i)ho uuison:
Da ni mac denne mak andremo helfan vora demo muspille.
denne daz preita uuasal allaz uarprinnit,
enti uugir enti luft iz allaz arfurpit,
uuar ist denne diu marha, dar man dar mit (e)o sinen magon piehc?
Diu marha ist farprunnan, (diu) sela stet pidungan,
ni u(ue)iz mit uuiu puaze, so u(e)urit si za uu(i)ze. (56–62)

71. Minis, *Handschrift, Form und Sprache des Muspilli,* 79.
72. Augustine, *De doct. chr.* 2.7.9–11.
73. Mohr, *Zweimal 'Muspilli,'* 18–19; see also Kartschoke, *Bibeldichtung,* 237.
74. Diu marha ist farprunnan, diu sela stet pidungan, / ni uueiz mit uuiu puaze: so uerit si za uuize (61–62). See Haug, *Zweimal 'Muspilli,'* 44. Haug translates: "Die mark ist verbrannt; die Seele steht benommen: Sie weiss nicht, wie sie sühnen könnte; so fährt sie in die Hölle."
75. Pidiu ist demo manne So guot, denner ze demo mahale quimit,
daz er rahono uueliha re(h)to arteile.
Denne ni darf er sorgen, denne er ze deru suonu qui (mit). (63-65)
76. Minis, *Handschrift, Form und Sprache des Muspilli,* 82-83; Haug, *Zweimal 'Muspilli,'* 47.
77.
ni uueiz der uuenago man, uuielihan uu(art)il er habet,
denner mit den miaton marrit d(a)s re(h)ta,
Daz der tiuual dar pi kit(arnit stentit).
(d)er hapet in ruouu rahono uueliha,
daz der man (er enti sid) upiles kifrumita,
daz er iz allas kisaget, denne er (ze) deru suonu quimit;
Ni scolta sid manno nohhein miatun intfahan. (66-72)

The weak and pitiable man, when he breaks the law through bribery, does not know who is shadowing him. (He knows not that) the devil is standing there in disguise, and is calmly noting everything, whatever evil one has ever done, so that he can present it all when he appears before the Last Judgment. For this reason, no one should take bribes. (translation mine)

78. Hans Robert Jauss, "Die klassische und die christliche Rechtfertigung des Hässlichen in mittelalterlicher Literatur," in *Die Nicht Mehr Schönen Künste,* (Munich: Fink, 1968), 159-60. In regard to the *ius talionis,* Jauss observes that the "edifying effect" does not arise out of what is represented as such, but rather from recognizing the relationship, in which the idea of divine justice manifests itself.

79. *Sermo de Symbolo (PL* 42, 1118): "Renuntiemus huic damnosae haereditati: pupilli effecti sumus. Antequam exactor veniat, tam pessimae haereditati, in qua sunt panni diaboli, pompae scilicet et angelis ejus si quis renuntiare neglexerit cum judex venerit, sicut Evangelium loquitur, tradetur debitor exactori, exactor autem debitorem in carcerem trudet." See also, for example, Scragg, *The Vercelli Homilies and Related Texts.*

80. *Sermo de Symbolo (PL* 42, 1119).

81. "Exsultabit ille adversarius in conspectu severissimi judicis, superiorem se esse clamans, agens talem causam apud talem judicem: Aequissime, inquit, judex juste, judica: Justitia et judicium praeparatio sedis tuae [Psalm 88:15]. Judica meum esse, qui tuus esse noluit : meus est, mecum damnandus est."

82. "Exspectatur enim dies judicii, aderit ille aequissimus judex, qui nullius potentis personam accipiet, cujus palatium auro argentove nemo corrumpet."

83. *Sermo de Symbolo (PL* 42, 1126) (emphasis mine). The *ius talionis* is also apparent in the acrostichon (*De civ.* 18, cap. 23.):
Judicii signum, tellus sudore madescet.

> E coelo Rex adveniet per saecla futurus.
> Scilicet in carne praesens ut judicet orbem.
> Unde Deum cernent, incredulus atque fidelis
> Celsum cum sanctis, aevi jam termino in ipso.
> Sic animae cum carne aderant, quas judicat ipse. . . .
>
> Sanctorum sed enim cunctae lux libera carni,
> Tradetur, sontes aeternaque flamma cremabit.
> Occultos actus retegens tunc quisque loquetur
> Secreta, atque Deus reserabit pectora luci.
> *Tunc erit et luctus, stridebunt dentibus omnes.* . . .
>
> Sed tuba tunc sonitum tristem demittet ab alto
> Orbe gemens facinus miserum variosque labores,
> Tartareumque chaos monstrabit terra dehiscens.
> Et coram hic Domina *reges* sistentur *ad unum.*
> Recidet e coelis ignisque et sulphuris amnis.

The Lesson of the Muspilli 75

In this instance it is those with authority: kings, princes and rulers who must stand before the Divine Judge.

84. Heinrich Fichtenau, "The Carolingian Empire, in *Studies in Medieval History*," ed. by Geoffrey Barraclough (Oxford: Blackwell, 1957), 9:1 12-117. Fichtenau refers to the critical poem of Theodulf of Orleans, *Versus contra iudices* in MGH, Poet. Lat. I, 493-517. Also see Finger, *Untersuchungen zum 'Muspilli,'* 106-111.

85. "Pro acquisitione pecuniae falsum testimonium dicis, mentiris, rapis aliena. Juras, perjuras, quae lex vetat. Cum haec omnia facis, quare non times, ne totus ardeas in aeternum?"

86. Alcuin, *De virtutibus et vitiis liber ad Widonem* (*PL* 101, 628). Alcuin notes: "Quapropter judex Deum judicem temeat, ne forte Deo judicante damnetur. Qui innocentes damnat, vel impios justificat pro muneribus; vel cujuslibet per - sonae amore vel odio (inique judicat, in Dei judicio vindictam subtinebit)." See also Roland Torkar, *Eine Altenglische Ubersetzung von Alcuins De Virtute et Vitiis* (Munich, Wilhelm Fink, 1981), 27-28, 237-38.

87. Alcuin, *De virtutibus et vitiis liber ad Widonem* (*PL* 101, 628): "Quatuor modis justitia in judiciis subvertitur: timore, cupiditate, odio, amore. Timore, dum metu potestatis alicujus veritatem (dicere vel) judicare quislibet pavescit; cupiditate, dum praemio muneris alicujus corrumpitur judex; odio, dum cujuslibet inimicitiae causa nocere alteri desiderat; amore, dum amicos vel propinquos contra justitiam defendit potentior. His quatuor modis saepe aequitas judicii subvertitur, et innocentia laeditur. Magis dolendi sunt qui opprimunt pauperes, quam qui patiuntur injuriam. Illi enim qui opprimuntur, temporalem miseriam cito finiunt: ille vero qui opprimunt eos per injustitiam, aeternis flammis deputabuntur."

88. Fichtenau, "The Carolingian Empire," 1 12.

89. *Gregorii Magni Dialogi, Libri IV,* ed. Umberto Moricca (Rome: Istituto Storico Italiano, 1924), 1-325. See Straw, *Gregory the Great,* 67-74.

90. In regard to negative models, see Le Gof f, "L'Exemplum," 49-50.

91. According to the Greek translation of Pope Zacharias from the year 654, *accepto pretio* (= crhmata).

92. *Gregorii Magni Dial.* 4.54.17-19 (Moricca, 312): "vade, et dic episcopo, proiciat hinc foetentes carnes, quas hic posuit; quia si non fecerit, die trecisimo ipse morietur."

93. "Ex qua re, Petre, collige quia hi quos peccata gravia deprimant, si in sacro loco sepeliri se faciant, restat ut etiam de sua praesumptione judicentur, quatenus eos sacra loca non liberent, sed etiam culpa temeritatis accuset" (4.53).

94. *Gregorii Magni Dial.* 4.62.10-15 (Moricca, 325): "igitur, dum per indulgentiae temporis spatium licet, dum iudex sustinet, dum conversationem nostram is, qui culpas examinat, expectat, conflemus in lacrimis duritiam mentis, formemus in proximis gratiam benignitatis, et fidenter dico quia salutari hostia post mortem non indigebimus, si ante mortem Deo hostia ipsi fuerimus." Also see *Dialogorum, Liber IV* (*PL* 77, 429).

95. Arno Borst, *Mönche am Bodensee* (Sigmaringen: Thorbecke, 1978), 56.
96. Walafrid Strabo, *De Visionibus Wettini (PL* 114, 1070).
97. Le Goff, *Purgatory,* 116-17.
98. Borst, *Mönche am Bodensee,* 54. Borst eloquently makes the point that pious manners and high office cannot offset inner failings: "In short, Wetti recognizes with horror the monastic reformers were right, that the dead abbots and benefactors of Reichenau cannot help him, that his monastic life is a failure. Neither do high-ranking offices nor does pious behavior save a person, if a person indulges in lust and self-centeredness in his heart" (translation mine).
99. Le Goff, *Purgatory,* 116-17.
100. Borst, *Mönche am Bodensee,* 48-66.
101. Strabo, *Visio Wettini (PL* 114, 1073).
102. Ibid., 1074.
103. Borst, *Mönche am Bodensee,* 54.
104. Strabo, *Visio Wettini (PL* 114, 1079).
105. Borst, *Mönche am Bodensee,* 55. Borst observes from Wetti's account of Gerold: "Er lebte und starb fast benediktinisch: für andere."
106. Norman Perrin, *Rediscovering the Teaching of Jesus* (New York: Harper and Row, 1976), 22-23.
107. Perrin, *Rediscovering,* 22. Perrin gives four examples: 1 Corinthians 3:17; 1 Corinthians 14:38; Mark 8:38; Matthew 6:15. "For if you forgive . . . your heavenly Father also will forgive you . . .If you do not forgive . . . neither will your heavenly Father forgive you." Also see Ernst Käsemann, in *Exegetische Versuche und Besinnungen* (Göttingen: Vandenhoeck and Ruprecht II, 1964), 69-82.
108. Perrin, *Rediscovering,* 151. Perrin notes this 'legalizing' effect in regard to the interpretation of Matthew 6:12 in the early Church.
109. *Sermo de Symbolo (PL* 42, 1117).
110. Grau, *Quellen und Verwandtschaften,* 254-56; also see Finger, *Untersuchungen zum 'Muspilli,'* 93-105.
111. A definition of *Symbolum* in Augustinian usage can be "Glaubensbekenntnis."
112. Theodulf of Orleans, *Versus contra iudices,* MGH, Poet Lat. I, 493-517.
113. Hans Mottek, *Wirtschaftsgeschichte Deutschlands* (Berlin: Volkseigener Betrieb, 1974), 78; also see Hans Planitz, *Deutsche (Germanische) Rechtsgeschichte,* 3d ed. (Berlin: Vahlen, 1944), 42.
114. Fleckenstein, *Die Bildungsreform Karls,* 10; Finger, *Untersuchungen zum 'Muspilli,'* 107-10.
115.
> So (daz hi)milisca horn kilutit uuirdit,
> enti sih der suanari ana(den) sind arheuit,
> der dar (s)uannan scal toten enti lepen(ten),
> Denne heuit sih mit imo herio meista,
> das ist allas so pa (ld), Daz imo nioman kip(a)gan ni mak.

The Lesson of the Muspilli 77

Denne uerit er (se d)er(u) mahalsteti, deru dar kimarchot ist:
dar uuirdit di(u suo)na, die man dar io sageta.
Denne u(a) rant engila uper (dio) marha,
uuechant deota, uuissant se dinge. (73-80)

116. Chase, "'Christ III,' 'The Dream of the Rood,' and Early Christian Passion Piety," 21.

117.
denne (scal) manno gilih fona deru moltu arsten,
lossan sih ar deru le(uuo) uaszon: (sca)l imo auar sin lip piqueman,
das er sin re(ht) alIaz kirahhon muozzi,
enti imo after sinen tatin art(eilit) uuerde. (81-84)

118.
Denne der gisizsit, der dar suonnan sca(l)
enti arteillan scal toten enti quekken.
denne stet dar umpi engilo menigi
guotero gomono: gart ist so m(ihhil). (85-88)

119.
dara qu(i)mit ze deru rihtungu so uilo dia dar ar (resti ar)stent,
so dar manno nohhein uuiht pimidan ni mak. (89-90)

120.
(dar sca)l denne hant sprehhan, houpit sagen,
aller(o) (lido) uuelihc unzi in den luzigun ui(n)ger,
uuaz er untar desen mannun mordes kifrumita. (91-93)

121. Johannis Singer, "Zu Muspilli," *Zeitschrift für Deutsches Philologie* 95 (1976): 449.

122. Singer, "Zu Muspilli," 44. Singer cites Heinrich Brunner, *Deutsche Rechtsgeschichte* (Leipzig: n.p., 1906), 254; Jacob Grimm, *Deutsche Rechtsaltertümer*, 4th ed. (Leipzig: Mayer and Müller, 1922), 3:521; and A. Quitzmann, *Die älteste Rechtsverfassung der Baiuwar en* (Nurenberg: n.p., 1866), 344.

123. Singer, "Zu Muspilli," 449. Singer notes that according to Germanic legal custom, victims of murder will testify against their murderers; this inescapability also applies to the Last Judgment: "The murder victim will also be among those at the Last Judgment, who arise from the sleep of death, *dia dar er resti arstent* (89), and as one snatched away from obscurity will, according to the old judicial custom, testify against his murderer. Where the deed, so to speak, raises up against the perpetrator, not even the omniscience of the divine judge or the perpetrator's own confession will be necessary: the Last Judgment will prove to be inescapable, for one will not be able to escape one's own deeds" (translation mine).

124. Minis, *Handschrift, Form und Sprache des Muspilli*, 87-88.

125.
Par ni is(t) eo so list(ic) man der dar iouuiht arliugan megi
daz er kit(arnan) megi tato dehheina,

niz al fora demo khunin(ge) (kichundit) uuerde,
Uzzan er is mit alamusanu fur(imegi)
enti mit fastun dio u(i)rina kipuazti. (94-98)

126. Minis, *Handschrift, Form und Sprache des Muspilli*, 97; Haug, *Zweimal 'Muspilli,'* 52; Schlosser, *Althochdeutsche Literatur*, 202.

127. uuirdit denne furi kitragan daz frono (chruchi),
dar de(r h)eligo Christ ana arhangan uua(rd).
denne augit (er) dio masun, dio er in deru m(enniski) anfienc,
dio er duruh desse mancunnes min(na) f(ardoleta) . . . (100-103)

128. Jacob Taubes, "Die Rechtfertigung des Hässlichen in urchristlicher Tradition," ed. Hans Robert Jauss, *Die Nicht Mehr Schönen Künste* (Munich: Fink, 1968), 108.

3

CHRISTIAN EDUCATION IN THE *MEMENTO MORI:* THE CALL TO JUDGMENT IN THE LATE ELEVENTH CENTURY

The *Memento Mori* is a vernacular work of religious poetry, chiefly tropological in design for the moral instruction of the learner.[1] It is a work written not for a monastic audience as an instrument of monastic reform, but rather for the immediate promotion of *conversio* and *vigilia* in a mainly aristocratic lay audience.[2] Within its eschatological context, the poem instructs the individual listener and member of the Christian community to uphold societal norms vigilantly and when necessary, to return to them by refraining from acts that imperil salvation. Although the lessons in the *Memento Mori* provided for "continual correction," they also affirmed the practice of already correct conduct, encouraged perseverance in the exercise of it and acted as a deterrent to potential error.[3]

There can be little doubt that the medieval Christian lay community generally lacked sufficient knowledge of Latin to permit its use as an instructional language. Indeed, even monks and clerics often commanded only a marginal knowledge of Latin. The religious and moral instruction of the illiterate Christian learner thus required the ongoing use of the vernacular.[4] The continual need for the edification of the major segment of learners, and among these in particular the lay aristocracy, is an indication of the continuity of a German vernacular instructional literature, if only as a meager stream, "ein schmales Bächlein," from the *Muspilli* to the *Memento Mori*.[5]

The poem, discovered in 1879 in a manuscript of Gregory the Great's *Moralia in Job*, first appeared some 800 years earlier amid the social and political upheaval of the Investiture Contest.[6] The right of the German emperor as the de facto head of both the German Church and state to invest loyal supporters as bishops with the religious and secular insignia of office[7] constituted an essential buttress of imperial interests.[8] The reform efforts of Pope Gregory VII for *libertas ecclesiae* aimed in particular at strengthening the papacy by asserting its claim to the sole right to select bishops and by forbidding the practice of imperial investiture. The excommunication of Henry IV, the election of a rival emperor, and the ensuing civil war provided large segments of the nobility with the opportunity to aggrandize its power and realize territorial aspirations at the expense of the emperor as well as of the *pauperes,* who lacked the power to defend themselves and their interests.[9] The disintegration of the traditional *ordo* undermined the efforts of Henry IV and his predecessors to establish a hereditary, dynastic rule and set centrifugal forces in motion that fostered the abuse of power and accordingly the violation of central tenets of Christian thought: *caritas, pax,* and *iustitia.*[10] The arguments of literary historians in placing the *Memento Mori* in either the papal or the imperial camp, or in a specific regional context, have not been convincing.[11] Francis G. Gentry has shown the attempt to construct a one-to-one correspondence between historical events and the *Memento Mori* has distorted rather than contributed to an understanding of the poem.[12] Accordingly, one may best examine the *Memento Mori* as a religious, pedagogical, and literary response to the violation of Christian principles within the turbulent empire of the late eleventh century.

The *Memento Mori* appears in an eleventh-century manuscript from the monastery of Ochsenhausen near the southern German town of Memmingen. The manuscript is of an earlier date than the poem, which is transcribed in compact form with strophes set off by capital letters.[13] This study retains the division of the poem by Friedrich Maurer into thematic groups of 6-(6)-6-2.[14] The author, Noker, of whom little is known with certainty but the name, was possibly a cleric or a monk, even an early abbot of the Hirsau-affiliated monastery of Zwiefalten in the Swabian Alps.[15] In any case, he appears to have had sufficient literary training and knowledge of biblical studies to execute a carefully composed religious instructional poem.[16] Noker begins the lesson perceptively:

1) Nu denchent, wib unde man, war ir sulint werdan.
ir minnont tisa brodemi unde wanint iemer hie sin.
si nedunchet iu nie so minnesam, eine churza wila sund ir sa han;
ir nelebint nie so gerno manegiu zit, ir muozent verwandelon
   disen lip.

Christian Education

Now think, men and women, what is to become of you.
you love this frailty [this life] and imagine always to be here.
however lovely it seems to you, you will have it for only
   a short while;
no matter how long you live, you [all] must die [in body].

The learner in a nonmonastic audience comprised of both women and men hears that regardless of how one loves the things of this world, one can possess them only briefly until death possesses and transforms the body itself.[17] The demand to anticipate and reflect upon the change from one's present to future condition, from one's presence in this world to one's absence after death, may have enabled the medieval learner to experience the narrative not as fiction but as immediate reality, that is, as though the transition from life to death, earthly existence to Judgment and eternity had already occurred. The immediacy of this transition could position the learner to regard his or her earthly reality *as if* it no longer existed.[18] In this mode of perception, the subsequent shock and saving terror may predispose the audience all the more to instruction:

2) Ta hina ist ein michel menegi, sie wandan iemer hie sin;
sie minneton tisa wencheit, iz ist in hiuto vil leit.
si neduhta sie nie so minnesam, si habent sie ie doh verlazan.
ich neweiz, war sie sint gevarn, got muozze so alle bewarn.

Gone are a great many, who imagined to be here always;
they loved this misery [this world], they are sorry for it today.
However lovely it seemed, they still had to leave it sometime.
I know not, whither they have gone, may God keep them all.

3) Sie hugeton hie ze lebinne, sie gedahton hin ze varne
ze der ewigin mendi, da sie iemer solton sin.
wie luzel sie des gedahton, war sie ze jungest varn solton.
nu habint siu iz bevunden: sie warin gerno erwunden.

They thought to live here, [yet] they [also] wished to travel
to eternal bliss, where they were meant to be forever.
How little they considered, whither they must go to Judgment.
Now that they have found out: they would gladly return.

The exemplary lesson in these strophes relates the error in conduct of those who love what is merely transitory and fail to consider their own transience on earth. The poem highlights the *affectus*—the sorrow, regret, and damaging persistence of the ones who erred—to persuade and move the listener not to imitate their damning conduct: "sie minnetan tisa wencheit, iz ist in hiuto vil leit." Although the sorrowful now regret their actions, it is too late. The poet as teacher and authority figure interjects in the first person that even he does not know their destination and may God protect them. This uncertainty serves to maintain anxiety in an audience already receptive to the early medieval fear of hell and possibly exposed to the more polemic varieties of the *Memento Mori* genre.[19]

To develop the lesson Noker elaborates on the error of the negative exemplary group. Those in this group thought to live in this world and to continue loving transitory things, yet they nevertheless expected eternal life. The eschatological dimension of their error becomes clear. Having thought little while on earth about the Last Judgment and the consequences for eternity, they now know and would gladly turn away from Judgment and return to this life.[20] The poet again draws attention to the *affectus* to move the audience to recognize and thereby avoid the conduct and misfortune of those who learned too late. Perhaps, too, the disorder arising from the Investiture Contest and the resulting disintegration of the empire's traditional, theocratic *ordo* imbued reference to the Last Judgment with particular relevance for the learner of the period. As salvation may depend on correct conduct and acts in the world, the emphasis Noker places on the brevity of earthly life and impending death and Judgment could combine with the apocalyptic mood of the late eleventh century to heighten the *as if* response of the learner.[21] Odo Marquard in his study of art as antifiction (*Kunst als Antifiktion*) demonstrates the importance of vsmh—the *as if* mode for the listener.[22] Within the eschatological context of the destruction of the world, he refers to the first epistle of Paul to the Corinthians (1 Cor. 7:29), where vsmh is expressed as "having as if one did not have" ("haben als hätte man nicht").[23] Marquard observes that with the two sentences: "Tempus breve est: reliquum est" and "praeterit enim figura huius mundi," Paul appeals to the Corinthians and, accordingly, to all Christians to heed the eschatological promise and prophecy that God will put an end to this world in favor of the world to come. Christians, therefore, ought to possess the things of this world in a manner as though they did not possess them, that is, they ought to lead their lives in anticipation as if this world had already ceased to exist.[24] From a pedagogical viewpoint, the

Christian listener—confronted by the resulting fear of the eschatological context—may experience the force of the narration as immediate reality and learn the rationale for accepting and implementing the lesson.[25] In accord with the continuous impact of eschatological thought on the Christian learner from the time of the early Church to the period of Gregory the Great and on to the era of Gregory VII, the audience of the *Memento Mori* was likely to be receptive to the *as if* mode.[26] The learner's confrontation with the reality of his or her own death and its eschatological dimension extends to the final three strophes [4–6] of the first group of six:

4) Paradysum daz ist verro hinnan, tar chom vil selten
   dehein man,
taz er her wider wunde unde er uns taz mare brunge,
ald er iu daz gesageti, weles libes siu dort lebetin.
sulnd ir iemer da genesen, ir muozint iu selbo die boten wesen.

Paradise is far away, and a man seldom
arrives there, who would return to bring us word,
or tell you what sort of life they lead there.
if you [all] are ever to be saved, you must become your
   own messengers.

5) Tisiu werlt ist also getan, swer zuo ir beginnet van,
si machot iz imo alse wunderliep, von ir chomen nemag er niet.
so begriffet er ro gnuoge, er habeti ir gerno mere.
taz tuot er uns an sin ende so nehabit er hie noh tenne.

This world is such, [that] whoever begins to be taken by it,
to him it endears itself all the more, so he can never be free of it.
though he understands right well, he likes it all the more.
this he does until he dies and so has neither here [this world]
   nor there [eternal life].

6) Ir wanint iemer hie lebin, ir muozt iz
   ze jungest reda ergebin.ir sulent all ersterben,
   ir nemugent is niewit uber werden.
ter man einer stuntwilo zergat, also skiero so diu brawa
   zesamine geslat.
tes wil ih mih vermezzen, so wirt sin skiero vergezzen.

You imagine to live here always, [yet] you must answer
  for your deeds at judgment. You will all die, you cannot
  escape it.
[For] a man is suddenly gone, as quickly as the blink of an eye,
I dare to say he will be forgotten just as quickly.

In strophe 6 as in strophe 1, the audience hears directly of its error: "You imagine to live here always." Strophe 6, however, aligns the error immediately with the demand for accountability at Judgment. The second half of the long line is preceptive: "You must answer for your deeds at the Final Judgment." Noker underscores the inevitability of death as the inescapable prelude to Judgment. When the final lines amplify the fleetingness of life, his assertion in the first person lends both authority and intensity to the argument: "I dare say one is forgotten just as quickly" ("so wirt sin skiero vergezzen").

Yet, in contrast to the *Muspilli,* the examined verses of the *Memento Mori* evidence less amplification of the horror of damnation. Though Noker may evoke fear and saving terror in the learner, the paraphrastic economy of the *Memento Mori* allows more scope in persuading the learner by reason.[27] Neither the fear of death and Judgment nor the torments of hell need be stated directly. The *as if* mode places the learner in the prescribed situation where he or she may experience it associatively as if earthly reality no longer existed and Judgment were at hand. And should the learner be predisposed to the lesson, the instructional use of the *affectus* can maintain a degree of saving terror to move the learner to implement the lesson, while paraphrastic economy facilitates the complementary process of persuasion by reason.

CHARITY AND THE EXERCISE OF POWER

Once the learner confronts his or her own accountability at Judgment, the use of the personal, collective *ir* form acquires a further eschatological dimension. By addressing the learner collectively as a member of a learning audience, Noker evokes the separation of humankind at Judgment into the saved and the damned. The *as if* response of the learner may then become intensified by identification with those in peril of damnation.[28] It is within this mood of heightened anxiety and fear of Judgment that the poet and teacher reveals the most serious error endangering the learner's salvation:

> 7) Got gescuof iuh alle, ir chomint von einim manne.
> to gebot er iu ze demo lebinne mit minnon hie ze wesinne,
> taz ir warint als ein man, taz hant ir ubergangan.
> habetint ir anders niewit getan, ir muosint is iemer scaden han.
>
> God created you all, you come from one man.
> He ordained [that] you dwell in this life with love,
> that you [all] would be as one man, this you have neglected
>   to do.
> If you have not done otherwise, you must pay for it forever.

To the biblical theme of the common origin of all humankind, Noker adds the universal command to live according to Christian charity.[29] He addresses the listener and learner collectively as belonging to one group characterized by one error in particular: the neglect of charity. This collective emphasis underscores both the common error and the damnation that awaits in common at Judgment. The learner may also experience the loss of the spiritual status shared by those who do practice charity and live *mit minnon*.[30] This sense of loss can complement and strengthen the fear of damnation. The learner confronts in the *as if* mode, namely, the prospect of forfeiting his or her spiritual equality with those who will number among the saved at Judgment.[31]

After presenting the fundamental lesson in strophe 7, the poet uses the exemplary strophes that follow to expand and clarify it:

> 8) Toh ir chomint alle von einim man, ir bint iedoh geskeidan
> mit manicvalten listen, mit michelen unchusten.
> ter eino ist wise unde vruot. . . .
>
> You all come from one man, [yet] you are separated
> by various skills, and by great vices.
> The one is wise and good . . .
>
> 9) . . . tes wirt er verdamnot.
> tes rehten bedarf ter armo man, tes mag er leidor niewit han
> er nechouf iz also tiuro, tes varn se al ze hello.
>
> Thus he will be damned.

The poor/powerless man needs rights, he cannot, alas,
   have them unless he pays dearly,
thus they will all go to hell.

10) Gedahtin siu denne, wie iz vert an dem ende!
so vert er hina dur not, so ist er iemer furder tot.
wanda er daz reht verchoufta, so vert er in die hella.
da muoz (er) iemer inne wesen, got selben hat er hin gegeben.

If they would only think about what will happen in the end!
[For] he must make the journey, and so he will be eternally dead.
For he has sold justice, and so he is going to hell.
Therein he must remain forever, [for] he has abandoned
   God Himself.

Strophe 8 begins by repeating the theme of the common origin from one person. This repetition accentuates by contrast the division of humankind—and the learning audience—according to abilities, wisdom and vices. It also accents the separation at Judgment according to the practice or neglect of charity in this life. The introductory lines of the strophe tell of the general state of humankind in the time that remains before Judgment. Within this eschatological framework, models of conduct as simplified rhetorical arguments can augment their power of persuasion by imbuing the lesson with a sense of urgency. The need to be vigilant in the practice of charity and to refrain from its abuse becomes immediate.

The presentation of instructional models for gaining salvation and avoiding damnation cannot, however, be rendered completely because of the *lacunae* between strophes 8 and 9. Regarding this difficulty, Gentry argues convincingly for the retention of the antithetical structure based on the plausible completion: "ter eino ist wise unde vruot" (the one is wise and good) and a conjectured "ter andere" (the other).[32] This view fits in well with the Call to Judgment that underlies the *Memento Mori* and its lessons. In the first exemplary argument, the listener hears of the man who is "wise unde vruot," presumably observes the precept of charity and lives in spiritual equality with those to be saved at Judgment. An antithetical model of conduct then follows in strophes 9 and 10. Yet before the poet describes the actions of the uncharitable man, the consequences are revealed: "tes wird er verdamnot." The announcement of the damning verdict may intensify both the *as if* reaction and the saving terror of the listener, who identifies already with those in danger of damnation. Noker skillfully maintains the narrative tension by an indirect exposition of the error. The specific act of the one who violates the precept of charity is not disclosed immediately. The learner first hears of the effects of the neglect of charity on the victim. In this case, it is "ter armo man," who does not necessarily lack financial means, but rather the power to protect his interests.[33] Thus the text positions the learner to participate in the lesson not only by anticipating the specific damning act, but also by deducing it from the narrative exposition and finally, by anticipating the damnation of the guilty in the *as if* mode. Accordingly, Noker presents the general error in strophe 7 indirectly in strophe 9 within the actual social context of the victim: "tes rehten bedarf ter armo man, tes mag er leidor niewit han, er nechouf iz also tiure." The listener learns that the "poor" man has to secure his *reht* at a high price.

The powerless person will not attain his "rights" unless he pays dearly. This does not have to refer to a monetary transaction or a barter. All that is being expressed is that the powerless are expected to render something in return for their *reht*, be that something money, goods, property, body or life and that because of this exchange they are being oppressed.[34]

The learner's understanding of *reht* stems directly from the fundamental lesson of strophe 7. Admonished for neglecting the central Christian tenet of charity, the loving of God and one's neighbor as oneself, the learner hears he or she must answer for this damning error at Judgment. The plight of the victim is clearly a consequence of the neglect of charity. Because the "poor" person is powerless, he or she must "buy" the charitable treatment—otherwise a right—at a price set by those who do have power. Thus, the text leads the learner from the effects on the victim to deduce the as yet unstated violation of charity, namely, the uncharitable exercise of power in the sale of *reht*. The poet then states the consequences of this specific form of the error unequivocally: "tes varn se al ze hello." Further, when Noker repeats the verdict of damnation at the end of strophe 9, he shifts from the third person singular ("tes wird er verdamnot") to the third-person plural.[35] Thus, all who have abused their power and are condemned for denying the powerless their *reht* are denoted collectively. Noker again confronts the learner with the accountability and separation of humankind and, in a more immediate sense, his own social group, the learning audience itself at Judgment.

Once the fear and collective risk of damnation has sharpened the listener's receptivity to affective instruction, Noker turns to the direct exposition of the error. He calls the audience's attention in the *as if* mode to the *affectus* (the spiritual, emotional, and physical state) of those who err. After he shows the plight of the victim, Noker demonstrates the impact of the error on the uncharitable themselves. The listeners hear that they have lost their spiritual orientation on the journey through this world and travel without thought of their final destination: "Gedahtin siu denne, wie iz vert an dem ende!" It is this emphatic wish that the uncharitable reflect on what awaits them, namely death and Judgment, that draws attention to their unwillingness or inability to look ahead. The text then directly reveals the consequences of such spiritual disorientation and the reason for it:

so vert er hina dur not, so ist er iemer furder tot.
wanda er daz reht verchoufta, so vert er in die hella. (70–71)

He must make the journey, and so he will be eternally dead.
For he has sold justice, and so he is going to hell.

Although eternal death and punishment lie ahead for those who sell *reht,* the person in these exemplary verses has committed the error without regard for the consequences. Thus, the text depicts him as acting contrary to reason by endangering his own spiritual welfare. Affected by his error and afflicted by sin, he has ignored norms of Christian conduct essential to salvation, namely the practice of charity and the consideration of death as a prelude to Judgment. The rhetorical force of the *affectus* to move and persuade the learner gains momentum by the juxtaposition of the damning error with the betrayal and sale of God.[36] In addition to the horror of eternal death and the anguish of hell, whoever sells *reht* is to be plagued by despair for having betrayed the only hope of salvation: "da muoz (er) iemer inne wesen, got selben hat er hin gegeben."[37] The *affectus* of the damned does not, however, require detailed description. The narrative context of judgment allows the learner to anticipate the fate of the uncharitable by way of familiar eschatological associations. Indeed, the poet's recourse to what would be familiar to his audience promotes persuasion.[38] In this manner, the economy of description can still maintain a high level of emotional intensity and saving terror, while foregrounding the appeal to reason as a combined means of moving and persuading the learner. At this point in the lesson, the preceptive verses of strophe 11 bolster the exemplary presentation of the central theme.

11) Ube ir alle einis rehtin lebitint, so wurdint ir alle geladet in
ze der mendin, da ir iemer soltint sin.
taz eina hant ir iu selben, daz ander gebent ir dien armen.
von diu so nemugen ir drin gen, ir muozint iemer dervor sten.

Lead your lives according to one form of justice, for in this
way you will all be invited to heaven, where you ought
to be forever.
[Yet] you have one [form of justice] for yourselves, the other
you practice towards the poor [less powerful].
Because of this you may not enter, you must remain outside
forever.

Noker collectively appeals in the *ir* form to the listener and learning audience to live in accord with the Christian norm of charity. Unlike strophes 7 through 10, however, where the listeners are positioned to identify with those in danger of damnation, they can now feel at one with those who might be saved. The shift in the *as if* mode from experiencing and identifying with the situation of the damned to that of the saved may bring a sudden resolution of the narrative tension by giving the learner a redeeming chance to implement the saving lesson. Thus, the experience of the damning affectation of spirit and potential damnation can be transformed into a readiness for correct conduct and a renewed hope for achieving salvation.[39] In addition, the learner may delight in recognizing the exemplary model of conduct and taking part in the *as if* mode as an active listener in a poetic work beneficial to his or her spiritual welfare. An implied pronouncement of judgment also legalizes the lesson: those who live and treat others in accord with Christian charity may expect similar treatment at Judgment. Because the listener and learning audience have power, they are obliged to exercise it charitably on the basis of a single standard for all.[40] Especially the powerless are to be granted *iustitia*, their right to charitable treatment without having to acquire it at a price. Thus, if the listeners and their kind abandon God by misusing their power for the sale of *reht*, they themselves will be abandoned by Him at Judgment and excluded from eternal happiness.[41]

The admonition at the close of strophe 11 alerts the listener to the consequences of disregarding the lesson. This reminder restores then a measure of narrative tension and saving terror to move the listener and learning audience toward *conversio*—a return to the correct practice of charity and a renewed vigilance in upholding it.

MODELS OF CONDUCT FOR THE JOURNEY

In the final major strophe group (12–17), Noker combines the lessons of the preceding two strophe groups; these encompass, namely, the view of life as a transitory journey, a pilgrimage, and preparation for judgment, and the charitable exercise of power in observing the rights of the powerless. The use of exemplary verses aims to compel the listener to recognize and experience both positive and negative models of conduct. First, the poet introduces the correct models as a means of positive orientation. A shift from the personal second-person plural form of address in strophe 11 to the third-person singular announces the exemplary character of the verses.

12) Gesah in got taz er ie wart, ter da
gedenchet an die langun vart,
der sih tar gewarnot, so got selbo gebot,
taz er gar ware, swa er sinen boten sahe.
taz sag ih in triwon, er chumit ie nohwennon.

Blessed is he, that ever he was born and who thinks
of the long journey, and
prepares himself as God Himself ordained,
so that he is ready, whenever he may encounter
His messenger [of death].
This I can say with certainty, He will come sometime.

13) Nechein man ter ne ist wise, ter sina vart wizze.
ter tot ter bezeichint ten tiep, iwer nelat er hie niet.
er ist ein ebenare, nechein man ist so here,
er nemuoze ersterbin, tes nemag imo der skaz ze guote werdin.

No man is so wise, [that] he knows when his journey will be.
Death signifies the thief, he will not let you stay here.
He [death] is the great leveller. No man is so mighty,
that he does not have to die. [for] riches cannot save him.

14) Habit er sinin richtuom so geleit, daz er vert an arbeit,
ze den sconen herbergon vindit er den suozzin lon.

des er in dirro werlte niewit gelebita, so luzil riwit iz in da.
in dunchit da bezzir ein tac, tenne hier tusinc, teist war.

> If he has used his wealth in such a way, that he journeys
> [in death] without care to the beautiful dwellings, he
> will find the sweet reward.
> Had he never lived in this world, he would scarcely regret
> it there.
> A single day will seem better to him there, verily, then a
> thousand days here.

Noker portrays the blessed man who thinks of the purpose of life's journey, lives accordingly, and is prepared for death and Judgment. He epitomizes, therefore, the correct orientation toward life in accord with reason, that is, Christian norms of conduct as prerequisites for salvation. The divine affirmation at the beginning of strophe 12: "Gesah in got taz er ie wart," highlights the correctness of the exemplary figure's spiritual state and conduct. Thus, the learner hears how reason manifests itself in the conduct of the person whose journey through life is at once a preparation for death. Noker's personification of death as a messenger announcing humankind's final journey is far removed from the descriptions of corporeal decay found in many Latin texts of the period and later vernacular works.[42] Indeed, as God's messenger, death serves an immediate eschatological function by bringing everyone to judgment and, ultimately, eternal bliss or punishment. In the three exemplary verses of strophe 12, it is to be the blessed man who is spiritually prepared. In the final verse of the strophe, Noker suddenly breaks the flow of the narration just as death itself breaks the flow of life: "I am saying this in truth, he is coming sometime." This interjection interrupts the *as if* response of the listener to call to mind and accentuate any discrepancy between the blessed man's and the learner's own spiritual condition.[43]

In strophe 13, a further description of death underscores the urgency of following the blessed man's example. Noker again takes up the theme of being unable to know when the final journey will begin. Not even a wise man can say with certainty. Death is then personified as a thief, a term designed to restore narrative tension and saving terror in a twofold manner. It steals not only life, but worldly treasures as well separating them from their owners without regard for their power and social position. This is particularly effective in reaching listeners who are themselves the powerful and profit from the "sale" of *reht*. Noker then abruptly shifts to the second-person form of address. He confronts the listener and learning audience with the uncompromising statement that they, too, will be taken: "iwer nelat er hie niet." ("he will not let you stay here" translation mine). The final personification of death as a leveller of all social degrees, *ein ebenare*, continues to focus directly on the wealthy and powerful. Wealth, *der skaz*, offers no protection from death. Death ensures the equality of everyone before God, where one must account for one's life and performance of charity irrespective of one's former station in life. In accord with the teaching strategy of the poem, the leveler theme as well as the entire depiction of death must needs serve to move and persuade the listener to correct those errors which immediately endanger salvation. These are the lack of forethought about death and imminent judgment and, the damning neglect of charity, in particular, in the double standard of justice that only grants the powerless their rights for a price. Nowhere does Noker advocate social equality within a new or revised social order as a necessary correction and condition for the listener's salvation. On the contrary, he appeals expressly to the powerful and wealthy to exercise their power by recognizing the claim of everyone to equal charitable treatment within the existing order. Because the grave error of violating the precept of charity is rooted in self-love as the *radix malorum*, it has priority of correction. The resulting errors imperiling the listener are an outgrowth of the lack of charity first stated in strophe 7. The correction of the uncharitable use of power in the sale of *reht* is then complemented by that of the uncharitable use of wealth. In the preceptive verses: "taz eina hant ir iu selben, daz ander gebint ir dien armen," the correction begins by admonishing the listeners to give of their wealth in such a fashion that they continue to maintain themselves while aiding those of lesser power and means. Thus, Noker clearly excludes a call to radical poverty, since it would destroy the material base required by the listeners to follow the given precept. Further, there is no inconsequence in not specifying exactly how much should be given. The poet leaves the decision to the listeners for he simply instructs them to use some part of their wealth in the spirit of charity, *mit minnon*.[44]

The transition from strophe 13 to 14 reveals a shift from the narrative tension evoked by wealth as a worthless deterrent to death to the release of tension by wealth as a means to salvation. If the exemplary figure in strophe 14 gives of his wealth so that it yields a sweet bounty of charitable acts in this life, he will be given a commensurate sweet reward, *den suozzin lon*, in the next.[45] The implied pronouncement of judgment provides the listener with a "legalized" condition for his or her salvation. Noker seeks to convince the listener that the given conduct is valid by emphasizing the rewarded man's *affectus*—his lack of grief in having left this world as well as his joy in heaven. As a result, the listener may identify out of admiration with the rewarded man and be disposed to imitate in the redeeming use of wealth.[46] Amplification conveys the urgency in observing the given condition.

15) Swes er hie verleibet, taz wirt imo ubilo geteilit.
habit er iet hina gegebin, tes muoz er iemer furdir lebin.
er tuo iz unz er wol mac, hie noh chumit der tac.
habit er is tenne niwit getan, so nemag er iz nie gebuozan

Whatever he neglects to do here, will be repaid to him in full.
If he has given something, he will live forever because of it.
May he do [give] as much as he can, the day is coming still.
If he has not done this by then, he will never be able
    to make amends.

Drawing the audience away from the joyful depiction of the reward and back to the necessity of choice, the shift in the narration redirects attention to create a momentary break in the approbatory identification with the positive model. The resulting distance allows the listeners to recognize their own peril and the immediacy of using their own wealth correctly.[47] Furthermore, the narrative direction in strophe 15 alternates from a negative model of conduct to a saving one and back again. The force of persuasion in this form of argumentation lies in a binary system, where only one alternative is provided to damnation, namely, salvation achieved by the practice of charity in the proper disposition of wealth.[48] Thus, the sequence of identification, break in identification, and reidentification heightens the narrative tension and may dispose the listener to resolve it by the imitation of the positive exemplary models. The poet ends the strophe on a note of unresolved tension in the reminder that the day of death and Judgment is still to come: "hie noch chumit der tac." The tension between the fear of damnation and the expectation of potential salvation may move the listener, therefore, to heed the lessons and act while time remains.[49] The final two strophes of the group (16–17) return to the theme of life as a journey and man as *viator.*

16) Ter man ter ist niwit wise, ter ist an einer verte,
einin boum vindet er sconen, tar undir gat er ruowen,
So truchit in der slafta ta, so vergizzit er dar er scolta;
als er denne uf springet, wie ser iz in denne riwit.

A man is not wise, if upon a journey he finds a lovely tree,
under which he goes to rest, for sleep so deceives him there,
he forgets where he should be going; and when he arises,
how greatly then he regrets it.

17) Ir bezeichint allo den man, ir muozint tur not hinnan.
ter boum bezeichint tisa werlt, ir bint etewaz hie vertwelt.
diu vart diu dunchit iuh sorcsam, ir chomint dannan obinan.
tar muozint ir bewindin, taz sund ir wol bevindin.

You all signify the man and you [all] must journey thither.
The tree signifies this world and you have dallied here
  somewhat.
The journey seems arduous to you, [but] since you come
  from up there
[Paradise, God], you must return. That you will discover
  well enough.

The poet, in the exemplary verses of strophe 16, clearly presents his listeners with a negative model of conduct, where the traveler neglects to use the journey through life wisely and awakens with bitter regret: "wie ser iz in denne riwit." The contrast with the saving model of the rewarded man, who has no regrets, is evident (strophe 14): "so luzil riwit iz in da." Strophe 16 further sustains the narrative tension from the previous strophe to dispose the listener to an even greater degree to resolve it. The simplified rhetorical argument admonishes the listeners to remain watchful, *vigilare,* while passing through this world. The image of sleep conveys this admonition *ex negativo:* "Sleep, thus, deceives him there, and he forgets where he should be going."

Noker then abruptly shifts from the third-person singular in the verses of strophe 16 to the collective *ir* form in strophe 17. This shift interrupts the *as if* mode, to transfer the identification with the previous model of damning conduct to the listener's own immediate spiritual condition. It is unmistakably a collective identification: "ir bezeichint allo den man, ir muozint tur not hinnan." Once reminded of death and the call to Judgment as the common destination, the listeners learn the metaphorical significance of strophe 16 in direct relation to themselves and those like themselves—the powerful who neglect charity and risk damnation.[50] And though this world has detained them and they have squandered their time, they still have to come to their journey's end whether prepared or not. The closing verse of strophe 17 appeals directly to the listener and learning audience to turn, *convertere*, to the proper course for salvation: "tar muozint ir bewindin." The lessons have shown the paths to damnation and salvation, and have attempted to persuade and move the listener to choose wisely. Of course, the decision whether to follow the correct path is for the listener to make. Yet, it is far from being a random one. According to the teaching strategy of the poem, the balanced presentation of rational arguments together with an underlying current of saving terror may largely determine the choice. Still, the immediate necessity of choosing is at once an impetus to act. Noker takes a further measure to assure the correct response by evoking the self-imposed collective control of the listener and learning audience as representatives of the Christian community and, in particular, of a privileged, lay community of power and wealth. This form of control may have proved especially effective as a legitimation of power—an issue which at the time of the *Memento Mori* it is of prime importance amid the Investiture Contest in the German Kingdom of the late eleventh century.[51]

The remaining strophes, possibly a later addition, contribute little to the lessons of the main three strophe groups and serve mainly as an epilogue.[52]

18) Ja du vil ubeler mundus, wie betriugist tu uns sus
du habist uns gerichin, des sin wir allo beswichin.
wir neverlazen dih ettelichiu zit, wir verliesen sele unde lip.
also lango so wir hie lebin, got habit inns selbwala gegebin.

Yes, you wicked world, how you tempt us.
you have given us riches, because of this we are all deceived.
If we do not leave you sometime, we will lose body and soul.
So for as long as we live here, God has given us a choice.

19) Trohtin, chinnic here, nobis miserere!
tu muozist uns gebin ten sin, tie churzun wila, so wir hie sin,
daz wir die sela bewarn, wanda wir dur not hinnan sulen varn.
fro so muozint ir wesin iemer, daz machot all ein Noker.

Lord, glorious king, be merciful to us!
Grant us understanding in the short time we are here,
that we save our souls, for we must journey thither.
May you be joyful always, all this Noker has written.

After repeating central themes of the poem, Noker reaffirms that the audience has been given the choice, *selbwala,* of acting in its own spiritual interest while on earth. Strophe 19 is then a plea to God that the listeners may also receive the understanding to use their brief time well for the salvation of their souls.[53]

The teaching objectives in the *Memento Mori* as in the *Muspilli* are to guide the listener and learner to *conversio* in correcting errors that immediately endanger salvation, and to foster *vigilia* in upholding norms of Christian conduct, especially Christian charity. In contrast to the ascent to wisdom and purification in the *Muspilli* with its emphasis on mounting amplication, culminating in the cathartic response of the listener, the teaching strategy in the *Memento Mori* stresses a balanced presentation of rational arguments and controlled emotional intensity. Within a framework of simplified rhetorical arguments in exemplary form, the *Memento Mori* aims to persuade and move the listener by appealing to reason as well as by eliciting various degrees of saving terror. Thus, *affect teaching* may predispose the listener to the imitation or rejection of exemplary models of conduct by virtue of whether or not the exemplary character acts in accord with reason, that is, the observance of prescribed norms of Christian conduct as a means of meriting salvation. The *affectus* of those in danger of damnation may be especially persuasive when strengthened by collective identification within the listener's own social group.[54] In addition, the context of impending death and the Call to Judgment may intensify the listeners' experience of the separating of the uncharitable as the potentially damned from the saved. For this reason, the sudden breaks in identification and the release of narrative tension provide the listeners with the necessary distance to the narration to assess their spiritual condition. And the momentary shock effect may compel the audience as members of a specific segment of the Christian community, the powerful lay nobility, to note any correspondence or lack of it between the given exemplary model and itself. This awareness of differences and similarities is a first step in a process of reflection that accompanies the implementation of the lessons of the *Memento Mori.* Noker further heightens the shock effect by interrupting the listeners' experience of recognizing and participating in the poetic

Christian Education

representation of the potential reality of damnation and salvation in the *as if* mode.

The balanced presentation evidences the controlled use of textual dynamics: the alternating shift in the listener's identification with positive and negative models of conduct together with the resulting evocation, release and restoration of narrative tension. This alternation could enable Noker to teach by *affectus* to persuade and move the learner both by reason and saving terror in a complementary fashion. Thus the dynamic quality of the narration plays an integral part in achieving the teaching objectives of the lesson by simulating the consequences of damning and saving conduct and perhaps disposing the learner to choose correctly and then act.

The chapters that follow examine concepts of learning and teaching in works which encompass the theme of Judgment from the early twelfth century until around 1170. We will look at how strategies of persuasion aimed to guide listeners to Christian edification, and ultimately, to the practice of conviction.

NOTES

1. For a discussion of the practical effect of tropological meaning on the believer, particularly in the sermon, see Freitag, *Die Theorie der allegorischen Schriftdeutung*, 35.
2. Heinz Rupp, *Deutsche religiöse Dichtungen des 11. und 12. Jahrhunderts*, 2d ed. (Bern: Franke, 1971), 261–95. See also Francis G. Gentry, "Noker's Memento Mori and the Desire for Peace," *Amsterdamer Beiträge zur Älteren Germanistik* 16 (1981): 37; and Erich Auerbach, *Literatursprache und Publikum in der lateinischen Spätantike und im Mittelalter* (Bern: Franke, 1958), 115.
3. Karl F. Morrison, *The Mimetic Tradition of Reform in the West* (Princeton: Princeton University Press, 1982), 160–77. In examining the history of mimesis in the West, Morrison speaks of the evolution of the idea of continual reform and the mimetic strategy for conversion from the period of Hincmar of Reims to the time of Gregory VII.
4. Auerbach, *Literatursprache und Publikum in der lateinischen Spätantike und im Mittelalter*, 215; Rupp, *Deutsche religiöse Dichtungen des 11. und 12. Jahrhunderts*, 275–77.
5. Rupp, *Deutsche religiöse Dichtungen des 11. und 12. Jahrhunderts*, 283.
6. Gentry, "Noker's Memento Mori," 52–62; see also Francis G. Gentry, "Vrout . . . Verdamnot? Memento Mori, vv. 61–62," *Zeitschrift für Deutsches Altertum und Deutsche Literatur* 4 (1979): 297–306. The poem discovered by K. A. Barack is designated as Barack, Nr. 1076. See *Bibliographie zur frühmittelhochdeutschen geistlichen Dichtung*, ed. Francis G. Gentry (Berlin: Erich Schmidt, 1992), 191.
7. Hauck, *Kirchengeschichte*, 3: 677.
8. Ibid., 784–86.
9. Karl Bosl, "Potens und Pauper: Begriffsgeschichtliche Studien zur gesellschaftlichen Differenzierung in frühformen der Gesellschaft im frühmittelalterlichen Europa," *Frühformen der Gesellschaft im frümittelalterlichen Europa* (Munich: Beck, 1964), 106–34.
10. Norbert Elias, *Der Prozess der Zivilisation*, 2d ed., 2 vols. (Bern: Francke, 1969), 2:131; Gentry, "Noker's Memento Mori," 45–53 and 60–62. See also Rudolf Schützeichel, *Das alemannische Memento Mori* (Tübingen: Niemeyer, 1962), 1–147; "Justitiam vendere," *Literaturwissenschaftliches Jahrbuch, Neue Folge* 5 (1964): 7.
11. Hugo Kuhn, "Minne und reht," *Dichtung und Welt im Mittelalter*, 2d ed. (Stuttgart: Metzler, 1969), 105–11. See also Gert Kaiser, "Das Memento Mori. Ein Beitrag zum sozialgeschichtlichen Verständnis der Gleichheitsforderung im frühen Mittelalter," *Euphorion* 68 (1974): 337–70.
12. Gentry, "Noker's Memento Mori," 35–36.
13. Marlies Dittrich, "Der Dichter des Memento Mori," *Zeitschrift für Deutsches Altertum und Deutsche Literatur* 72 (1935): 58.

14. Friedrich Maurer, *Die religiösen Dichtungen des 11. und 12. Jahrhunderts*, 3 vols. (Tübingen: Niemeyer, 1964), 1:249.
15. Dittrich, "Der Dichter des Memento Mori," 65–67. See also Gentry, "Noker's Memento Mori," 25.
16. Noker's accomplishment may be contrasted with the "miraculous" *paraphrasis* of biblical verse into Germanic heroic verse by an untrained Caedmon. Noker's work is a select composite of biblical themes designed for instructional purposes within the medium of vernacular literature. A list of possible themes and excerpts incorporated by Noker appears in Karl Bertau's *Deutsche Literatur in europäischen Mittelalter*, 2 vols. (Munich: Beck, 1972), 1: 213. The theme of simony is, however, unlikely. See Gentry, "Noker's Memento Mori," 32, 46.
17. Gentry, "Noker's Memento Mori," 37.
18. Odo Marquardt, "Kunst als Antifiktion," in *Funktionen Des Fiktiven*, ed. Wolfgang Iser (Munich: Fink, 1983), 38–39.
19. Gerhild Scholz–Williams, *The Vision of Death: A Study of the "Memento Mori" Expressions in some Latin, German, and French Didactic Texts of the 11th and 12th Centuries* (Göppingen: Kümmerle, 1976), 12–13. See also Jacques Le Goff, *The Birth of Purgatory*, 116–17; Arno Borst, *Mönche am Bodensee*, 54–56; Walafrid Strabo, *De Visionibus Wettini* (*PL* 114, 1070–79). See also Gentry, "Noker's Memento Mori," 38–39.
20. In "sie warin gerno erwunden" (strophe 3) Lexer translates "erwinden" as "zurückkehren, –treten," that is, as to turn back, return.
21. Gentry, "Noker's Memento Mori," 53.
22. Marquard, "Kunst als Antifiktion," 36–51.
23. Ibid., 39. Marquard refers to the passage (I Cor. 7:29–31): "Hoc itaque dico, fratres: 'Tempus breve est: reliquum est, ut et qui habent uxores, tanquam non habentes sint: et qui flent, tanquam non flentes: et qui gaudent, tanquam non guadentes: et qui emunt, tanquam non possidentes: et qui utuntur hoc mundo, tanquam non utantur: praeterit enim figura huis mundi."
24. Ibid. In Paul's appeal to the Corinthians, Marquard views the *as if* mode (der Modus des Als-ob; vsmh in relation to the Christian anticipation of the eschatological end of the world (die Vorwegnahme der eschatologischen Weltvernichtung).
25. Ibid., 40.
26. Alois M. Haas, *Todesbilder im Mittelalter*, 101–11, 118.
27. Gentry, "Noker's Memento Mori": "Although there can be no doubt that the individuals to whom Noker is referring will suffer eternal torment, he does not state it directly. That is a feature of the first part of the 'Memento Mori'. Although the topic is the death of the body and the salavation of the soul, Noker does not indulge in drastic, black/white depictions of heaven and hell. He avoids hyperbolic descriptions of the deceptive joys of the world and the terrors of eternal punishment. He is presenting general theses about the meaning of existence taken from traditional theology. It is not his main purpose to stir up the

emotions of his listeners, to frighten them into a better life, but rather to appeal to their reason" (38).

28. Wilfried Kettler, *Das Jüngste Gericht* (Berlin: De Gruyter, 1977). Kettler comments on the separation of humankind at Judgment in regard to the centrality of Matthew 25:31–46.:

> Für die frühmittelalterlichen eschatologischen Dichtungen ist wie für die althochdeutschen die biblische Darstellung des Jüngsten Gerichtes in Matt. 25,V. 31–46 *die* zentrale Quelle. Immer wieder treffen wir auch in ihnen auf Vorstellungen, die aus diesem Bibeltext entnommen sind.

For the early medieval eschatological poems and, as it were, the Old High German ones, the biblical depiction of the Last Judgment in Matthew 25:31–40, is the central source. Again and again we encounter images in them taken from this biblical text. (2.4.5)

29. Gentry, "Noker's Memento Mori," 40–41.
30. Norman Cohn, *The Pursuit of the Millennium* (New York: Oxford University Press, 1971), 183–86.
31. This prospect must not be construed as a question of social equality. See Gentry, "Noker's Memento Mori," 34–37.
32. Gentry, "Noker's Memento Mori," 42–43. See also Gentry, "Vruot . . . Verdamnot?" 299–306.
33. Karl Bosl, "Potens und Pauper," 106–34.
34. Gentry, "Noker's Memento Mori," 46–47.
35. Ibid., 47.
36. Schützeichel, "Justitiam vendere," 7. The theme of selling God is not, however, related to simony in the *Memento Mori*. The theme serves instead to intensify the narrative tension in predisposing the listener to be receptive to the lesson.
37. The theme of the despair of the damned in hell is rendered associatively in the *Memento Mori* as compared to the explicit depiction in the *Muspilli*.
38. Averil Cameron, *Christianity and the Rhetoric of Empire: The Development of Christian Discourse* (Berkeley and Los Angeles: University of California Press, 1991). Cameron, in speaking of early Christianity, comments on one aspect of the nexus between pedagogy and rhetoric as follows: "An answer to the question of how this pedagogic action (for the reproduction of Christianity's own ideas) was achieved in rhetorical terms might well be found by looking along the same lines as those observed by anthropologists studying political rhetoric in other traditional societies. I shall argue, therefore, that Christian discourse too made its way in the wider world less by revolutionary novelty than by the procedure of working through the familiar, by appealing from the known to the unknown" (24–25). See also 40–41.
39. Hans Robert Jauss, *Ästhetische Erfahrung und literarische Hermeneutik* (Munich: Fink, 1977), 1:147. Although the release of narrative tension in the shift from strophes 10 to 11 in the Memento Mori is not specifically catharsis,

the text aims to move the learner towards the *imitatio Christi*. In commenting on "das geistliche Spiel" of the twelfth century, Jauss observes that the cathartic experience is not purgation, but rather the transformation of the aroused emotions (*Affekte*) into a dispositional readiness to follow Christ: "Die hier geforderte kathartische Erfahrung ist nicht Reinigung, sondern Verwandlung der aufgerührten Affekte in die Gemütsbereitschaft zur Nachfolge Christi" (47).

40. Gentry, "Noker's Memento Mori," 49.

41. An implied "eschatological judgment pronouncement" to legalize the lesson is also evident when we view power as legal jurisdiction. The listeners who misuse their power in the sale of *reht* also misuse their jurisdiction and authority as judge. Thus, their conduct would be rewarded or punished commensurately in what was perceived to be a legal act. For comments on the early medieval perception of the Last Judgment as a legal proceeding and judicial gathering see Kettler, *Das Jüngste Gericht*, 380. Though Noker makes no explicit mention of a gathering (*Versammlung*) at the Last Judgment, this does not preclude an appeal to the listeners' feelings of collectivity with their own social group.

42. Scholtz-Williams, *The Vision of Death*, 12–13, 40.

43. For a discussion of the importance of the interchange between narrative distance, 'Distanznahme,' and identification, see Jauss, *Ästhetische Erfahrung*, 221. Jauss highlights in particular the back and forth motion, "die Hin-und-her-Bewegung," of the listener in testing him/herself in relation to the fate of the 'other': "das Erproben seiner selbst am vorgestellten Schicksal des anderen, macht das eigentümliche Vergnügen am Schwebezustand einer ästhetischen Identifikation aus" (221).

44. Gentry, "Noker's Memento Mori," 50–53.

45. Friedrich Ohly, "Geistige Süsse bei Otfried," *Schriften zur mittelalterlichen Bedeutungsforschung* (Darmstadt: Wissenschaftliche Buchgesellschaft, 1977), 93–127. We can also trace the influence of the theme: "geistige Süsse" to the "sweet reward" in the *Memento Mori*.

46. Jauss, *Ästhetische Erfahrung*, 220, 231–37.

47. Ibid., 221.

48. Niklas Luhmann, "Über die Funktion der Negation in sinnkonstituierenden Systemen," *Positionen der Negativität*, ed. Harald Weinrich (Munich: Fink, 1975), 201–18. Luhmann discusses the use of a binary schema wherein a given position posits only one alternative which can be dismissed as erring.

49. For a discussion of the difference between the "historical" and the "Christian" experience of time in early Christianity, see Gerhard Hergt, "Christentum und Weltanschauung," *Terror und Spiel*, ed. Manfred Fuhrmann (Munich: Fink, 1971), 357–68. Accordingly, the Fathers of the Church could experience "their immediate reality as (the) eschatological present." Luhmann notes: "Für den Christen gibt es wohl Zeiten, aber keine Zeit" (358). The Augustinian perception of time is also applicable to the medieval period: "tempora sunt tria, praes-

ens de praeteritis, praesens de presentibus, praesens de futuris." *Confessiones,* 11.20.

50. Gentry, "Noker's Memento Mori," 52.
51. Ibid., 53–62.
52. Maurer, 1:249–52. Also see Gentry, "Noker's Memento Mori," 53.
53. Kettler, *Das Jüngste Gericht,* 212, 215–16. See also Psalm 50 (51), *Peccatoris paenitentis confessio, promissio, preces.*
54. Karl Schmidt, "Über das Verhältnis von Personen und Gemeinschaft im früheren Mittelalter," *Frühmittelalterliche Studien* 1 (1967): 225–49. See also Walter Ullmann, *The Individual and Society in the Middle Ages* (Baltimore: Johns Hopkins University Press, 1966), 48–49.

4

PERSUASION AND PEDAGOGY IN THE WORKS OF FRAU AVA

The early twelfth-century poems of Frau Ava are comprised, when taken together, as one *oeuvre*,[1] in that the poems evince a unified pedagogical thrust based on the *ascensus* pattern, whereby the learner's purifying ascent to wisdom culminates in the last poem of the series, *Das Jüngste Gericht.* The concepts of learning and teaching that convey the call to Judgment in Ava's work were influenced by the rise of twelfth-century spirituality. Indeed, as we have seen, the *Memento Mori* at the end of the eleventh century gives evidence of a heightened responsibility for neighbor and charitable service in the world.[2] This practice was but one expression of the new "concern for neighbor" characteristic of the religious revival of the early twelfth century.[3]

In her study *Docere Verbo Et Exemplo,* Caroline Walker Bynum reveals similar and differing expressions by examining twelfth-century treatises of spiritual advice to determine the "monastic and canonical senses of vocation."[4] She shows that the regular canons viewed the Christian responsibility for neighbor differently from the new monastic orders. The canons were clergy who saw Christian service to others as "an obligation to edify."[5] They perceived themselves and the community they served as both givers and receivers of edification. Bynum observes: "Regular canons elaborate the idea of literal imitation of patterns of behavior and see in the offering of example *coram Deo, coram hominibus* a way of loving God and serving humankind."[6] Monks, however, did not regard the edification of others as a goal of their vocation, although they did at times perform pastoral duties.[7] The representatives of the new monasticism, in particular the Cistercians, saw themselves as learners in the search for God. Love of neighbor was chiefly an emotional identification with the conduct (*exemplum*) of others in their community. Their example then provided an "emotional catalyst" to affect the spiritual life of the individual learner.[8] Bynum concludes:

> The Cistercian understanding of example as affecting heart and will is in striking contrast to the canonical conception of example as pattern. Whereas the canonical idea focuses the reader's attention outward, toward horizontal relationships between people, the Cistercian idea turns attention inward, toward emotional and psychological development, and upward, toward the vertical relationship between human beings and God.[9]

THE ACTIVE AND CONTEMPLATIVE LIFE

We can answer the question as to the role Ava played within the framework of early twelfth-century spirituality by examining her religious status. Her name appears in numerous necrologies as Ava *inclusa* for the year 1127.[10] A study of the religious institution to which Ava belonged has been made by Otmar Doerr, and in his work, *Das Institut der Inclusen in Süddeutschland,* he calls attention to the rules that governed this institution.[11] The most renowned of these is the *Regula Solitariorum* of Grimlaicus, which enjoyed a continual reception from the ninth to the fifteenth century.[12]

The daily routine of the recluse encompassed not only the contemplative life, but the active life as well.[13] In Chapter 8, *Quid sit proprie activa, quidve contemplativa vita,* Grimlaicus defines both ways of life. He begins with the active life that teaches how to give guidance and show Christian love to those who live within the religious community.[14] As such, the active life advocates the exercise of charity, the giving of instruction and the correction of error:

> The active life itself distributes bread to the hungry person, teaches the word of wisdom to the ignorant person, corrects the erring person, recalls the proud person to the way of humility, takes care of the sick person. It hands out to each of these what they require and carefully provides for the transgressors in so far as they are able to take it.[15]

Grimlaicus now turns to the contemplative life, which focuses on the learner's relationship with God in transcending the material world out of the desire for heaven.[16] Although the contemplative life will ultimately supersede the active life, both are complementary and necessary for the spiritual growth of the recluse.

> From these [lives but] one [life] is signified; the one by Martha is the active, the other by Mary is the contemplative: [and] yet Martha is indeed a relative of Mary.[17]

After stating the duties of the recluse to provide pastoral care, Grimlaicus takes up the theme of teaching by example.[18] In chapter 21, *Ut solitarii lucis exempla omnibus dent*, references to the authority of Paul, Gregory the Great, and Jerome stress the importance of this traditional form of instruction. Those who choose the life of the religious recluse were to shine as examples of virtue to others:

> These, however, who put examples of virtue to the fore, as well as light through a life lived well, who demonstrate the preached word to others, are rightly called "lamps."[19]

Although Grimlaicus's rule is dedicated to a priest, "venerabili sacerdoti," pastoral care was not the exclusive domain of the clergy.[20] Doerr notes that women who led the religious life of a recluse were often active in the care of souls.[21] In addition, the *inclusa* advised people of varied walks of life and social rank.[22] It can be stated with some degree of certainty, therefore, that Ava's work was in large measure an expression of the *activa vita* and her concern for the spiritual welfare of her fellow human beings.

Richard Kienast has examined the source material that Ava used in her work to express her particular spirituality. In his *Ava-Studien I*, Kienast points out that each of the poems in Ava's text stems from various sources commensurate with its genre: *Johannes* and *Das Leben Jesu* as "epic narratives"; *Die Sieben Gaben des Heiliges Geistes* as a tractate, and *Der Antichrist* and *Das Jüngste Gericht* as prophetic-visionary literature.[23]

In her study *Die Gedichte der Frau Ava, Untersuchungen zur Quellenfrage*, Eoliba Greinemann both affirms and refines Kienast's observation.[24] In so doing, she shows that the source material suggested by him evidences many similarities with literary genres found in the liturgy.[25] In fact, the important role of the liturgy and liturgical literature in the life of the recluse lends credence to Greinemann's findings.[26] She thus argues that Ava's major source material stems from liturgical pericopes.[27] Yet Greinemann is careful to note that Ava does not always adhere to the standard chronological order of lections. Instead, Ava deals selectively with the source material as an expression of major feast days in the liturgical cycle. And although Ava's poems, in particular, *Das Leben Jesu,* do exhibit a liturgical dimension that contributes to an understanding of specific passages and the work as a history of salvation, the reliance on pericopes alone cannot fully explain the teaching strategy in Ava's poems or the rhetorical means of persuasion at work in them.[28]

In analyzing the major poem of the series, *Das Leben Jesu,* Greinemann calls attention to the graduated instruction—Stufenlehre geistlichen Lebens—in the section entitled *Die Gaben des Heiligen Geistes.*[29] In accord with Kienast, she notes the similarity of Ava's seven-step ascent pattern with that of Augustine.[30] Although Greinemann conjectures that Ava may have been familiar with Augustinian sermons, especially *De sermone Domini in monte,* both she and Kienast accurately observe that direct dependence on Augustinian texts as immediate source material cannot be established.[31] Thus, it is on the basis of traditions of learning and teaching that we may seek further evidence for the influence of the *ascensus* pattern as a unifying pedagogical and poetic force in Ava's work.

Johannes

In the series of four poems written between 1120 and 1125, Ava seeks to instruct and delight her listeners with a poetic rendering of the history of salvation. The first poem, *Johannes,* portrays the life of John the Baptist as a *figura* of Christ and a transitional figure from the Old to the New Testament.[32] Greinemann makes the important observation that Ava's treatment of the annunciation and birth of the Baptist, his public ministry, and martyrdom, differ proportionally from that of Luke. Of all the Gospel authors, only Luke provides a history of the events surrounding the Baptist's birth (Luke 1:5-25; 26-38; 39-56; and 57-80). This account is more than twice the number of verses dedicated to the public ministry of the Baptist (Luke 3:1-20; 21-22; 7:18-23, 24-35). Only two

Persuasion and Pedagogy

verses recount his death (Luke 9: 7-9). In contrast, while Ava's account of the annunciation and birth of the Baptist is proportionally greater in length than the remaining accounts, she also provides an extensive narration of both his public ministry and martyrdom.[33] Greinemann notes that the liturgical celebration of the Baptist on the feast days of his birth (July 24), and death (August 29), highlights two aspects, namely, his function as a precursor in the history of salvation, and the positive example of his character.[34] This fits in well with the pedagogical thrust of the lesson.

At the outset of the poem, the listeners immediately learn both aspects. After Ava has introduced the Baptist's aged parents, Zacharias and Elizabeth (13-14), she tells of the precursor:

in ir alter si gewan   den aller grozzisten man,
der was ze ware   gotes vorloufare.
er was ein herhorn des himeles   unde ein vaner des ewigen
    chuniges. (33-38)

In their old age, they received
the greatest man of all,
[the man] who truly was God's precursor.
He was a herald of heaven and a standard bearer of the
    eternal king.

The listeners next experience the annunciation of the Baptist's birth to Zacharias, whereby angelic authority affirms the Baptist's virtuous traits:

niht nefurhte du dir,   ze ware ich sage iz dir,
du solt einen sune gewinnen,   des sich manige mendent.
wines trinchet er niht   unde von diu trunchenhait gesciht.
ze ware sage ich dir daz,   sin tugent ist alse Helyas.
du solt des gewis sin: Johannes ist der name sin. (51-60)

Be not afraid, [for] in truth I say to you, you will have a son,
[and] because of him many people will be glad.
He will neither drink wine nor take part in drunkenness.
In truth I say to you; his fame will be like [that of] Hellas.
Of this you may be certain: John will be his name.

Because of his lack of faith in the angelic message (65-66), Zacharias is punished by the loss of speech (67-72). Ava thus instructs her listeners in both the fear of God and the need for piety—the initial steps in the ascent to wisdom.

As a parallel to the annunciation of the Baptist's birth, the poem turns to the annunciation to Mary (137-52). In contrast to the doubting Zacharias, Maria acknowledges her faith in God and goes to dwell with Elizabeth until the birth of John.[35] The poem then emphasizes the exemplary character of both mothers: "There dwelt the good [and] purest of mothers" (163).[36] Maria's absolute faith in God remains highlighted as her central virtue: "I have no doubt about God. I believe in His power over young and old" (154-56).[37] After the Baptist's birth and circumcision, and doubting Zacharias' regaining of speech by the intercession of the Holy Spirit, the poem recounts the exemplary character of the Baptist himself. Paraphrastic amplification in strophes 14 and 15 accentuates the account: "One reads [and hears] of John, the holy man . . . " ("Man liset von Johanne, deme heiligen manne").[38] The general subject one (*man*) in strophes 14 and 15 then shifts to the first-person plural form of address, *wir*. This shift evokes a collective identification that unites both the author and audience as members of an edified Christian community. Ava now directs the communal attention of the learning audience to the words of the Baptist:

> Wir lesen von Johanne,   deme heiligen manne:
> er gie in der wuoste,   di menige er troste.
> er sprach: "swer mit der riwe   besuochet gotes triwe,
> dem nahent waerliche   diu himeliscen riche." (233-40)

> We read [and hear] of John, the holy man:
> he went into the desert, [and] gave solace to a great many.
> He spoke [thus]: "Whoever seeks God's love with repentance,
> to him the kingdom of heaven draws near."

This theme of repentance sets the tenor of the first poem to predispose the listener to the correction of his or her own error and to vigilance in preventing its reoccurrence.

As would be expected, Ava depicts the child Johannes as exemplary in seeking consolation and strength in God:

> Nu wuohs daz chint, daz ist war, unz iz chom vur ahte jar.
> do huob er sich in die wuoste, got nam er ze troste.
> daz was ein michel wunder an eineme jungen chinde,

> niewan daz in erliuhte der gotes scin, daz iz wol mohte
> sin. (195-202).
>
> Now when the child had grown to be eight years old,
> he set out into the desert, [and] took courage in God.
> It was a great wonder in a child so young,
> that he wanted only to be illuminated by God's light.

Johannes also struggles to control the desires of the flesh by the practice of ascetic discipline (203-6). In sharp contrast, the listener hears of the lascivity of King Herod:

> Herodes was ein ubel man, ich waene in lusten began
> sines bruoder wibes minne, daz waren unsinne. (295-98)
>
> Herod was an evil man, I [Ava] think he began to desire
> the love
> of his brother's wife. That was a foolish thing.

By the affective teaching in these antithetical models of conduct, the listeners may learn, therefore, how Herod subjects reason to erotic passion while John upholds the rule of reason and bridles sensual desire. The final strophe of the poem depicts the Baptist joyfully entrusting his soul to God in the face of his impending death (427-30). Ava then affirms the validity and blessedness of John's conduct and concludes by underscoring his role as a helper to the Christian listener and learning audience: "ane alle rede ze ware/uns ein helfare" (445-46). The correct spiritual orientation enables John to serve God and humankind, bear the ultimate witness of martyrdom, and merit the praise of the angels in heaven and of all Christendom. Once Ava has concluded the example of the Baptist's purifying ascent to wisdom and holiness—and perhaps disposed her listeners to repentence and renewed resolve, she provides the lessons of the major poem of the series, *Das Leben Jesu*.

THE PRACTICE OF CHARITY

At the beginning of *Das Leben Jesu,* Ava recapitulates the themes of the annunciation, the mission and witness of John the Baptist, and the machinations of Herod. This repetition not only maintains thematic continuity and forms a narrative bridge, it also recalls and reinforces the positive and negative models of conduct already presented. After the reintroduction of positive models, Ava elaborates on the negative model of Herod: "He was the son of eternal death" (208). The audience hears how Herod abuses his power and office to plot against the Christ child as a potential rival and threat to his kingship. In contrast, the appearance of an angelic messenger to the wise men affirms their saving and meritorious conduct. The poem thus shows the force of reason, the power to decide to learn God's will and act in accord with it, to be deficient in Herod. In doing the devil's bidding, he is himself deceived:

> Do si do gebeteten,   eine naht si sich enthabeten,
> ein sconer engel in erscein,   er zeiget in einen anderen
>   wech hine heim,
> daz si niene chomen hine widere   ze dem ungetriuwen chunege,
> der mit sinem liste   wolde slahen Cristen,
> der sich gezechinet hat   an des tieveles getat,
> der alle die wirret   unde vil vlizechlichen irret
> di der ze guote gent   unde sin dienest bestent. (283-96)

> Because they [the Magi] prayed, they remained for the night,
> [and] a beautiful angel appeared to them. He showed them
>   another way home,
> [so] that they would never return to the deceitful king,
> who by way of his cunning wished to slay the Christians,
> [and] who subjected himself to the devil's work; [for]
> [he, the devil] brings confusion to all those [like Herod],
> and diligently leads many astray who have given themselves
>   to [his] work, and have done his bidding.

The exemplary verses of this strophe (27) are then reinforced by the preceptive verses of strophe 28. The interjection of the author and teacher, Frau Ava, is at once a signal to the aristocratic listener to take particular note of the lesson to follow:

> Lieben mine herren,   des scult ir got flegen, daz wir den
>   vermiden,   so wir heim ilen. (298-300)

> My dear lords, you ought thus to beseech God, that we may
>   avoid that one [the devil], so [that] we will hurry home.

Persuasion and Pedagogy 111

Addressing those who do exercise power, *lieben mine herren,* Ava admonishes them to orient themselves toward God, so that they, too, may be led safely as were the wise men, and not astray as was Herod. Ava's use of the *wir* form evinces a collective and communal appeal to members of an aristocratic audience and the Christian community:

so megen wir mit gesunde   chomen heim ze lande
hin ze paradyse   uzer dirre freise. (301-4)

For in this way we can journey home to the [heavenly] land,
to paradise [and] away from this horrid danger.

When the narration resumes and relates Jesus' baptism in the Jordan (438-39), the listeners learn of the major antithetical models of Christ fasting in the desert and of Satan his tempter. In the exchange between Satan and Christ, the magisterial replies of Jesus offer counter-instructions to the devil who is the ultimate model of evil conduct and spiritual misorientation:

. . . der tievel want ob er in des genote,
daz er ime ouch mer volgete   an deme ime wol behagete.

Do antwurte ime do got,   di heiligen scrift er ime do bot:
"es newirt ouch niht al ein genote   gefuort mit deme brote
der lip noch diu sele,   sunder sie frout diu gotes lere,
diu von gotes munde get,   vil saelich ist der si verstet." (482-92)

The devil thought that if he could compel Him
    (to change stone into bread),
that He would become his follower from that time on,
    [and] that would please him well.

God then answered him by way of the Holy Scriptures:
"Neither the body nor the soul shall be tempted by manna,
instead they delight in the divine teachings,
which come from the mouth of God; blessed is he who
    understands them."

Jesus' final replies to Satan are expressly preceptive in tone: "You should not tempt the Lord your God at all, [and] thus you will surely be damned."[39] The poet complements and intensifies this initial defeat of Satan, "da wart der tievel gescendet" (526), by the actual subjection of the devil during Christ's triumphal harrowing of hell (strophes 160 and 161). Ava amplifies the picture of the devil being bound as an introduction to the theme of penance. The listeners hear how Christ casts down the "hellhound" and forces its mouth to remain open: "er leit ime einen bouch in sinen munt" (1752). Those who come into the grasp of his jaws because of their sins may escape by way of penance:

> daz der freisliche hunt niht geluchen mege den munt,
> daz er in durch bihte unde durch buoze sines undanches
>   muozze lasen. (1757-60)

> [So] that the horrid hound may not close its mouth,
> [and] would have to release him from his accursedness
> through confession and through penance.

After the scenes of Jesus' temptation in the desert, the narration continues the ascent toward the Crucifixion, Resurrection, and Ascension. As Ava recounts Jesus' miracles, it is the restoration of the blind man's sight (strophes 91 and 92) which particularly emphasizes the transformation of the healed into witnesses for Christ. Yet, the failure to bear perfect witness to Christ underscores the need for continual penance. Judas Iscariot's premeditated betrayal finds its complement in Peter's triple denial of Christ (strophes 127, 128, 137, 138). Peter's insistence on his unshakable loyalty only magnifies his failure (strophe 138):

> der hane iesa crate, Peter sich verdahte,
> waz er habete getan, do ilt er weinende danne gan.
> mit biterme sere so chlaget er iz iemer mere. (1487-92)

> As soon as the cock had crowed, Peter thought about
> what he had done, [and] he hurried forth weeping.
> With bitter anguish he lamented it evermore.

The figure of Peter as the rock on which the church was founded further demonstrates the need for continual vigilance.[40] His failure to keep awake on the Mount of Olives illustrates this point for the listeners. Jesus admonishes Peter:

Persuasion and Pedagogy 113

er sprach: "Peter, trut min,   du newil niht wachende sin
eine luzel wile;   wie harte si ilent,
die mich gebent sciere   in die hende der sundare." (1387-92)

He spoke: "Peter, my dear [friend], you do not care to keep watch for [even] a short while; how eager they are to deliver me into the hands of the sinners."

Prior to the account of the capture, trial, and crucifixion of Jesus, the listeners learn God's central precept to his disciples:

Zuo zin choset aver got: "iz nist nehein merre gebot,
denne daz ir iuch underminnet, also ich iuch han geminnet.
doch nist nehein merre minne vone wibe noch vone manne,
danne man durch sines vriuntes not den lip gebe in den tot.
daz han ich durch iuch getan, daz sult ir vor iuweren ougen han." (1319-28)

To the chosen God declared: "there is no greater command than that you love one another as I have loved you. For there is no greater love of a woman or a man, than [when] one gives one's life out of love for a friend. This I have done for you, [and] you ought to keep it in mind."

Ava clearly places the precept of charity into an exemplary context—the sacrifice of one's life freely out of love for a friend. The preceptive verse, "daz sult ir vor iuweren ougen han" (1328), stresses the immediacy of the precept. Hearing how Christ suffers for their sins in their place, the listeners may not principally experience the *gloria passionis*,[41] Christ's triumph over death and sin, but rather the supreme act of charity performed for their benefit:[42]

Daz criuce si gestahten,   sine hende si im gerahten.
da wurden vier nagele   durch Cristen geslagene;
durch sine hende,   daz *laid er* durch unser sunde;
durch die fuoze sine,   daz wolt er durch unsich liden.
    (1605-12, emphasis mine)

They made firm the cross, [and] they raised him by his hands.
Four nails were driven through Christ:

[both] through his hands—this he suffered for our sins,
[and] through his feet—this he chose to suffer for us [in our place].

The dialogue between the two thieves crucified on either side of Christ further accentuates the act of charity in these exemplary verses. After Christ has granted the good thief's wish to be remembered,[43] the bad thief mockingly replies:

> Do sprach der ander scachman: "diu rede was ubel getan.
> mohte er iemer frum wesen, so waere er selbe genesen."
> des antwurte ime sare der guote scachaere:
> "swaz so ich lide, daz ist umbe min sunde.
> daz er lidet den tot, des netwinget in nehein not
> wan sin einvaltigiu guote durch des menscen note." (1637-48)

> Then the other thief spoke: "The speech was ill made!
> [For] had He always been honest and god-fearing, He would be saved himself."
> The good thief answered him thus:
> "whatever I suffer in this way, it is because of my sins.
> [But] that He suffers death—nothing compels Him
> other than His simple kindness towards the plight of humankind!"

These simplified rhetorical arguments in exemplary form aim to move and persuade the listeners to confession and penance and thus to the practice of charity. The poet augments the force of *compunctio* through saving terror in the image of escaping the hellhound's jaws "durch bihte unde durch buoze" (1759). She then illustrates Christ's charity in the redeeming of those who loved God from hell:

> "ich han durch iuwere not erliten einen grimmechlichen tot.
> die mich habent geminnet, di wil ich fuoren hinnen." (1769-72)

> "I have suffered a horrible death because of your plight.
> [All] those who have loved me I wish to lead forth from here."

The listeners' ascent to purification and wisdom continues from the account of the resurrection to Jesus' appearance before the disciples in the sealed room (strophes 181-92). After a brief account of the ascension, the narration remains focused on the upper room where the Holy

Spirit brings the fear of God and the concomitant gifts of understanding, strength of expression, good judgment, and the power of reason: "er brahte in forhte jouch guote gewizzen, sterche, rat unde vernunst" (2150-51). The qualities which the Holy Spirit imparts do not remain abstract or theoretical in expression. The poem translates them into practice. That is to say, the seven gifts of the Holy Spirit were to be used for the benefit of others—*ad utilitaten*.[44]

The listeners discover, then, that the recipients of the divine gifts immediately teach their saving wisdom to others: "vil rehte si lerten" (2160). Furthermore, the new wisdom transforms the teachers themselves (2172-74). Their success in converting others to wisdom from error is then confirmed by an interjection from Frau Ava:

an dem anderen tage,   also ich vernomen habe,
du becherten si an der stunt   mere denne driu tusunt,
manne unde wibe,   got hete gesterchet die sine. (2179-84)

On the following day, as I have heard told,
they converted in [but] an hour more than three thousand
men and women. [For] God nourishes [strengthens] his own.

The final strophes of the poem, *Das leben Jesu*, briefly recall the negative exemplary figure of Judas Iscariot, *der trugenare*, as they inform the listeners that Matthias has taken his place. And to heighten the contrast, Ava makes known the command of Peter to the faithful disciples:

daz si solten ilen,   tihten unt scriben,
die cristenheit leren   de vita unseres herren. (2195-98)

that they should make haste to put [their belief] into words and
on to paper, [and] to teach the Christian belief in the life
of our Lord.

As Ava introduces the positive exemplary figures of the four evangelists, her listeners hear how each figure bears witness to the life of Christ by recording it and thereby providing instructional material for conversion. In the accounts of Matthew and John eschatological references appear; the *evangelicum* of Matthew encompasses the Last Judgment:

Matheus bublicanus   der dihtote alsus,
der guote hirte,   vone gotes geburte.
er zalt uns vil rehte   Cristes geslahte
von anegenge unze jungist,   er screip liber generationis. (2209-16)

Matthew the Publican wrote in this way
of the good shepherd and of the birth of God.
He told us rightly of Christ's ancestry
from the Creation to Judgment Day;
[for] he wrote the *liber generationis.*

After the gospel of John, the listeners hear of the Apocalypse:

da sah er menegiu wunter,   diu screip er besunter.
des muget ir sin vil gewis,   er screip ein buoch deist a
    pocalypsis. (2249-52)

There [in the heavens] he saw many wonders,
[and] these he wrote down one by one.
[For] of this you may be certain;
he wrote a book called the Apocalypse.

The main body of the *Das Leben Jesu* ends with the exemplary figure of Peter teaching the *Evangelicum* and furthering conversion during his tenure as bishop in Antioch and Rome.

The strophes 210 to 218, known as "The Seven Gifts of the Holy Spirit," provide Ava's listeners with a recapitulation and a catalogue of Christian virtues given by Jesus to his disciples (strophe 197). The beginning and end of the cycle of virtues, coming from and leading back to God, is the fear of God:

Unser fleiskich erde   diu sol getemperot werden
mit dem geiste der forhte,   also er uns vor worte,
wil er unsich iteniuwen: so leitet er unsich ze der heiligen riuwe.
diu sol uns leren,   wie wir got sulen phlegen. (2279-86)

Our earthly abode of flesh must be tempered
By the Spirit through fear [of the Lord].
For just as He promised us, He wishes to renew us:
thus He leads us to blessed penance.

Persuasion and Pedagogy

[For] it will teach us, how we ought to revere God.

Fear of God as the beginning of all wisdom (Psalm 110:10) leads to regret for sins committed and eventually to other saving virtues. Again, the expression of these virtues is not theoretical, but practical in nature, through the observance of the precept of charity:

> Ein gebe vil tiure diu misket sich zuo unserem fiure.
> daz ist geist der guote, der zuntet unser gemuote,
> daz iz uf zuo gote get, also daz fiur in siner nature gestet.
> daz bringet uns froude unde gedingen, daz wir den nahisten minne. (2293-2300)

A gift most precious which becomes part of our fire:
this is the Spirit of Goodness, which lights our minds and hearts,
so they may ascend to God, [and] the fire remains within them.
This [gift] brings us joy and hope, so that we may love [our] neighbor.

And it is the saving virtue of reason, *spiritus intellectus,* as the correct orientation to God (2357-72) that fosters charity as a bulwark against ungodly teachings (strophe 218). The negative exemplary figure of the Antichrist in the poem that follows *Das Leben Jesu* is thus in sharp contrast to Christ's disciples who manifest the seven gifts of the Holy Spirit. As a result, Ava's listeners may clearly perceive the conduct of the Antichrist as the direct antithesis to that of the virtuous.

Furthermore, the beginning of "The Seven Gifts of the Holy Spirit," implies a collective and communal identification between the virtuous original recipients of the seven gifts and the learning audience itself:

> Nu sculen wir bevinden in dirre heiligen gotes minne,
> wie sich der geist von der hohe misket in unser brode;
> wie er her nider zuo uns gat, alse diu gescephede gestat
> an dem libe unde an der sele, daz wellen wir iuch leren.
> nu tuot uf die inneren oren, diu uzeren sulen iz horen. (2269-78)

Now we ought to discover in this blessed love of God
how the Spirit from on high shows concern for our weaknesses;
how He came down to us, for [His] work brings succor
to the body and to the soul; these things we wish to teach to you.

Now open your inner ear [your hearts and minds],
[that] your outer ear may hear them!

Preceptive verses direct the listeners to take to heart the lessons which follow (2277-78).[45] But it is the identification of the listeners as fellow recipients, with the disciples, of the seven gifts that allows for a direct confrontation in the *as if* mode with the Antichrist and imbues the eschatological poems of the series with additional narrative intensity.

In the final strophe of "The Seven Gifts of the Holy Spirit," the poet recalls that the fear of God, is the beginning and end of wisdom. This reminder serves both to amplify and strengthen the given instructional pattern. More precisely, Ava is describing the seven gifts of the Holy Spirit as a seven-step pattern of ascent to wisdom and purification. As such, it is not a "theologisch dogmatischer Traktat" as Kienast has conjectured.[46] And, unlike Augustine's emphasis on faith at the sixth level (*De doct. chr.* 2.7.11), Ava stresses the use of reason as an instrument of meditation and a means of ascending to the seventh and final level:

So bringet uns diu vernunst zuo   daz heizet meditacio.
diu leret denne,   daz wir got erchennen.
So beginnen wir in minnen   mit liehteme sinne;
so haben wir das lutere gewizede,   daz ist daz reine herze.
    (2381-88)

So reason perfects us—it is called meditation.
It teaches so that we may know God.
For in this way we begin to love Him with an enlightened mind;
And so we have a clear conscience,
[for] that is purity of heart.

Thus Ava provides a pattern that is compatible with her religious vocation as *inclusa*. Greinemann observes that the virtues associated with the seven gifts point to a "cloistered milieu."[47] She further notes that the arrangement of the gifts forms two groups. The first group comprises *timor, pietas, scientia,* and *fortitudo,* and corresponds to the virtues of the *vita activa.* The second group consists of *consilium, intellectus,* and *sapientia* and corresponds to the *vita contemplativa.*[48] We may view Ava's use of the ascent pattern, therefore, as an expression of Grimlaicus's *Regula Solitariorum* in leading both an active and a contemplative life. Yet, in respect to the active life, Ava's edifying works extend beyond the

Persuasion and Pedagogy 119

"klösterliches Milieu," for she clearly addresses an audience comprised at least, in part, of members of the nobility who will have exercised some degree of power and influence in the world.[49]

THE PRACTICE OF VIGILANCE

In the twelve strophes of *Der Antichrist,* Ava next offers the learning audience a lesson that may be given separately, yet when considered in the context of the entire work as a history of salvation, provides an extension of the previous lessons and a narrative transition to the concluding poem of the series, *das Jüngste Gericht.* And, as we will note, Ava continues to rely on traditional concepts of learning and teaching. By identifying, for instance, with the disciples and recipients of the Holy Spirit, the listener and learning audience may confront the approaching reign of the Antichrist as members of one community: "In dem jungisten zite so nahet uns des Antechristes riche" (1-2). The first two strophes state that the Antichrist will overthrow the existing order and take possession of the entire world. Particularly moving for Frau Ava's aristocratic audience may have been the *as if* experience of the disintegration of familiar administrative and judicial units amid a universal struggle for power. The resulting chaos is an eschatological portent for the listener to take heed:

So stent uf al geliche   mit gestrite diu riche.
nehein lant ist so chleine,   man nemuoze in denne teilen.
marche unde bistuom,   grascefte unde herzochtuom
daz teilet man chleine,   iz niezent zwene oder dri vur einen.
mit grimme unde mit sere,   so stet iz darnach iemer mere. (9-18)

For all kingdoms alike rise up in struggle.
No land is so small, that one does not have to divide it.
Margravate and bishopric, earldom and dukedom—[these]
One carves up thoroughly, until two or three are there
   instead of one.

Ava, in the next three strophes, makes a collective appeal to the listener to respond to the impending danger as a vigilant community.[50] Preceptive verses clearly emphasize the constant necessity of vigilance in achieving salvation:

So hevet iuwer houbet unde iuwer hende, so nahet uns diu
    ware urstende.
so sul wir alle unseren herren   vil innechlichen flegen,
daz wir in dem wige   niht verlazen an dem ewigen libe. (27-32)

So lift up your head and hands, for the true resurrection
    draws near.
Thus we all should beseech our Lord devotedly,
[so] that we do not neglect the battle for eternal life.

Throughout the entirety of der *Antichrist,* the poem aims to maintain the listeners' identification with a vigilant community. Consequently, the final strophes 6-12 present the learning audience as a united front against the Antichrist. And, apart from the biblical admonition of Elias and Enoch (strophe 7), the initial warning in strophes 1 and 2 is complemented by the exemplary verses that demonstrate qualities antithetical to the Seven Gifts of the Holy Spirit. The poem thus alerts the listener and learning audience, *ex negativo,* to the real nature of the Antichrist and his apparent miracles. Those who lack the correct orientation to God are deceived by false signs: "So beginnet er zeichenon, si wanent er si gotesun" ("For he begins to give signs, [that] they believe he is the son of God") (87-88). The listeners then learn that the reign of the Antichrist is to be four and one half years, and will bring terrible persecution to all Christians (111-12). The persecution ends with the fall and death of the Antichrist precipitated by his fatal spiritual error of *superbia:* "sin ubermuot in vellet, der tot in bechrellet" (115-16).

The teaching objectives in der *Antichrist* are twofold: to dispose the listeners to vigilance in upholding the virtues imparted by the Holy Spirit to the community of the faithful, and to enable them to recognize the deceptions of the Antichrist. Ava undertakes, therefore, to prepare her learning audience to withstand the final onslaught of Satan and the reign of his representatives before the Second Coming and the day of Judgment. Accordingly, the teaching strategy of the poem is to emphasize the collective identification of the audience with the virtuous community of the saved by confronting it with the conduct and threatening reign of the Antichrist. Thus, the instructional juxtaposition of positive and negative qualities not only accentuates the differences but also encourages the learners to preserve Christian qualities—in particular, the gifts of the Holy Spirit that enable them to remain within the saved community.

THE CALL TO JUDGMENT

The major theme in *das Jüngste Gericht,* Ava's final poem of the series comprising "dizze buoch," is the call to Judgment. Ava relates the culmination of salvation history in thirty-four strophes, of which the first seventeen recount the signs that are to precede the Second Coming of Christ and Judgment day. The use of the entire first part of the poem to teach the portents of the Last Judgment serves the pedagogical aim of predisposing the listeners to the major lessons of the second half. Thus, hearing what each of the fifteen days and their corresponding signs bring, and how those awaiting judgment, *wib unde man,* react, the listeners may experience heightened narrative tension. In fact, Ava does not hesitate to evoke a tone of salutary terror together with the hope of salvation at the outset of the poem:

Nu sol ich rede errechen   vil vorhtlichen
von dem jungisten tage,   als ich vernomen habe,
unde von der ewigen corone,   die got gibet ze lone
swelhe wole gestriten   an dem jungisten zite. (1-8)

Now I am bound to tell [one by one]
of the last days most fearful, as I have heard told,
and of the eternal crown [of life],
that God shall grant as a reward
to whomever has fought well in the final time
   [before Judgment].

After the poet affirms in the first-person singular that her narrative is founded on sources, "als ich vernomen habe," and affirms the importance of fighting the good fight as the criterion for salvation, she begins the actual account of the fearful signs. Ava does so by a general reference to authority, and by commentaries from which she has learned of the events that herald the coming of Judgment:[51]

Finfsehen zeichen gescehent,   so die wisten jehent.
wir nevernamen nie niht mere   von so bitterme sere.
so bibenet allez daz der ist, so nahet uns der heilige Crist. (9-14)

Fifteen signs [portents] shall occur, for so say the wise.
[And] we will never again hear of such bitter suffering.

For everything there is shall quake, when the Holy Christ
draws near to us.

The learning audience can experience in the *as if* mode the imminent Parousia—the Second Coming of Christ. In this case, each successive strophe introduces a new portent bringing the listeners another day closer to Judgment. During the first three days the listeners hear how the waters of the earth decrease, and then swell and flood the earth. In the fourth strophe Ava shifts to the collective *wir* form and addresses her audience with the personal, collective *iu:* "On the second day—we must tell you [all], . . . "(23-24). In this way, Ava fosters the listeners' identification with the potentially saved, her community of the faithful, while teaching them lessons beneficial to their salvation.

Beginning with the fifth strophe, Ava gradually makes use of *affect teaching* to acquaint her listeners with the reactions of those who face imminent destruction; all who are present, *wip unde man,* to witness the terrible signs feel sorrow for what will be lost as the Last Judgment, *daz urteile,* draws near (31-38). The listeners further experience how the cries of sorrow intensify as the signs of the fourth, fifth, and sixth days foretell the end of the world. The chaotic behavior of fish and fowl, the turning of the sky blood red, and wonders regarding the sun and the moon all serve to promote the fear of God.

The first differentiation in the *affectus* of those experiencing the portents of Judgment appears on the seventh day (67-80). For when the winds rage on this day, the pitiable, unrepentant sinner whose conscience tells of the loss of God's favor will rage in fear and sorrow: "so grimmet sich ze ware der arme suntare . . ." (77-80). Thus the plight and error of the sinner in these exemplary verses may evoke in the listeners a brief identification with the group of the potentially damned. And strophes 10 and 11 do not dispel this identification. It is in this frame of mind, therefore, that the listeners could learn of the eighth and ninth days. The inability to stand and seek refuge as the earth begins to quake serves to heighten the anxiety (81-88). The ninth day, too, amplifies the theme of inescapable judgment. The interjection of the author in referring to her sources lends emphasis to the account:

> An dem niuten tage, alse ich vernomen habe,
> brestent die steine, daz gescihet vor dem urteile. (89-92)

On the ninth day, as I have heard told,
Stones will burst asunder—[for] this is to happen before Judgment.

Yet, on the tenth day, the poem restores the identification with the community of the potentially saved (strophe 12). In addressing an aristocratic learning audience already predisposed by salutary terror to affirm its place among the saved, Ava prescribes the correct and saving response to the ruin of castles as symbols of vainglory. A signal for the restoration of the listeners' saving identity is the reintroduction of the collective *wir* form of address in conjunction with a theme of particular relevance to aristocratic listeners:

An dem zehenten tage,   vil luzel sul wir daz chlagen,
so zevallent die burge,   die durch ruom geworht wurden.
berge unde veste   daz muoz allez zebresten.
so ist got ze ware   ein rehter ebenaere. (97-104)

On the tenth day, we should complain very little [of these things],
for the castles built by fame will fade away.
[and] mountains and fortresses—they all must crumble.
For God is truly a just leveler.

By upholding the correct, saving orientation to God, namely, by acting in accord with reason and wisdom, the listeners need not be troubled by the loss of worldly acclaim and power at the approaching day of Judgment. Indeed, the former seats of power and privilege are of no importance before the Judge and their loss does not warrant lamentation. By leveling the castles and fortresses as portents of the tenth day before Judgment, God, as *ein rehter ebenaere*, is the just leveler in testing the faith of everyone, regardless of their former social status.

Strophe 13 and the sign of the eleventh day amplify and underscore the importance of the correct orientation to God and the things of this world. Ava admonishes her listeners as members of the potentially saved community to be unperturbed when gold, silver, and precious objects are destroyed—among these things, the "clasps and brooches, the jewelery of the women" ("nusken unde bouge, daz gesmide der frouwen") (111-12). Again, it can be said with some certainty that Ava is addressing an aristocratic audience. Not surprisingly, even the material wealth of the Church is no longer required, and it too will pass away. Indeed, all that has been fashioned by humankind must perish. Ava exhorts her audience in the personal collective *ir* form to take heed of the transitory nature of the world: "know that it is true, it passes away and turns to dust and ash" (118).

On the twelfth day both domesticated and untamed animals run about wildly, collide, and bellow. The panic of the animals and the unnatural phenomena augment the fear of God and impending Judgment. The narrative tension increases as the graves open and the dead come forth to be judged on the thirteenth day. No witness to this event is likely to be unmoved. The poem, in the final two lines of the strophe, emphasizes the *affectus* of those who have not done penance for their sins: "It is dreadful for all of those, who know they are guilty of sin" (133-34). The result of unperformed penance is exclusion from the saved. Saving terror may strengthen, then, the listeners' resolve to perform necessary penance and remain within the community of the potentially saved, especially while they witness the plight of the impenitent in the *as if* mode.

The fourteenth day brings the most bitter lament. The poem powerfully amplifies the *affectus,* the spiritual, emotional, and physical state of all those who know they are afflicted with sin and have not done penance:

si wuofent unde weinent   mit luteme gescreige.
in dem selben dinge   so zergent in die sinne. (139-42)

They grieve and weep with loud lamentation.
[And] at the same time, in truth, they lose their minds.

Thus, the cries of the terrified who are still alive on the day before Judgment demonstrate the consequences of the loss of the correct spiritual orientation. They no longer possess the ability to act in accord with reason, that is, to perform penance and gain hope of salvation.

The fifteenth day arrives as the harbinger of death: "so nahet uns der gotes slach" (148). The audience, perhaps already disposed by affect teaching to avoid the error of unrepented sins, learns what must occur before appearing at Judgment:

so sculn alle die ersterben,   die der ie geborn wurden,
alle gemeine   vor dem urteile. (149-52)

Thus all shall die, who ever were born,
all alike before Judgment [Day].

The listeners may then experience in the *as if* mode the final destruction and purification of the world by fire, and the arrival of Judgment within "the wink of an eye."

With strophe 17, the first half of the poem comes to an end, as does the history of salvation itself. *Affect teaching* and textual dynamics complement the pedagogical use of escalating narrative tension in effectively alternating the listeners' identification between the saved and the damned. The linear flow of the salvation history depicted in the fifteen signs and the fifteen days provides a simplified rhetorical vehicle that carries the listener toward Judgment. Thus, Ava endeavors to predispose her listeners to the culminating lessons of the four poem series.

The second half of the poem begins appropriately with the actual Parousia. The rhetorical repetition of the verb *chomen,* starting at the beginning of strophes 17, 18, 19, and 20 denotes the final moment before Judgment and aims to increase the already high level of narrative tension. Christ is preceded by the four evangelists, who awaken the dead. And, though the listeners hear that "the good shine like the sun," the depiction of the angels bearing the cross and crown to the appointed site of Judgment serves to heighten the narrative tension and maintain saving terror. Ava then confronts her audience with the arrival of Christ in might and majesty. The emphasis she places on Christ's power accentuates the punishment to be dealt to those who made him suffer. In sum, the poem amplifies the theme of Christ's awesome arrival as Lord (*in siner magencrefte*). The paraphrastic amplification of the theme of Christ as the mighty Lord and just judge forcefully demonstrates to an aristocratic audience, *wip unde man,* that all are to be judged according to their spiritual orientation and subsequent actions, not according to their former social status: "Thus He judges justly [both] the lord and the servant, the lady and the maid" ("so rihtet er rehte dem herren unde dem chnehte, der frouwen unde der diuwe") (185-87).

The listener next learns that the fulfillment of this essential criterion for achieving salvation is not possible after the coming of Christ. The time for repentance has passed. This recognition intensifies the fear of being numbered among those who caused Christ to suffer by their sins, and of facing the imminent wrath of God. The preceptive lines 189 and 190 then break the listeners' identification with the damned by again addressing the listeners in the collective *wir* form and telling of the need for repentance, *riuwe,* for gaining salvation: "(*riuwe*) die wir haben solden, ob wir genesen wolden." The textual dynamics allow the audience to experience another chance for their salvation in an otherwise hopeless situation. Thus, the identification, and subsequent break from the identification with the damned, creates a momentum that may dispose the listeners to make use of the redeeming opportunity and implement the saving lesson. Once the poem has reinstated the listeners in the community of the potentially saved, they at once learn of a series of redeeming virtues:

> so werdent die vil harte geret, die hie von der werlt cherent.
> die sizent da ineben gote in der scare der zwelfpoten.
> wande si durch gotes minne verchurn werltliche wunne.
> die sint alle geheiligot, die wirseren sint erteilot. (191-98)

> They shall truly receive great honor, they who turn now from the world.
> They shall sit next to God among the group of the twelve apostles,
> for they have renounced worldly pleasures for the love of God.
> They all are blessed, [but] the evil are damned.

Underlying these virtues is a binary classification. Those who turn from the world and do not esteem worldly pleasure will be honored. And yet, this act does not demand a cloistered life, or a life as a recluse as was Ava's, but primarily one that is led in accordance with the precept of charity as the correct spiritual orientation. All who observe this precept will join the group centered about the twelve apostles in the presence of God. Furthermore, the association with the apostles as exemplary models of conduct and active Christianity emphasizes the practice of their positive spiritual orientation and charity. Consequently, those who do not adopt this orientation face damnation: "die wirseren sint erteilot" (198).

Ava interrupts the narrative by introducing a catalogue of virtues in strophe 21. In so doing, she again reminds her listeners of the apostles as models of conduct. The poet then strengthens the exemplary message with preceptive verses, telling her audience that she will now give instructions on how to lead a virtuous life: "doch wil ich iu sagen da bi, wie der leben sol getan sin" (203-4). The strophe that follows begins with the central Christian precept of charity. Speaking of those who practice charity, Ava announces:

> Si sulen got minnen von allen ir sinnen,
> von allem ir herzen, in allen ir werchen. (205-8)

They shall love God with all their mind,
with all their heart, and in all their works.

After she has exhorted the learning audience to do likewise, she presents them with a list of saving virtues:

> si sulen warheit phlege,   ir almuosen wol geben,
> mit mazen ir gewant tragen,   mit chiuske ir e haben,
> bescirmen die weisen,   die gevangen losen.
> si sulen den vianden vergeben,   gerihtes ane miete phlegen,
> den armen tuon gnade,   die ellenden phahen.
> si sulen ze chirchen gerne gen,   bihte unde buoze besten.
> (209-20)

They shall keep the truth, give their alms well,
attire themselves modestly, lead their married lives chastely,
protect and succor orphans, and ransom the imprisoned.
They shall forgive their enemies, render justice without bribery,
show mercy to the poor [the powerless], [and] care for strangers.
They shall gladly go to church, confession, and do penance.

The specific virtues given are particularly applicable to an aristocratic audience capable of exercising power to ransom prisoners, hold court, and to protect and show mercy to those of lesser power, *den armen*. Such listeners will also have commanded a sufficient degree of material wealth to give alms generously and to aid the destitute. The exercise of these redeeming virtues corresponds at once to the performance of the listeners' representational duties as a member of a powerful societal group and privileged Christian community. The final preceptive verses in the catalogue admonish the listeners not only to go to church with a willing heart, but to repent and do penance—the essential criterion for salvation that must be fulfilled before the Last Judgment.

In an epilogue to the catalogue of redeeming virtues, the listeners learn that if they are unable to fast, then they are to exercise charity by the giving of alms. And, when possible, self-mortification by scourging is advocated, whereby the penitent assumes the place of the scourged Christ. With the final emphasis placed upon an extreme physical expression of atonement, the narration of the Last Judgment resumes and the listeners learn the consequences of heeding or ignoring the "good advice." Who ever has done these things wholeheartedly, thus offers much good advice:

> Swer daz mit triwen begat,   des wirt da vil guot rat.
> ze dem sprichet der gotesun: "var ze miner zeswen!
> venite benedicti,   mines vater riche ist iu gerihtet." (225-30)
>
> To him the Son of God shall speak: "come [sit] at my right hand!
> Venite benedicti, my father's kingdom is made ready for you. "

The saving results of practicing the catalogue of virtues are immediately confirmed by God, whose testimony as the divine witness serves as a guarantee for the reality of the depiction.[52] The listeners then experience as a members of the community of the potentially saved the spoken words of Christ in the *as if* mode. In the words that comprise the pronouncement of Judgment, the listeners hear that they are saved: Christ tells them to join the blessed on the right, for whom the kingdom of God has been prepared. The next four strophes (25-28) provide amplification of the condemnation and punishment of the damned. After the separation of the wheat from the chaff, the blessed from damned, the poem makes known the wrath of God (234). On the left, the damned then turn to the Holy One. A brief preceptive verse underscores the terror of the moment: "Think of it, if you will" ("dar denche, swer so welle") (240). The audience next hears the verdict given to the damned. The evocation of the testimony of God as divine witness, and the use of the collective, personal *ir* form of address allow the listeners to experience their personal damnation as the consequence of ignoring the good advice of practicing the given virtues.

> So sprichet got mit grimme   ze sinen widerwinnen.
> er zeiget in sine wunden   an den vuosen unde an den henden.
> vil harte si bluotent,   si nemegan da niht widere gebieten.
> von sineme rehte sprichet er in zuo: "mines willen newolt ir
>   niht tuon.
> ir hetet min vergezzen,   ir negabet mir trinchen noch ezzen,
> selede noch gewate,   ubel waren iuwere getate.
> dem tievele dienotet ir mit flize,   mit im habet diu ewigen
>   wize." (241-54)
>
> Thus God shall speak with rage to His enemies.
> He shall show them the wounds on His hands and on His feet.
> How they bleed! They [His enemies] cannot deny anything there.

Persuasion and Pedagogy

He shall rightly speak to them: "My will you did not chose to do.
You [all] have denied me, you gave to me neither food nor drink,
shelter nor clothing—evil were your deeds!
You served the devil with diligence,
[and so] with him shall you have hellfire."

Because they failed to observe the precept of charity and made no atonement, the damned are consigned to the devil, whom they have served instead of God. The poem then amplifies the torments of hell to bolster salutary terror, and in so doing, the listeners' resolve to follow the good advice. The description of the agonies experienced in the *as if* mode, moreover, are the antithesis of charity and forcibly aim to move and persuade the listeners to avoid the errors and spiritual orientation of the damned. If they had only considered their ways while time remained for correction:

Da nehilfet golt noch scaz,   e bedahten wir iz baz!
da ist viur unde swebel,   wir sturben gerne unde muosen
   leben. (267-70)

[For] gold and treasure cannot help [here], had we only thought
   more about it earlier!
[Here] there is fire and sulphur—how gladly we would die and
   [yet still] have to live.

The poem now breaks the collective identification of the learning audience with the damned to restore the identification with the saved. As a signal of this transition, the devil departs: "So der tievel danne gevert, vile wol unser dinch vert" (315-16). The sudden release of narrative tension can thus magnify the joys of salvation to evoke a cathartic experience of redemption and euphoria that extends throughout the remaining seven strophes of the poem.[53] In identifying with the damned at Judgment and experiencing the consequences of their own potential error, the listeners may be moved and persuaded, *ex negativo*, not to imitate the negative model of conduct in which they themselves have participated in the *as if* mode. The break of identification with the damned and the reidentification with the saved may then free the listeners to make the necessary correction in their spiritual orientation and conduct. In the cathartic experience of *Das Jüngste Gericht*, the teaching strategy is first to manipulate the listeners into the role of the hopeless damned, who lack all opportunity to correct their errors and atone for their sins, and then to release them from the negative identification and lead them to identify with the saved. There is no central cathartic heroic figure in *Das Jüngste Gericht,* written in the early twelfth century, as there is in the ninth-century *Muspilli,* where the resurrected Christ can purify and move the listeners by compunction to imitate his charity. Thus, in comparison with the *Muspilli,* where it is Christ's sacrifice as the supreme exemplary expression of charity that directs the listeners toward *imitatio Christi, Das Jüngste Gericht* leads the listeners away from potential damnation and frees them to implement a catalogue of virtues, the "good advice." In so doing, Ava reinforces the general exemplary lessons in *Johannes, Das Leben Jesu,* and *Der Antichrist.*

Having experienced the deathless terror of hell (287-88), the listeners also learn of the blessings of heaven:

> so scinet uns scone   diu edele persone.
> sich zaiget got mit minnen   allen sinen chinden. (317-20)

> [And] so the noble personage [of the Trinity] shall shine for us
> in a beautiful way.
> God reveals Himself with love to all His children.

After the poem has demonstrated the consequences of the correct spiritual orientation and the exercise of positive conduct, the account of the Last Judgment concludes. The remaining five strophes of the poem provide a final confirmation and recapitulation of the lesson. Strophe 30 commemorates the beginning of the liturgical year at Easter, an appropriate time for necessary spiritual reorientation and renewed vigilance:[54]

> Do vahet ane, daz ist war,   Jubileus, das guote wunnejar.
> so beginne wir minnen   di inren sinne,
> vernunst unde ratio,   diu edele meditatio.
> da mit erchenne wir Crist,   das er iz allez ist. (327-34)

> Then, in truth, Jubileus—the good and joyful year—shall commence.
>   [And] so we shall begin to appreciate our powers of mind:
> the ability to think and reason, [and] noble meditation.
> [For] in this way we can know of Christ—that He is everything.

The end of the poem, *Das Jüngste Gericht*, and, accordingly, the end of the series comprising *dizze buoch*, encourages the learning audience to reflect and meditate on the given lessons. Indeed, as an additional incentive in persuading her listeners—perhaps already predisposed—to do so, Ava gives an account of the remarkable benefits:

so habe wir vil michel wunne, so si wir siben stunde sconer
denne der sunne.
zuo der selber scone so gibet uns got ze lone
eine vil statige jugende unde manige herliche tugende.
(335-40)

So we shall have great joy, for we will be seven times
brighter than the sun.
[And] together with this brightness, God shall give us
everlasting youth and many glorious virtues.

Plainly, the rewards consist of more than the enticing notion of eternal youth:

Do habe wir das ewige lieht, neheines siechtuomes nieht.
da ist diu veste winescaft, diu milteste trutscaft,
diu chunechlich ere, die haben wir iemer mere. (347-52)

Then we shall have eternal light, [and] no sickness at all.
There is constant happiness, the most pious loving union,
[and] kingly praise, which we shall have for ever more.

In fact, Ava collectively informs her listeners that they shall easily be able to flee from all sin: "[for] we shall be swifter than the wind" (357-58).

Her exhortation in strophe 32 serves as a pedagogical signal to take heed:

So vernemet alle da bi: da sit ir edele unde fri,
da nedwinget iuch sunde noch leit, daz ist diu ganze friheit,
da ergezet uns got sciere aller der sere,
die wir manege stunden liten in ellende. (359-66)

So listen, all who are here: there you would be nobel and free,
there neither sin nor sorrow would bother you, [for] that is the
   perfect freedom.
There God shall repay us at once for all the tribulations
that we have suffered in misery for many an hour.

The aristocratic audience learns that where they are free of sin and sorrow, namely among the saved at Judgment, there is the true freedom and nobility of the blessed of God. The prominent wordplay and juxtaposition of "edele unde fri" with "diu ganze friheit" effectively highlights this point for the listeners. Ava then amplifies the theme of nobility in the strophe that follows:

Da ist daz ewige leben,   daz ist uns alzoges gegeben,
Crist, unser hertuom,   unser vernunst unde unser wistuom.
der ist gecheret an in,   vil edele ist unser sin. (367-72)

There is the eternal life, which has well and truly been given to us:
Christ, our ruling power, our reason and our wisdom.
Since He has come to it—our understanding is noble indeed.

The catalogue of virtues, *der vil guot rat,* now reappears in condensed form (strophe 34). The poem recapitulates the virtues, but this time without preceptive verses. Ava simply relates them as qualities of the children of God. Although these verses are exemplary, they are at once a summary listing of the virtues that were presented preceptively in strophe 22. The teaching strategy of *Das Jüngste Gericht* gives evidence of, therefore, a circular pattern imposed upon a linear pattern of the ascent to wisdom and purification.[55] The linear progression simulates the continual forward motion toward the day of Judgment. Thus, Ava guides her learners to experience the successive stages that mark the arrival of the Last Judgment, and herewith their own judgment. The circular pattern then provides additional support. After the poem has introduced the redeeming virtues, the consequences of practicing them, or not, are revealed by positive and negative models of conduct. Ava completes the circular pattern by selective recapitulation; the theoretical exposition of essential qualities for achieving salvation given in strophe 22 finds concrete expression in strophes 24 to 29. After Christ the Judge has given his verdict to those who practiced the catalogue of virtues, he renders his verdict to the damned. In so doing, Christ substantiates the verdict by describing in exemplary verses how the damned have ignored the precept of charity and, accordingly, the observance of the given virtues. The paraphrastic amplification of their torments in hell then emphasizes the consequences of their error.

The poem, *Das Jüngste Gericht,* and the entire series concludes with the author's request to her audience for its prayers:

Dizze buoch dihtote   zweier chinde muoter.
diu sageten ir disen sin,   michel mandunge was under in.
der muoter waren diu chint liep,   der eine von der werlt sciet.
nu bitte ich iuch gemeine,   michel unde chleine,
swer dize buoch lese,   daz er siner sele gnaden wunskende wese.
umbe den einen, der noch lebet   unde er in den arbeiten strebet,
dem wunsket gnaden und der muoter,   daz ist AVA. (393-406)

This [was] the book [that] the mother of two children wrote.
[It was] they [who] told her of the meaning. Great joy was
    among them. The mother loved her children, [but] one
    [son] has [since] departed from this world.
Now I beseech you all in common, [both] great and small,
[that] whoever reads this book, would wish for mercy on his
    [the deceased son's] soul.
[And] for the one who still lives and strives in his work,
wish [that] mercy be shown to him and to his mother, Ava.

By a common appeal, "nu bitte ich iuch gemeine," Ava makes provision for the spiritual welfare of her sons and herself, while at once emphasizing the communal and collective identity of those whom she entreats, the learning audience.

Thus, the individual learner neither learns nor is taught in isolation. He or she learns as an active participant in a community characterized by its observance of either positive or negative examples of conduct. The poet guides each learner to experience a collective identification with a group that is actively meriting salvation or damnation according to its observance of charity and its exercise of vigilance in the face of trial. At the same time, Ava seeks to move and persuade the listener to take individual initiative in implementing the lesson. It remains for each learner, therefore, to attain his or her own salvation.

NOTES

1. Richard Keinast, "Ava–Studien I," *Zeitschrift für Deutsches Altertum und Deutsche Literatur* 74 (1937): 34. Although Kienast views Ava's work as a compositional unity, "als wohlkomponierte Einheit," he does so on the basis of Wilhelm Scherer's overinterpretation of the major part of *Das Leben Jesu* as a history of the Church. See *Geistliche Poeten der deutschen Kaiserzeit* (Strassburg: n.p., 1876), 2:64–77 (*QF* VII). See also Eoliba Greinemann, *Die Gedichte der Frau Ava, Untersuchungen zur Quellenfrage* (Ph.D. diss., University of Freiburg, 1968), 14–19. In upholding the unity of Ava's poems, Greinemann notes the high degree of agreement between the structure of the poems and the order of pericopes within the liturgical cycle. See Peter K. Stein, "Stil, Struktur, Historischer Ort und Funktion–Literaturhistorische Beobachtungen und methodologische Überlegungen zu den Dichtungen der Frau Ava," in *Festschrift für Adelbert Schmidt zum 70. Geburtstag,* ed. Gerlinde Weiss (Stuttgart: Akademischer Verlag Hans Dieter Heinz, 1976), 38–44. Although Stein also views Ava's poems as constituting a "unity," he does not accept Kienast's premise of the history of the Church, nor does he embrace the pericope-based view of Greinemann, noting that Ava also utilized knowledge of the Bible. Instead, Stein highlights the depiction of salvation history under two perspectives: the historical-chronological *sensus litteralis,* and the mystical-dogmatic aspect of the *septem sigilla* (Apoc. 5) with respect to the life of Christ. See also Wiebke Freytag, "Geistliches Leben und christliche Bildung. Hrotsvit and andere Autorinnen des frühen Mittelalters," in *Deutsche Literatur von Frauen,* ed. Gisela Brinker–Gabler (Munich: Verlag C. H. Beck, 1988), 1: 74–75. In a brief overview of Ava's work, Freytag offers a feminist perspective—the theme of subjective experience as an important characteristic of the literary activity of medieval women. See also my "Frau Ava," in *Dictionary of Literary Biography,* ed. Will Hasty and James Hardin (Charleston, S.C.: Bruccoli, Clark, and Layman, 1995), 148:39–44; and my "Frau Ava," in *Semper idem et Novus: Festschrift für Frank Banta,* ed. Francis G. Gentry (Göppingen: Kümmerle Verlag, 1988), 209–30.

2. Gentry, "Noker's Memento Mori," 53.

3. The term "concern for neighbor" is from the work of Caroline Walker Bynum, *Docere Verbo Et Exemplo: An Aspect of Twelfth–Century Spirituality,* HarvardTheological Studies 31 (Missoula, Mont.: Scholars Press, 1979), 1–2.

4. Bynum, *Docere Verbo Et Exemplo,* 1–226.

5. Ibid., 195.

6. Ibid., 196.

7. Ibid., 137. See Hauck, *Kirchengeschichte 4,* 335. See also Philip Hofmeister, "Mönchtum und Seelsorge bis zum 13. Jahrhundert," *Studien und Mitteilungen zur Geschichte des Benediktiner Ordens und seiner Zweige* 65 (1955): 209–73.

8. Bynum, *Docere Verbo Et Exemplo,* 191.

9. Ibid.

Persuasion and Pedagogy   135

10. Otmar Doerr, *Das Institut der Inclusen in Süddeutschland* (Münster in Westf.: Aschendorff, 1934), 99–100 (Lambach); and 103–4 (Melk). See also *Ancrene Wisse—Guide for Anchoresses*, ed. and trans. Hugh White (London: Penguin Classics, 1993). The introduction, vii–xxiii, provides a particularly useful overview of the institution.

11. Doerr, *Das Institut der Inclusen in Süddeutschland*, 1–168. See also Stein, *Stil, Struktur, Historischer Ort Und Funktion*, 45–46.

12. Doerr, *Das Institut der Inclusen in Süddeutschland*, 5–8. See also Grimlaicus, *Regula Solitariorum* (*PL* 103, 573–662).

13. Doerr, *Das Institut der Inclusen in Süddeutschland*, 55.

14. Grimlaicus, *Regula Solitariorum*, c. VIII: "Activa scilicet vita est conversatio religiosa, quae docet quomodo Praepositi sub se regant viventes ac diligant."

15. Grimlaicus, *Regula Solitariorum*, c.VIII: "Ipsa namque actualis vita panem esurienti tribuit, verbo sapientiae nescientem docet, errantem corrigit, superbientem ad humilitatis viam revocat, infirmantis curam gerit; quae singulis quibusque expediunt dispensat, et commissis sibi qualiter subsistere valeant, sollicite providet" (*PL* 103, 586). See also Doerr, *Das Institut der Inclusen in Süddeutschland*, 56–57.

16. Grimlaicus, *Regula Solitariorum*, c.VIII: "Contemplativa quoque vita est dilectionem Dei et proximi tota mente retinere, transitoria cuncta despicere, visibilia postponere, tantummodo quae coelestia sunt desiderare."

17. Grimlaicus refers in c.VIII to Luke 10:38–42: "Ex his enim signatur una, id est activa per Martham; et altera, id est contemplativa, per Mariam: sed necessaria est omnino Martha Mariae."

18. Grimlaicus, *Regula Solitariorum*, c.XX, *Quomodo solitarii debeant esse docti, et qualiter alios doceant*.

19. Grimlaicus, *Regula Solitariorum*, c. XXI: "Hi autem qui exempla virtutum praerogant, et lumen per vitam boni operis, et verbum praedicationis aliis demonstrant, jure lampades appelantur."

20. Grimlaicus, *Regula Solitariorum, Prologus* (*PL* 103, 575).

21. Doerr, *Das Institut der Inclusen in Süddeutschland*, 66.

22. Ibid., 67. In regard to the social rank of those who may have sought counsel with a religious recluse, Doerr notes: "Wir finden nicht nur gewöhnliches Volk, sondern auch Ritter, Bischofe, Abte an die Zelle herantreten, um in irgendeiner Lebensfrage die Incluse um Rat zu fragen."

23. Kienast, *Ava–Studien I*, 28.

24. Greinemann, *Die Gedichte der Frau Ava*, 5–24.

25. Ibid., 25–193.

26. See Doerr, *Das Institut der Inclusen in Süddeutschland*, 54.

27. Greinemann, *Die Gedichte der Frau Ava*, 119.

28. Ibid., 24. Greinemann regards pericopes as a "Gesamtquelle" for Ava's work. See Stein, *Stil, Struktur, Historischer Ort und Funktion*, for a further reservation on Greinemann's focus on pericopes as the comprehensive source

of Ava's work, 34. Remarking on Ava's chronology, Stein notes that she utilizes the entire Bible and does not rely solely on pericopes: "Ava wertet also die gesamte Bibel, nicht nur das liturgische Perikopensystem für ihre Chronologie aus."

29. Greinemann, *Die Gedichte der Frau Ava*, 137–40.
30. Ibid., 142–44. See also Kienast, *Ava–Studien III*, 94., also in *Zeitschrift für Deutsches Altertum und Deutsche Literatur* 77 (1940).
31. Greinemann, *Die Gedichte der Frau Ava*, 143–44. See Keinast, *Ava–Studien III*, 94
32. Erich Auerbach, *Mimesis*, 118–19. See Heinz G. Jantsch, *Studien zum Symbolischen in Frühmittelhochdeutscher Literatur* (Tübingen: Niemeyer,1959), 31–40.
33. Greinemann, *Die Gedichte der Frau Ava*, 25–28.
34. Luke 1:18–20.
35. Ibid.
36. "da woneten di guoten, di reinisten muoter" (163).
37. "an gote bin ich zwiveles vrie. /ich geloube sinen gewalt uber junge unde uber alt" (154–56).
38. "du solt dinen herren/niht gar se verre/mit cheinen dingen bechorn, des wirdestu lihte verlorn" (507–10).
39. The negative model of unwatchfulness that Peter offers in strophe 131 is preceded by another negative model of conduct in strophes 127 and 128. Peter receives a reprimandfor his prideful self-assurance that he will never deny Christ. Also see Greinemann, *Die Gedichte der Frau Ava*, 96–97.
40. Hans Robert Jauss, *Die nicht mehr schönen Künste*, 159. See also Auerbach, *Literatursprache*, 53–54.
41. Jantsch, *Studien zum Symbolischen*, 232–33. Jantsch calls attention to the "Holz"–formular in strophes 148–49: "Ava realisiert also die Kreuztragung als Aufsichnehmen der 'Bürde' und bezieht die Opfertat Christi zugleich zurück auf die erste Sünde" (232).
42. Jantsch notes the typological dimension of the conversation between Christ and the two thieves in strophes 152–53, whereby it is Christ as the "new Adam" whose guiltless death is in atonement for humankind's first sin. Jantsch also refers to the Abel–motif.
43. Eckart Conrad Lutz, *Rhetorica divina* (Berlin: De Gruyter, 1984), 174–75.
44. Greinemann, *Die Gedichte der Frau Ava*, 137–38. See also Kienast, *Ava–Studien III*, 97.
45. Kienast, *Ava–Studien I*, 28; *Ava–Studien III*, 93–96.
46. Regarding the "klösterliches Milieu," see Greinemann, *Die Gedichte der Frau Ava*, 150–52
47. Greinemann, *Die Gedichte der Frau Ava*, 137.
48. In his valuable study, Peter Stein considers lay brothers at Benedictine monasteries to have been the chief audience of Ava's works. Indeed, her audi-

ence, at least in part, may well have been lay brothers at the monastery of Melk, who, during their meals, might have heard her poems as a source of meditation and edification. Yet, in this regard, a study of the social standing of lay brothers at Melk and other relevant monasteries would be useful in determining how many were members of nobility, and, if so, what power or control did they exercise in their society—either before or even during their lay brotherhood. See Stein, *Stil, Struktur, Historischer Ort und Funktion*, 46–52. Furthermore, Stein's emphasis on *meditatio* in the Benedictine tradition, especially as *lectio continua*, fails to consider the importance of the *vita activa* as the counterpart to the *vita contemplativa* in Ava's work.

49. Ava again underscores the communal aspect through the expulsion and flight of the good:

> So hore wir dann banne uber banne, wir horen alle stunde
>   vermainsamunge.
> des wirt daz riche allez vol, so vliehent die guoten ze walde in diu
>   steinhol. (19–24)

> For we hear of banishment upon banishment, we hear of expulsion
>   every hour.
> The kingdom becomes filled with these [things], so the good flee
>   into the forest to the caves.

50. Kienast, *Ava–Studien I*, 33–34. See also Grau, *Quellen und Verwandtschaften*, 261.

51. Hans Blumenberg notes that the "dritte Instanz," the testimony of God, was a traditional device in use since the time of Augustine and throughout the Middle Ages to confirm the reliability of a given aspect of human understanding: "Gott als der verantwortliche Bürge für die Zuverlässigkeit der menschlichen Erkenntnis, dieses Schema der *dritten Instanz*, des absoluten Zeugen, ist in der ganzen Geschichte der mittelalterlichen Selbstauffassung des menschlichen Geistes seit Augustin vorbereitet." ("This scheme of God as the guarantor for the reliability of human knowledge, as the absolute witness, as the arbitrating authority, became established throughout the entire history of the medieval understanding of the human mind since Augustine." See Hans Blumenberg, "Wirklichkeit und Möglichkeit des Romans," *Nachahmung und Illusion*, ed. Hans Robert Jauss (Munich: Fink, 1969), 12.

52. Hans Robert Jauss, *Ästhetische Erfahrung*, 136–61.

53. Helmut De Boor, *Die Deutsche Literatur* (Munich: Beck, 1949), 162. See also Keinast, *Ava–Studien I*, 31–32.

54. Kenneth Burke, *A Grammar of Motives* (New York: Prentice–Hall, 1945), 222.

55. Wolfhart Pannenberg, "Person und Subjekt," *Identität, Poetik und Hermeneutik*, eds. Odo Marquard and Karlheinz Stierle (Munich: Fink, 1979), 7: 408–22. See further Bynum, *Docere Verbo Et Exemplo*, 192–97. Also Detlef Illmer, *Formen der Erziehung*, 167.

5

THE CALL TO JUDGMENT IN
VON DEN LETZTEN DINGEN
(DER LINZER ANTICHRIST)

Ava's final poem, *Das Jüngste Gericht*, evidences many similarities, "especially parallel elements in composition," with the so-called *Linzer Antichrist*.[1] This tripartite work of an unknown author from the latter part of the twelfth century depicts the reign of the Antichrist as a prelude to Judgment. The title, *Linzer Antichrist*, however, is misleading.[2] Although the major segment of the poem deals with the origin, arrival, and demise of the Antichrist, it is but one part of the whole. A title more representative of the entire work, therefore, is *Von den Letzten Dingen*.[3] Together, its three parts reveal a unified poetic and pedagogical concept, whereby the *ascensus* pattern pedagogically complements the poetic narration of salvation history.

Preserved in a thirteenth-century manuscript from the former monastery of Gleink,[4] *Von den Letzen Dingen* is an eschatological poem of disputed origin. Written in 1170 by an anonymous author, the poem is comprised of three sections designated by the Latin descriptions: *De antichristo: Elia et Enoch; De signis XV dierum ante diem iudicii;* and *De adventu Christi ad iudicium.*

LEARNING TO BE WATCHFUL

The first strophe of section 1 immediately introduces narrative tension. Addressed in the collective *wir* form, the listeners discover that they are counted among those privy to the Pauline admonition against succumbing to false teachings, and that the perilous time foreseen by Saint Paul is at hand: "Wir han zehant daz zit, von dem Paulus sus kit" (1-2). A German vernacular rendition of verses from Paul's

Second Epistle to Timothy depicts the antithesis of saving conversion,[5] namely, the actions of those who turn from the teachings of Scripture, the *nüziu rede.*

> ir orin kerint sie von der warheit,
> nüziu rede ist in leit.
> spellir unt niwe maere,
> sin si joch ungewaere,
> horint si allir gernist. (3-7)

> They turn their ears from the truth,
> [for] useful speech is an affliction to them.
> Storytellers and new fables,
> [especially] when mendacious,
> they hear all the more.

In these exemplary verses, *affect teaching* demonstrates the error of those who act contrary to reason by endangering their own salvation. The erring are adverse to *nüziu rede,* the very lessons beneficial to their spiritual well-being. Instead of scriptural truths, they seek and enjoy the fables and false teachings that lead to damnation. The vernacular rendering of Paul's authoritative warning underscores both the futility and spiritual danger of such a preoccupation. If the erring persist, they will have nothing to show for their efforts before God (8-10). Predisposed, perhaps, to shun the damning model of conduct, the listeners immediately learn of the saving orientation of the vigilant who deem it good to know of things to come:

> Och hant gnuge den muot
> daz sie duhte vil guot,
> swer in sagte oder sunge
> von kunftigin dingen,
> daz hetin sie ze grozin minnin. (11-15)

> Also enough [people] are of the mind that they
> would deem good, whoever speaks or sings of
> future things, [and] for this they would be
> thankful.

Because enough people care to learn of the future, the poet begins to

The Call to Judgment

tell of the Antichrist and the suffering that will befall the world. As a member of the collective *wir* group in strophe 1, the poet proceeds in the *ich* form to instruct the listeners and fellow members of the Christian community in eschatological revelation. This instruction observes the principle of charity, fulfilling the obligation of Christians to teach the spiritual truths they have learned to others.[6] It is only after the poet has set the tenor of the lesson by fostering an identification with the watchful community of the saved, and a recognition of the need for vigilance, that the listeners hear of the lives of Christ and the Antichrist.

The Old Testament prophecy given by Jacob on his deathbed relates the lineage of the antithetical figures. The listeners hear first of the tribe of Judah, which will bring forth the Virgin Mary and mother of Christ. The poet's authority attests to Jacob's prophecy that its descendants will gain the strength of a lion (34-35). Yet it is Jacob's curse that reveals the origin of the Antichrist: "fiat Dan coluber in via" (40). The poet provides the listeners at once with a vernacular translation of Genesis 49:16-17: "Dan iudicabit populum suum sicut et alia tribus in Israel. Fiat Dan coluber in via, cerastes in semina, mordens ungulas equi."

> daz chit: Dan der muoze ligen
> sam der slange an dem wege.
> damite dete er *uns* chunt,
> daz der leidigi hunt
> in sim chunne
> muoter giwunne. (41-46, emphasis mine)

> That is to say: Dan must lie along the way like
> the serpent.
> Thus he [Jacob] makes known to us,
> that the miserable dog would find a mother
> from its own kind [its own lineage/tribe].

In addition, the reference: "damit dete er *uns* chunt" (43) promotes the common spiritual bond of poet and listeners with the community of the vigilant.

After recounting the accursed heritage of the Antichrist, the poet paraphrastically amplifies the serpent metaphor. The listeners not only learn of the Antichrist's serpentine nature and his opposition to God, but also of the error of his victims. These are the unwary who on their pilgrimage through this world fall victim to the serpent Satan and his representative from the tribe of Dan. The image of the lurking serpent thus conveys a feeling of imminent danger while accentuating the importance of immediate vigilance:

> Des wurmis nature
> hat her ungehure:
> er bizet die ungewarn
> die den wec wellint varn.
> sam tuot der entecrist,
> wan er wider got ist. (47-52)

> The beast has the nature
> of the serpent: [for] he bites the unwary who
> wish to travel the way [through this world].
> So, too, does the Antichrist
> for he is against [an enemy of] God.

When the listeners hear of the consequences of unwatchfulness, they may momentarily experience, in the *as if* mode, the terror of separation from the vigilant community. Thus, the poet uses saving terror in a simplified rhetorical argument in exemplary form to dissuade the learning audience from imitating the unwary and committing their error. With the preparation for the next part of the lesson completed, the learners hear how in the time before Judgment the Antichrist will severely test the followers of Christ:

> die mit Criste wellint bestan
> unt den rehtin wec gan,
> den tuot er vil michil not
> unt ze jungist den tot,
> oder sie muozin
> den selbin wec lazin. (53-58)

> Those who wish to remain with Christ and
> follow the right path, to these he shall do great
> harm and bring death at Judgment, or they
> must leave [that] same path.

In the face of persecution and death by the Antichrist, the fear of separation from the watchful community "die mit Criste wellint bestan," may move the listeners to strengthen their ties through a greater vigilance and resolve to travel the path of salvation, "den rehtin wec." Textual dynamics, therefore, direct the listener away from the damning conduct of the unwary and toward the saving conduct of those who travel the way with Christ.

The listeners hear next of the antithetical natures of Christ and the Antichrist, in accord with the Pauline tradition, in 2 Thessalonians 2-3, where the Antichrist appears as an actual individual.[7] The poet refers to Saint Jerome as an authoritative source in introducing an account of the Antichrist's childhood: "Sante Iheronimus *uns* seit, von sinir geburte di warheit" (59-60, emphasis mine).[8] The use of the collective *uns* form may motivate the listener further to heed the lesson of vigilance. The poet then depicts the childhood of the Antichrist in opposition to that of Christ.[9] The Antichrist is to be born of a man and a woman, not from a virgin, "niut von einer magit" (63). And the keeper of hell, "der ubel hellewart," will watch over his charge as did the Holy Spirit the son of Mary (69-72).

Yet before the contrasting depiction of childhood continues, the Latin term *anticristus* is translated into the vernacular:

> Der name anticristus
> wirt betiutet sus:
> Christe widirwerdic
> wirt alliz sin dinc. (73-76)

> The name Antichrist means:
> All his doing shall be against Christ.

The emphasis placed on such a translation demonstrates the religious pedagogical importance of providing a clear point of reference and clear alternatives when deliberative action is required of the learner. If the poem is to foster vigilance, it must empower listeners to distinguish truth and honest intent from falsehood and deception. This discernment is particularly important in the eschatological context of the lesson. The vernacular translation of *anticristus* acts as a signal to alert the audience to the Antichrist's intent. His activities are therefore contrary to conduct founded on wisdom, that is, meritorious of salvation. The translation also serves as a propaedeutic for *affect teaching* by highlighting the Antichrist's inability to act in accord with saving wisdom the *affectus* that will betray him and his damning conduct to the vigilant.

The account of the antithetical childhoods resumes and tells how the angels and the Holy Spirit protected the Word of God in the Virgin's womb. A comparison follows with the mother of the Antichrist. In contrast to the Virgin Mary, the mother of the Antichrist will be filled with death (84-88). And though the son she bears will be a son of the devil, the child's nature will not be identical with that of Satan.[10] The Antichrist, as a *filius perditionis,* incurs damnation through his *tobehait,* his senseless rage in acts devoid of saving merit:

> wan den siu da gebirt,
> ain sun er divels wirt
> niut an der menschait,
> sunder *an allir slahte tobehait.* (89-92, emphasis mine)

> For the one whom she bears will be a son of
> the devil—
> not because of his human form or nature,
> but by all manner of [his] senseless raging.

Consequently, by sealing his damnation not by birth, but rather by deed, the Antichrist retains his human nature. Indeed, a major source of the poem emphasizes the prominance of this theme.[11] In *De ortu et tempore Antichristi* (c. 950), Adso of Montier-en-Der writes that as much as the Antichrist, *ille homo,* may try to destroy his human nature, he cannot do it completely and will himself be destroyed.[12] For as a human being, the Antichrist becomes diabolical "non per naturam, sed per imitationem."[13] The author of the German poem was acquainted, then, with the traditional depiction of the Antichrist as the one who will do the devil's bidding and be Satan's son by imitation.[14]

The poem highlights the damning qualities that constitute the Antichrist's imitation. To achieve this amplication, the poet first provides the listeners with a contrasting point of reference in the saving quality of humility embodied by Christ, who chose Bethlehem as the humble site of his birth. By sharpening the contrast with the Antichrist's birthplace of Babylon, the lesson of strophe 8 confronts the listener with two distinct and conflicting qualities, namely the saving virtue of humility in Christ and the vice of pride characteristic of Satan and his son, the Antichrist. The eschatological contrast offers clear guidelines to the listeners for distinguishing the deceptive teachings and deeds of the Antichrist from Christ's own and, accordingly, for upholding and heighten-

The Call to Judgment 145

ing vigilance. The negative example of the accursed towns of Chorozaim and Bethseda further stress the importance of being able to recognize the true Christ, and the consequences of associating with his imposter. After the Antichrist is born in the pagan's mighty city, Babylon, he leaves for these two towns where he is to be educated. It is there that the Antichrist is to learn the arts of deception, in the very towns that Christ's miracles could not persuade to do penance (Matt. 11: 20-24; Luke 10: 13-16). The two cities then typify the damnation that awaits those who do not recognize and accept the truth of God. The words attributed to Christ lend weight to the curse:

> in den stetin Crist manigin beruohte,
> iedoch er sie beide virfluohte:
> er sprach "we dir Bethsayda unt Chorazaim."
> da wirt derselbe wuotgrim
> ein junger zware
> der ubiln goucgelaere:
> ir liste wirt er so vol,
> wan er si alle habin sol. (105-12)

> In these cities, Christ cared for many [people],
> yet He cursed both [towns]: saying "Woe to you Bethsaida and Chorazaim!"
> [It is] there the same rampant one shall become a follower of [an apprentice to] the magicians: [yet] he is to become so filled with [the art of] their deceptions,
> that he shall have [mastery of] them all.

While hearing that the subject matter of the Antichrist's training is deception, the listeners learn that practitioners of magic themselves pose a threat to salvation.[15] The Johannine concept of many Antichrists serves to bolster the argument for increased vigilance. The plurality of the *goucgelaere* and their association with Satan's son as his mentors alerts the listeners to the magnitude of the threat, and the need to be watchful and critical of those who seek to persuade by signs. Strophe 8 thus acquaints the learning audience with the contrasting qualities of Christ and the Antichrist. In so doing, the lesson provides the criteria of humility and pride as a guide to distinguishing divine miracles from demonic deception.

The lesson of strophe 9 shifts from the conception and childhood of the Antichrist to the eschatological portents of his coming. Pauline authority and a reference to the *discessio* theme begins the strophe (2 Thess. 2-4).[16]

> Paulus der guote man,
> do er redin began
> von der werlt ende
> unt ouch von der urstende,
> do sprach er also
> nisi venerit primum discessio".
> daz kit: gewalt geswiche
> dem romiscin riche
> unt werde och iroffenot
> mit der grimmen not
> der sun der verlornisse,
> der mit allim sime liste
> widir gote wil sten,
> e mac diu werlt zergen. (113-26)

> Paul the good man began then to speak of the end of the world and also of the resurrection. He then spoke thus:"nisi venerit primum discessio."That means: "Power and authority must vanish [depart] from the Roman Empire, and the son of perdition, who with all his deceptions would stand against God, also be made known with terrible might—before the world may end.

After the authority of Paul attests to the truth of the lesson, his words rendered in Latin rhetorically enhance the impact upon the listeners. The use of one of the three holy languages and that of the Western Church provides an additional expression of authority, especially to an audience unversed in Latin. Set off from the vernacular, the highlighted verse alerts the listeners to its importance, perhaps disposing them to learn its meaning. The poet then makes them privy to the saving lesson. The Pauline verse becomes accessible and intelligible in the vernacular by biblical paraphrasis. Consequently, without hearing a direct translation of 2 Thessalonians 1-7, the listeners learn of an essential condition for the ascendancy of the Antichrist:

da bi hat uns gekundit,
doch er iz niwit habe irgrundit,
wie daz romisce riche zerge garliche,
e der selbe valant werde chunt ubir lant. (127-33)

In this way [Paul] has informed us—though
he did not explain how [it shall occur]—
that the Roman Empire would wholly pass
away before the same fiendish being would
become known thoughout the land.

Thus, the *discessio* theme introduces a retarding element into the narration.[17] While acquiring a tangible guideline with which to sharpen their vigilance, the listeners find assurance in the *translatio imperii* that time remains before the coming of the Antichrist.[18] Indeed, as a bulwark the empire granted the listener and learning audience a final preparatory period to be used wisely in correcting error and perfecting vigilance. Furthermore, the lesson of the *discessio* theme provides an additional guideline for discerning false eschatological teachings.

Once the poet has reaffirmed the listeners' identification with the vigilant community of the saved (127), they receive further instruction on the authority of Saint Jerome:

Ieronimus der scribaere
sagit uns ze maere,
wie er ze Rome vunde,
wan er iz gesuochin chunde,
an aim buoche gescribin stan
wie disiu dinc suln irgan. (133-38)

Jerome the learned writer told to us the tale, how he
found written in a book in Rome, as he could seek it
out, how this thing would come to pass.

The *discessio* lesson acquires contour in the description of the Frankish king.[19] Epideictic verses praise him in regard to his standing at the Last Judgment, where he is to be first among all the rulers who went before him. His influence will even extend to Rome and the Lateran, which will be subject to him. The envisioned restoration of the dominance of German kingship over papal authority, that is, of conditions prior to the Investiture Contest of the eleventh century, provides yet another bulwark against the coming of the Antichrist. The king's power will be so great than even "Rome unt Lateran" must comply (145).[20] The rich, moreover, must pay tribute: "sie muozin im zins gebin" (149). Yet, though the life of the Frankish king will be long and blessed, his reign of peace must reach its climax in the *discessio*. The prelude is the final crusade:

> Ze jungist er sich wol bewart,
> so gebiutit er eine hervart
> ze Jherusalem in daz lant.
> daz keiserliche gewant,
> sper, swert unt crone
> unt daz cruce vrone
> bringit er mit dar. (12 vv. 152-59)

> At the Last Judgment he shall commend himself well, for he will order a crusade to Jerusalem, into the [Holy] Land . [And] the imperial robes [and armor], spear, sword and crown, he shall bring thither.

The armed pilgrimage then fulfills the king's eschatological mission. Once the listener has been able to dwell on the wise use of the remaining interim before the *discessio,* the theme as a retarding element is rapidly pushed aside by the increasing narrative momentum of the forward-moving crusade. The amplification that follows may enable the listeners to experience the approaching *discessio* in the *as if* mode as immediate reality:

> so groz wirt diu selbe var,
> daz nie keine me
> so creftic wart e.
> daz volc daz er leitet,
> daz gevilde is bespreitet
> sam die vogil die seti. (160-65)

> So great will be this very campaign,
> that never was there one so mighty.

The Call to Judgment 149

The people whom he shall lead, will be spread over
the plain like birds upon seeded fields.

The general economy of description also provides the "empty space" in the narration, which may induce the listeners to complete and amplify the account by way of their own fantasy.[21] And because the subject matter, namely a crusade to Jerusalem, is readily believable, it may further activate the phantasy of each listener to evoke familiar associations and supply the missing details. Thus, as the *as if* experience intensifies, the learning audience may actively participate in forming the narrative.

At the Mount of Olives, the Frankish king consummates the history of the empire by offering the imperial diadem to God in a gesture of *commendatio*.[22] This offering, then, removes the final barrier that shields the listeners from the Antichrist and the coming of Judgment. The narrative momentum that dispels the *discessio* theme as a retarding element continues into the following strophe. Thus, the poem channels the forward narrative motion of the crusade account into the progression of events that signal the reign of the Antichrist.

In the lesson of strophe 13, the listener learns immediately that the Apocalypse is at hand: "Sam drate ist daz zit, von dem Johannes in apocalypsi kit" (171-72). And with the narrative tension restored, the Johannine account amplifies the events that precede the imminent approach of the Antichrist. Furthermore, "empty spaces" serve to compel the listeners to experience the rising tension by the free play of associations. First, the earth will be rocked by earthquakes:

> diu erde elliu irwagit,
> wan vil maniger danne clagit
> daz im nieman vor si,
> er si scalc odir vri,
> wan iegelicher danne tuot
> als in leitet sin muot
> und als erz bringen mac. (173-79)

> The earth will quake dreadfully,
> so a great many will then lament,
> that no one is [there] to lead them,
> be he servant or freeman, each shall do only as he
> sees fit and is able to perform.

The resulting upheaval will further weaken the social order by disrupting hierarchical structures. Although these remain unspecified, the lament of both servant and nobility alike, "scalc odir vri," connotes a general collapse of authority. In the ensuing anarchy, each person acts without social restraints and concern for his neighbor. By experiencing the terrifying disorder in the *as if* mode, the listeners actively contribute to the lesson and strengthen its persuasive force. In verses 173-79, therefore, the completion of the narrative picture by the listener can magnify and complement the saving terror already evoked by the description in the text itself.

The narrative tension then increases by additional amplification. When the sun turns black and disappears, Christ, too, will be hidden from view:

> swarz wirt der sunne sam ein wullin sac.
> der heligi Crist
> der ein sunne des rehtin ist,
> der wirt virholin danne
> beide wib unt manne. (180-84)

> The sun will blacken like a woolen sack [penitent's shirt]. Holy Christ, He who is a sun of righteousness, shall be concealed both to man and to woman.

The wordplay of sun (sunne) and Christ as "ein sunne des rehtin" emphasizes the terror of imminent disorder. The imagery of darkness, namely the disappearance of the light of day, and of Christ as the light of the world, heightens the tenor of the strophe. The poem directly aligns the difficulty in seeing with the decline of watchfulness. The clergy, having fallen victim to sleep, no longer perform the pastoral duty of watching over the congregation on its pilgrimage through the world (185-87).[23] Learning of the impending loss of pastoral care, the listener audience suddenly hears the poet speaking in the first person that whoever lives in accord with God's law will be subjected to tribulation:

> ob och iemin nach gote lebet,
> ich weiz er die not lidit,
> von der der wissag it scribit,
> des gotis wurtis durst unt hunger. (188-91)

If anyone should live by [the fear of] God, I know that he shall meet with suffering. For the prophet writes that for the sake of God there was hunger and thirst.

The *ich* interjection of the poet momentarily suspends the *as if* mode and thereby accentuates the account. An additional appeal to the authority of Saint John, *der wissag,* further highlights the passage. Thus, the theme of vigilance in the approaching period of the Antichrist finds its complement in the theme of the suffering servant of God. In enduring travail out of fear of God, none of the faithful regardless of their social standing wish to incur God's wrath. Consequently, the God-fearing master and pupil alike, "der meister odir der junger," must not be adverse to the passing of the world, whereby their suffering, too, will pass (192-96).

Because the listeners' identification with the vigilant community in earlier strophes (127, 134) remains unbroken, the model of the suffering servant may readily move and persuade them to uphold their spiritual status. Once the poem has reaffirmed the resolve to remain vigilant, the listeners are ready for the lesson of the following two strophes.

Although the Antichrist will remain hidden from view until he reaches age thirty, he will secretly send false prophets, "sine vorbotin wise," to prepare his way (201-4). The Johannine notion of many Antichrists evinces, then, the urgent need for increased watchfulness. The false and clever prophets, portrayed in a traditional manner as wolves in sheep's clothing, are the deceivers, *truginaere,* who would pass for the God-fearing, *guote liute* (205-9).[24] From the vantage point of the vigilant, the listeners learn first of the bitter pain of the unwatchful who choose to follow the pseudoprophets (210-12). Indeed, the *grex* image of the flock of sheep may further strengthen the listeners' resolve to vigilance by emphasizing the danger to the community from within.

Another simplified rhetorical argument for remaining watchful appears in strophe 15. Although the poet cites John's Apocalypse as the source, the poem does not strictly adhere to the Johannine account of the scorpion-like locusts that are to befall humankind, and sting to punish without killing.[25] The listeners discover that it is the nature of the locusts—like the false prophets—to move erratically, namely, to deviate from the straight path of virtue: "sin wellint niut rehte gan" (216). The locusts are also said to bite in a concealed fashion (217-18). Regardless of how sweet they sing or high they jump, they quickly fall to earth. Their bad wings, *ir bose gevidir,* will not sustain them (226). The allegorical potential is chiefly restricted to the tropological level. The false prophets who live and teach to deceive others will themselves succumb to their own deceptions:

> die ouch die trugihait begant,
> die selbin site sie hant:
> wan sie des wenic gedenkint,
> waz diu vetach bezechinint
> daz si got rehte wellin minnin,
> vur den vluoc muozin sie springin. (227-32, emphasis mine)
>
> They who commit the deception share the same trait:
> how little they consider what the wings signify—that
> they may want to love God rightly, [yet] instead of
> flight they have to hop miserably.

Although the messengers of the Antichrist enjoy great success, they commit a betraying error by overlooking the fact that Christian teachings as *moralis scientia* should be as spiritually and morally uplifting wings.[26] Their short hops cannot feign the true ascending flight of charitable love to God. As good as the words of the false prophets may sound, they commit murder, *mort,* by bringing spiritual death and damnation to the simple and unwary, "an den einvaltin muotin" (233-35). Thus, in avoiding the plight of the unwary, the vigilant must first learn to recognize false prophets and their teachings. The watchful Christian must take note of more than how sweetly the prophets sing. Poetic beauty and rhetorical eloquence alone are not to be blindly accepted as a guarantee of truth. Of greater importance is the test of charity. If any prophet's personal conduct and message disregard charity and do violence to the Christian community, the listener must be wary of deception.

The strophe concludes with an admonition that many of the unwary shall fall victim to the false prophets: "ir wirt vil uz der zal, so grozi craft hant sie ubiral" (237-38). Thus, exemplary verses *ex negativo* warn the learning audience that it, too, may be numbered among the victims. The threat of separation from the community of the potentially saved then restores narrative tension and combats the possible waning of vigilance out of complacency. Although vigilance requires frequent renewal, it also fulfills the pedagogical function of sustaining a correction once made for as long as possible. The sustaining force of vigilance is strengthened, therefore, by the introduction of a confrontational situation to evoke narrative tension and alert the listener to the immediate danger of false teaching and damning error.

LEARNING THROUGH CONFRONTATION

Yet the encounter with the Antichrist's cunning messengers pales before the confrontation of God's prophets, Elias and Enoch, with the Antichrist himself. The account encompasses nearly half of part 1: *De anticristo, Elia et Enoch,* and a third of the poem in its entirety.

Before the confrontation begins, the poet informs the listeners that God, to preserve his faithful, has saved the two prophets until then as a foil to the Antichrist (239-42). Elias and Enoch are to defend the faithful to prevent the Antichrist by his deception from leading them completely astray "daz er mit sime liste unt mit lere daz liut betalle niut verkere" (248-50). The threat of false conversion, namely, the turning from the saving path of truth to that of false teachings and damnation, maintains the undercurrent of narrative tension.

The danger of erring from *den rehtin wec* (54) and falling prey to the lurking serpent of the tribe of Dan also elicits narrative tension in conjunction with the pilgrimage theme. The forward sequential motion of the narration evokes the journey of humankind as pilgrims along the path of life. Each listener as *viator* traverses the successive stations which, in contrast to the *Memento Mori,* culminate in the Last Judgment. This sequential narrative form is that which Conrad of Hirsau designated in the *Dialogus super auctores* (c. 1100) as the *ordo naturalis,* as opposed to the nonsequential *ordo artificialis*.[27] By conveying a sense of irreversible narrative motion, the textual dynamics compel the listener to confront and surmount a series of threatening false conversions. Thus, the confrontational thrust of the poem not only heightens the narrative tension and perhaps the impact of the lesson, it also affords an opportunity to practice vigilance within the narrative as a controlled learning exercise. Indeed, the delight of listeners in the poetic account of the confrontation may further promote their receptiveness to the saving exercise.

Yet preceding the account of Elias and Enoch is a repeated reference to Johannine authority: "Als uns santde Johannes diutet" (251). The collective *uns* form encompasses the listeners and the poet alike as those who are privy to the saving teachings of John. Thus, besides the saving terror of false conversion, the desire to retain an identification with the community of the potentially saved may forcefully move the listeners to heed the lesson, especially as an active affirmation of vigilance and of membership in that community.

The listener next hears a brief allegorical description of Elias and Enoch as the two olive trees in Apocalypse 11:1-14. The allegorical potential remains in large part unrealized:

> die zwene gotis druten
> sint zwein olboumin gelich,
> wan si der minne sint so rich,
> sie luhtint sam zwei kerzestal. (252-55)
>
> The two beloved [servants] of God are like two olive trees, for they are so ripe with love [Christian charity] that they shine like two candlesticks.

Instead of the fear of God evoked at once in Apocalypse 11:5, where whoever would harm God's prophets is to be consumed by fire from their mouths, the poet first emphasizes the charity of the prophets' deeds. Their love of God and humankind is manifest both in preaching and in miracles:

> Ir predige ist suoze unt guot.
> got durch ir willin tuot
> vil creftigiu wunder.
> manic ungesunder
> gat von in heil.
> mit dem divil hant sie kain teil. (263-68)
>
> Their preaching is sweet and good. God does many powerful miracles through their will [and intercession]. [And] many an inflicted person takes leave of them cured and well. They have no part in the devil.

The exemplary verses in strophes 17 and 18 present Elias and Enoch as models of charity and vigilance. Their actions support the criteria by which the listeners are to distinguish saving teachings and miracles from the spurious. The binary system of saving charity and damning cupidity provides a clear frame of reference, by which the listeners can prepare for the trial test of vigilance in the narrative to follow, and for deliberation at the imminent encounter with the teachings and deceptions of the Antichrist.

The Call to Judgment

After strophe 18 has reaffirmed that it is God who enables Elias and Enoch to change water into blood (269-90), the listeners hear that the prophets will quickly overcome their adversaries (271-72). The paraphrasis of the Johannine account of the two witnesses ends by repeating the collective *uns* and referring to biblical authority: "ir predige werit vierdehalb jar, so sagint *uns* diu bouch vur war" (273-74, emphasis mine). These concluding verses form the counterpart to the initial verse of the account: "Als *uns* sandte Johannes diutet" (251, emphasis mine). Strophes 17 and 18 illustrate the the tendency toward the use of small units of discourse in medieval rhetoric.[28] In fact, the use of small narrative, rhetorical units also serves pedagogical aims by directing the listeners' attention to a particular point of instruction within the overall lesson and teaching strategy of the poem. The listener may then master the material more rapidly in a smaller format. Such units of discourse in *Von den letzten Dingen* may vary, retard, or quicken the sequential narrative flow of the *ordo naturalis,* and thus contribute to the compositional unity as dynamic, intergral parts of the whole.

The narrative bridge leading to the first confrontation with the Antichrist and his means of false conversion appears in strophe 19. Upon hearing of the two prophets, the Jews begin to return to Jerusalem and rejoice at the coming of the promised Messiah (275-88). It is at this junction in the narrative that the Antichrist appears:

> Sa zuo dere stunde
> wirt dem hellehunde
> abe gezuckit daz seil:
> des wirt vil maniger ungeil. (289-92)

> So at that hour the hellhound shall slip forth from its leash: this shall bring to many despair and sorrow.

The first major confrontation with the Antichrist's efforts at false conversion and, accordingly, the listeners' first exercise in vigilance occurs in strophes 20 through 23. The listeners learn of the acceptance of the Antichrist by the Jews: "den Judin wirt er ein wile trut" (296). The deceiver swearing to be the Messiah promises to deliver them from their sufferings, restore their land and rebuild the Temple of Solomon (293-309). Furthermore, the Antichrist undergoes the rite of circumcision as a sign of compliance with Old Testament law and proof of his sworn claim (305-6). This action evokes the biblical theme of blindness (Matt.

23:1-39; and Exod. 34:33), in particular, the patristic theme of *Synagoga* blindly adhering to the law.[29] The poem depicts the blindness of the Jews to saving conversion, namely to the wonders and deeds of Christ, by their vulnerability to damning conversion.[30] Consequently, strophes 19 and 20 present an admonitory account; the Jews fail to heed their prophets and blindly turn to the Antichrist. Thus, the learning audience hears the warning against unwatchfulness and inadequate deliberation as a prelude to its own exercise in vigilance.[31]

Strophe 20 concludes with affect teaching. The Antichrist reveals the telling *affectus,* his disregard for the truth of Christianity:

> wan daz ist alliu sin ger,
> wie er die altin e
> mit ir gesezidi bege:
> uf hebit er die judischeit,
> daz er zerstorin mege die cristinheit. (310-14)

> For it is his greatest desire [and demand] to fulfill
> the Old Testament and its laws: he shall raise up the
> Jewish people that he may destroy Christendom.

Although the purpose for his deception of the Jews is to serve his aim of destroying Christianity, the further depiction of the Antichrist's deeds reveals his contempt for both the Old and the New Covenant. Thus, upon failing to persuade and overcome the vigilant, he slays Elias and Enoch with his sword (577-82) and puts to death whoever refuses to worship his image (714-31).

The listeners next confront the Antichrist's three means of false conversion: false miracles, bribes, and persecution (strophes 21-23).[32] The first means of false conversion comprises deceptive wonders (319-21). Nevertheless, his conjuring of natural phenomena such as storms and lightening will have the power to appeal to the hearts and minds of God's chosen (330-32).[33] The listeners discover, namely, that even the potentially saved will be vulnerable unless God protects them. It is God's prophets Elias and Enoch, however, who will be the instruments of divine protection (strophe 16). Without vigilance, the listeners jeopardize their ability to distinguish the godly work of the prophets from the deceptions of the Antichrist. Yet, the fear of succumbing to the Antichrist may result in heightened narrative tension, and in turn a greater resolve on the part of the listeners to remain watchful.

Exemplary verses amplify the false conversion theme by the negative model of bribery. The learning audience hears that the Antichrist will bribe in a twofold manner: first, by offering material wealth representative of power and social status, and second, by granting worldly honor (333-41). The model of damning conduct for both the giver and taker of bribes follows at once:

> alsus ubirkumit er mere,
> ez insi daz diu buoch habin glogin.
> kunige unt herzogin,
> biscoffe unt phaffin,
> *die da soldin biwachin*
> de vil arme cristinheit,
> di gewinnit er vil gereit
> mit sus getanin gebin:
> bose wirt der rehtin lebin. (340-48, emphasis mine)

> In this way he shall overcome [gain power over] more [people], if the sources do not lie. Kings and dukes, bishops and priests—they who ought to watch over poor Christendom—he shall win over easily with such gifts [bribes]: [and] the life of the righteous shall be terrible.

Clearly, the failure of both secular rulers and clergy to resist bribery by the Antichrist leads to their false conversion. Blinded by corruption, the defenders of the Christian community endanger those in their charge. And, because they who should be watchful are not, it is for each listener to be vigilant in their stead. Thus, the loss of protection and pastoral care augments the force of persuasion already elicited by saving terror and narrative tension. Further augmentation occurs by the absence of specific historical references, which provides an "empty space" conducive to the listeners' fantasy. The impact of the lesson is enhanced by association, whereby the listeners may complete the narrative references by calling to mind specific corrupt practices current to the given period. The extent of such practices around 1170 is evident in eschatalogical works contemporary to *Von den letzten Dingen,* namely in Heinrich von Melk's *Vom Priesterleben* and *Von des todes gehugede,* as well as in the works of Gerhoch von Reichersberg and Hildegard von Bingen.[34] The lesson concludes by warning the listeners that the life of the just, in this case those who resist bribery, will be one of tribulation: "bose wirt der rehtin lebin" (348).

The Antichrist's final means of false conversion magnifies the salutary terror: "Whomever he cannot overcome, to that person he shall reveal his third trait: his grim rage" (349-50). The theme of persecution does not, however, receive immediate amplification in the text. Instead, the lack of detail again creates an "empty space" which invites the listeners to participate in the narrative process and supply the missing amplification.

The cause of the persecution lies in the damning error of the Antichrist and those who imitate him. The poet uses affect teaching to guide the listeners to the error without delay. The *affectus* of the persecutor and his servants is clearly envy, that is, their envy of the potentially saved fosters hate and intensifies the persecution (351-56).

Once the lesson on the means of false conversion has raised the level of narrative tension and saving terror, the resulting narrative momentum brings the listeners closer to a confrontational situation. Elias and Enoch denounce the Antichrist's deeds and teachings as satanic deception (361-62). Again, the poem intensifies saving terror. The listeners hear that whoever chooses to follow the Antichrist must toil in hell, "swer ouch im volgin welle der muoze buwin di helle" (363-64). Only after this point in the narration, however, do the listeners learn of the prophets' victories in the area of saving conversation. Their oratory—"mit rede so gevuoger"—not only increases the ranks of the chosen, but also converts the Jews to Christianity (365-68).[35] Indeed, the very act of preaching, namely, moving and persuading the erring to convert to the path of salvation, is itself an act of charity. Thus, the saving conversion carried out by Elias and Enoch affirms their purpose as stated in strophe 16 and demonstrates God's provision for pastoral care. Even when the people of God, of the Old and New Covenant alike, are unwatchful and blinded by deception, God's charity provides the prophets in order that they may be saved.

The listeners next hear of the effects of saving conversion. In the spirit of the *Concordia Veteris et Novi Testamenti,* the converted Jews become staunch defenders of the Christian faith and a bulwark against the Antichrist (373-76).[36] Although this scene lacks the dramatic amplification found in the *Ludus de Antichristo,* whereby Elias and Enoch remove the veil from *Synagoga,* the conversion of the Jews clearly ends their blindness. They proceed then from a veiled state of spiritual knowledge, *velatio,* to *revelatio.*[37]

In accord with the teaching strategy of preparation and confrontation, the poem forewarns the listeners of the next encounter. Strophes 25 through 35 amplify the Antichrist's damning conduct on the basis of Apocalypse 13:1-4. The Johannine vision of the beast rising out of the sea begins the lesson. First, however, a collective *uns* evokes identification with the vigilant community of the potentially saved: "Johannes ewangeliste scribit uns von dem entecriste" (377-78). The listeners then learn of John's vision. As in the depiction of the two witnesses as olive trees (strophe 17), the allegorical potential of the account remains largely undeveloped. After the preceptive verse: "Now hear what this means" (400), an exegesis chiefly restricted to the tropological level follows. The listeners immediately hear an interpretation of the vision, whereby a compendium of damning characteristics highlights the *affectus* of the Antichrist and his followers (401-8). The Antichrist's words bring about the antithesis of charity, namely murder (*mort*). The raging beast's speech like that of the lion swells with pride (415-41). Indeed, in the verses that follow, the Antichrist even claims to be the Creator (427-28). This boast complements and amplifies his blasphemy from strophe 20: "er sprichit, daz er si Crist" (297).

The shift in sources that supplement the Johannine account from Adso's treatise in strophe 20,[38] to either multiple sources as Wundrack believed,[39] or a possible unknown commentary as Kursawa conjectures, does not, however, pose a problem for the author or the listeners. In fact, the second blasphemy provides a pedagogically useful repetition, which the narrative purposely accentuates. There is no attempt made by the poet to tone down the repetition as Kursawa maintains.[40] And, although strophes 20 and 27a each depict blasphemy in the "tempil Salomonis" (20), "in templo domini" (27a), the blasphemous claims made are not identical, nor are they addressed to the same group within the given narrative context. The Antichrist's claim to be the Messiah, "der in so lange geheizin ist" (298), aims at the false conversion of the Jews. By strophe 27a, however, Elias and Enoch have already achieved the saving conversion of the Jews. At this point in the narrative progression, the listeners hear that "the next falsehood [false oath] shall be great" (424). It is the next blasphemy of the raging Antichrist, the *wuotgrimme* (425), who falsely swears he has created everything through his power and majesty, "mit siner magincrefte" (429). Not only does he claim authority over the angels, but omnipotence as well.

    die engil in dem lufte
    muozin im sin undertan,
    kein got meg och gegin im gestan. (430-32)

The angels in the sky must be obedient unto him,
[and] no god may stand against him.

Those targeted for deception by the blasphemy in strophe 27a cannot be the converted Jews alone, who have since joined the ranks of the chosen and actively oppose the Antichrist: "in der irweltin scar, wider dem entecriste sezint sie sich gar" (375-76). The blasphemous claim must aim, therefore, at a larger group, namely the community of the potentially saved in its entirety. The impending confrontation then reinforces the listeners' own bond with the embattled community of the vigilant.

Thus, there is no need for the poet to arrange the material cleverly in order to conceal repetition, for the repetition of the blasphemy theme occurs within two different, yet complementary contexts. By divorcing the pedagogical from the poetic function of the work, Kursawa underestimates in this case the importance of deliberate repetition as a confirmation, and by varying the context, an extension of the lesson. The listener next hears that no shelter will remain so that even Christ himself would have no place to stay (433-34). The destruction will be unmerciful: "be it church or [town]wall, the monster will destroy it" (437-38).

In the strophe that follows, the collective *wir* encompasses the listeners as potential members of the vigilant community. This acknowledgement may sharpen the learning audience's receptivity to the further interpretation of the Johannine vision (443-48). It is within this frame of mind that the listeners hear of the bitter treatment that the bear-like claws of the beast will inflict on all opponents. The teachings of the Antichrist, *misliche lere* (451), are like the deceptive manner of the leopard—at first mild and then ravaging, "nu demuote, denne here" (452). The poet employs negative exemplary verses to describe how the erring followers seek praise and fame by fostering error, and thus the false conversion of others:

> sie bringint manigin irretuom,
> des wellint sie habin ruom,
> welher mit sime sinne
> mengirn volger gewinne. (455-58)

> They bring many a [harmful] error, because they
> wish to have praise [fame], which through his
> cunning may win over a great many followers.

The Call to Judgment

After elements of the beast have been explained in relation to the Antichrist's damning attributes, the poem teaches the listeners the meaning of the seven heads of the beast. These signify the seven evil spirits that desecrate all things and wound the soul (459-64).[41] The saving conversion of Mary Magdalene depicts the confrontation of the evil spirits with Christ. The listener first hears of the consequences of forgetting God:

> mit den och was besezin
> *diu da gotis hete vergizin*
> Maria Magdalena.
> universis viciis plena
> aller meine was siu vol,
> iedoch bedahte siu sich wol. (465-70, emphasis mine)

> By those [demons] Mary Magdalene was also
> posssessed—she who had forgotten [forsaken] God;
> universis viciis [vitiis] plena—filled with all manner of
> falsehoods, she did well however to think about it!

It is God's grace that breaks the demonic possession (471-74). The listeners bear witness to Mary Magdalene's gestures of repentance and gratitude: the washing of Christ's feet with her tears and the drying of his feet with her hair. The very use of her long tresses, once a source of damning pride, highlights her performance of penance (478-79). In addition to providing an exemplary account of the true spirit of penance, the depiction also reminds the listeners that they cannot rely on a direct intercession of Christ during the reign of the Antichrist (181-84). The only recourse is to vigilance. God's intercession in the person of his representatives, Elias and Enoch, can only benefit the watchful—those who are able to distinguish the teachings and deeds of the prophets from the deceptions of the Antichrist and his followers.

The insertion of the Mary Magdalene episode into the eschatological context of the narrative acts as a retarding element. That is, as the nonapocalyptic theme amplifies the threat of the seven demons, it also slows the sequential narrative motion toward the Last Judgment. In this way, the poet grants the listeners an opportunity to reflect on the need for watchfulness in the immediate present. At the close of the strophe, however, the retarding element vanishes. After Mary's release from possession, the listeners again hear of the Antichrist.

> Von Criste wart siu do wol bewart,
> mit sinin gnadin er sie droste,
> von sibin diveln er sie loste.
> daz sint diu sibin houbit,
> des divels kint vil wol irougit
> der ungehiure entecrist,
> daz er ir allir vol ist. (483-86)[42]

> Through Christ she was saved, with his grace he consoled her, [and] from the seven devils he released her. They are [signify] the seven heads, [and] the monstrous Antichrist reveals right well the devil's child, for he is filled with them all.

The restored narrative momentum directs the listener to the impending confrontation with the Antichrist's next effort at deception.

In the vision of the Apocalypse, the mortally wounded head of the beast becomes whole again (487-88). The listeners learn at once that the feigned wound signifies deception (489-91). Exemplary verses present the damning conduct of the deceivers who feign the Antichrist's resurrection. And it is he who teaches his followers to perform the fraud: "er lerit sie wie sie werbin unt wie si in suln began" (494-95). The listeners witness both the deception and its consequences. The Antichrist's followers, themselves deceived, revel in the words of the seemingly arisen one:

> er sprichit er welle iemer lebin,
> der gewalt si im gigebin
> in himil unt erde:
> des vrouwint sich die sine so werde. (511-14)

> He says he wishes to live forever, [and] the power is given unto him in heaven and earth: because [of these things] his followers take great delight.

Affect teaching clearly accentuates the blindness of the deceivers to their own damning acts.[43] Their empty happiness, therefore, contrasts powerfully with Mary Magdalene's repentant tears of joy (475-79).

The conflict of good and evil escalates with each successive confrontation. Strophes 32 through 34 advance the narrative to the encoun-

The Call to Judgment 163

ter between the Antichrist and the two witnesses, Elias and Enoch. Before the listeners experience this conflict, however, the poet aims to strengthen their identification with the community of the potentially saved:

> Die altin scribaere
> sagint uns ze maere:
> (*wir* vindinz an den bouchin,
> welle wirz suochin:) (515-18, emphasis mine)

> The [learned] writers of old tell us the story:
> (we will find it in the books [Scriptures], should we but wish to look for it).

The Antichrist's conquest of the ten kings, the envisioned horns of the beast, turns them into instruments for the persecution of all Christians (546-52). Meanwhile, as members of the vigilant community, the listeners in the *as if* mode may also experience the reprisals of the Antichrist against God's two witnesses. In addition, the vague depiction of the Antichrist's cunning and wrath invites the listeners to fill the resulting "empty spaces" through their own powers of association.

Further, when the rulers in each land, as horns of the beast and instruments of its fury, become persecutors themselves, the listeners may also experience the lack of possible refuge and the inevitability of persecution (552). Thus, the teaching strategy directs the listeners to anticipate confrontation, and in so doing, would persuade them to prepare actively for the trials of vigilance and persecution.

The next confrontation occurs as Elias and Enoch oppose the Antichrist in their preaching (553-56). Exemplary verses describe their conduct. Their sorrow, *ir herzeleit* (557), at the magnitude of the Antichrist's deceit moves them to preach unrelentingly (557-58). Because they strive to protect God's people from false conversion, Elias's and Enoch's sacrifice is at once an act of charity. They are so steadfast in their opposition, that they disregard their personal welfare (559-61).

In the ensuing debate, the Antichrist is hard pressed by their grand style of oratory and rhetorical prowess:

> samint beginnint sie limmin
> mit rede gnuoger,
> dieffir unt gefuoger.

> so creftig wirt der strit,
> daz unz an daz zit
> nie kein gelert man
> so getanez began
> noch ie mohte vurbringin:
> mit den wortin beginnint sie in twingin. (562-70)
>
> Together they began to cry out strongly with speech more
> abundent, greater in depth, and more artful. So mighty
> shall be the dispute that never did a learned man till that
> time begin [to speak] in that fashion or could have
> brought it to a conclusion: [and] with their words they
> began to subdue him.

And yet, the poet does not give the specific subject matter of the debate. Consequently, the account of the verbal contest emphasizes the power and eloquence of Elias's and Enoch's rhetoric in combatting their foe.

As soon as the Antichrist begins to lose the battle of words, he seeks to weaken the prophets' spirits by a show of miracles (571-73). Elias and Enoch are assisted by God, however, in performing even greater works. Once angered, the Antichrist quickly reveals his true nature:

> wan in diu rede niut virfeht,
> von diu grifit er an daz swert:
> sie sint die eristin den er tuot den dot,
> vil groz wirt denne not.
> abeslahin heizit er in diu houbet:
> so ist ubir die cristan irloubet. (577-82)
>
> When the talking no longer suited him, he reached for his
> sword: they were the first whom he put to death, [and]
> great then shall be the distress. He shall order their heads
> be cut off: [and] so [these things] will be allowed to
> befall the Christians.

Thus, he openly displays his true nature in his contempt for the sanctity of life by the murder of the prophets.

As the first martyrs at the hands of the Antichrist, the prophets offer a model of saving conduct. The narrative momentum then increases as the poem amplifies the martyrdom and its consequences. The listeners

The Call to Judgment

hear first of the damning *affectus* of the Antichrist's followers (583-89). Unable to discern their error, his followers are deceived by their damning belief in the Antichrist and delight in their seeming victory. Their model of damning conduct is characterized by their blindness to their self-deception; they delude themselves that the prophets' demise and the end of the tormenting preaching will bring a comfortable life. Indeed, the sin of gluttony further amplifies their damning conduct: "sie vlizint sich deste mere ir vrowede mit gefraeze" (590-91). After affect teaching has demonstrated the shallowness of their victory, the learning audience hears that no one in Jerusalem dares to bury the bodies of the slain prophets (592-94).

The listeners are immediately privy to God's response: "God shall vent his anger: because the two will be lost [in the encounter], He shall not let it go unavenged" (595-97). Thus, God intervenes as the God of Judgment, avenging the prophets according to the *ius talionis* (598-601), and destroying a third of the city by thunder and earthquake (602-4). The poet's interjection in the first-person singular affirms that the unjust who dwell there will be subjected to a divine Judgment: "daz ist ein gotis gerihte" (605-6).

The poet contrasts the saving terror evoked by judgment and damnation with the rewards of the martyred. A shift to the collective *wir* form of address occurs as the poem relates the prophets' resurrection and ascension (609-14). Once Elias and Enoch have been carried to heaven, a voice resounds to invite them to their reward: "siu ladit die herrin als in wol gezimit" (618). The poet then amplies the theme of the martyred witnesses in the strophe that follows.

The preceptive verses of strophe 39 call upon the listeners to take note of the exegesis of other teachers, *leraere* (619-22). These teachers believe that Elias and Enoch will lie unburied during the entire reign of the Antichrist (625-26). The corpses of the prophets will face the people as though appearing at Judgment (635-37). Nevertheless, the listeners, addressed collectively, gain assurance that God will care for the two witnesses regardless of the duration which their bodies might lie unburied (638-40). By presenting an additional version of the martyred witnesses, the poet retards the narrative motion in the eschatological sequence of events.[44] This technique reduces the narrative tension by momentarily sheltering the listeners from the account of inevitable persecution. In this manner, the textual dynamics allow the listeners a final respite before the onslaught of the Antichrist.

Yet, preceptive verses (641-43) soon direct the listeners to the impending confrontation, whereby a renewed campaign of false conversion envelopes the learning audience.[45] First, the audience hears that the Antichrist has gained dominion over all the world: "Be it kingdom or bishopric, he has it in his hand. Conquered has he every land" (644-46). The poem next teaches that the Antichrist orders everyone, regardless of social standing, to forsake Christ:

> er gebiutit swa dehein gotis holdi si,
> er si scalc odir vri,
> lege odir phaffe,
> daz man daz scaffe
> mit guote odir mit leide
> daz er von Criste sceide. (647-52)

> He orders [that] wherever anyone faithful to God may be, whether he be serf or freeborn, layperson or priest, he must see to it for better or worse, that he abandons Christ.

The only alternative is to flee (653-55). Yet, even if flight were impossible, it matters little for scarcely anyone will escape (656-58).

As the Antichrist's followers set forth on their mission of false conversion, they not only perform false wonders, but also announce the resurrection of their Lord. In addition to their blasphemy, their mockery of Christ further reminds the listeners of their damning *affectus:* "vil manigvalt wirt der spot den si tribint von Criste" (668-69). The deceivers resemble the animal with the horns of a lamb in the Johannine vision, for they, too, conceal their duplicity by appearing to be harmless (678-82).

The poem next provides the listeners with an exercise in vigilance, whereby it calls upon them to recognize the error in a sample lesson of false conversion:

> Nu wellin wir iu ouch sagin,
> wirn megin iz niut verdagin,
> ein deil von ir lere,
> da bi gedenkit irre mere. (683-86)

> Now we also wish to tell you about a part of their teaching—[for] we may not keep silent about it.
> Hereby think about [consider] erring pronouncements.

The Call to Judgment

The false lesson begins by denouncing Jesus: "He who is called Jesus was a grim and horrid man," *ein grimir man* (688-89). It attacks Christ, in particular, for his lack of charity in wishing suffering and death upon his friends (690-92). In contrast, the erring lesson protrays the Antichrist as showing mercy to all who approach him: "Be he meek and merciful or a thief, they are all dear to him in equal measure" (700-701). At the close of the lesson, the listeners discover the result of such conversion. Those who choose to become subject to the Antichrist may do as they please and yet remain his followers (704). This argument contrasts sharply with the argument given to the recalcitrant who oppose the lesson; they who resist hazard the same fate as the two prophets (709-13). The threat of murder violates the precept of charity and thus highlights the spurious nature of the lesson.

Once the vigilant listeners have heard the arguments desinged for false conversion, they confront the Antichrist's final means of persuasion. Death awaits all who refuse to worship his image (720-31). Further, whoever does not bear the mark of the Antichrist, *des entdecristis bustabe,* on his or her right hand must perish. Yet, those who do are also marked for damnation—by the devil at Judgment (740-43).

The listeners hear the rhetorical question whether or not there ever existed such adversity (744-46). The ensuing exclamation that many begin to wish for death introduces additional amplification of the persecution theme. Indeed, a reference to words of Christ from Matthew 24:16-19 lends authority to the account and heightens the narrative tension in strophes 45a and 46. And yet the poet soon checks the increase in tension (strophe 47). Together with the vigilant community, the listeners gain the consolation that the Antichrist's persecution of the chosen will end after three and a half years (772-85). A reference to Pauline authority begins the account of the Antichrist's punishment.[46]

> Daz muoz er douwin sere,
> nach santde Paulis lere,
> in sleht daz gotiswort,
> zerstiebin muoz er *als ein*
> *stinkindiz mort*
> vor gotis gesihte. (786-90, emphasis mine)

> He must pay dearly [for] that (disobedience to God), [for] according to the teaching of Saint Paul, the word of God shall slay him, [and] he must dissolve [like dust] before

God's countenance as would an act of foul murder.

Judgment for the Antichrist is to be on the Mount of Olives, where his "just reward" is according to the *ius talionis:* "he shall receive eternal death"(798-99).[47] Upon hearing of the Antichrist's fate, the listeners immediately learn of the controversy surrounding the form of his execution.[48] The introduction of this dispute provides a retarding element to allow for amplification:

> Similiche stritent dar umbe,
> wie in der engil wunde:
> er sla in mit eim swerte.
> similiche widerredint daz geverte,
> sie sprechint in sla des donris slac. (800-804)

> Many argue about how the angel shall wound him: [some say that] he will slay him with a sword. Others deny [this is] the way, saying a clap of thunder will slay him.

The poet settles the dispute by an appeal to Johannine authority. A reference to Apocalypse 20:9-10 affirms that the Antichrist will be struck down not by sword, but by lightning:

> vil wol daz wesin mac,
> wir megin wol geloubin daz iz war si,
> wan Johannes sprichit in apocalypsy,
> daz da von swebile unt viure
> vurwerde der ungehiure,
> er unt sine holdin,
> wan si got hant irbolgin. (805-11)

> Be that as it may, we may well believe that it is true, for John speaks in Apocalypse that the beast shall be destroyed by fire and brimstone—he and his followers alike, for they have raged against God.

The demise of the Antichrist and his followers receives additional amplification in the depiction of the rain of fire (812-17). None will escape (818-820). The account ends with a reaffirmation of God's wrath, *gotis zorn* (821-25).

The Call to Judgment

Once the Antichrist's reign has passed, the listeners learn of the great silence that will engulf the world: "ein silencium quasi media hora" (834-36). The vernacular translation that follows refers to it as the middle hour: "between the death of the unjust and the divine joy of Christendom" (842-43). The first part of the poem concludes by slowly increasing the narrative motion in the depiction of the interim before Judgment (strophe 50). The learning audience hears the cries for mercy of those who wish to return to God. These are the ones who submitted to the Antichrist under great duress, "durch die grimmin not" (848); hence God grants them forty days for penance to prepare for Judgment (853-58). This final reprieve serves briefly to retard the increasing narrative momentum. In this way, the poet evokes a sense of immediacy and to dispose the listeners to use the remaining time for penance wisely.

After a reference to the prophet Daniel (859-60), strophe 50 ends with the admonition that no one can know how long the world will endure (861-62). The authority of Christ underscores this warning. And, in the final verses of the strophe, the listeners experience Christ's testimony:

> Crist sprach selbe durch sinin munt: ez insoltde
> wizzin der junde noch der alte daz der vater hat in
> sime gewalte. (863-65)

> Christ himself spoke saying: neither the young nor the
> old may know what the Father can do in His power.

With the listeners possibly disposed to do penance and exercise vigilance, the poet now prepares them for the Call to Judgment. The second part of the poem, *De signis XV dierum ante diem iudicii,* intensifies both narrative motion and tension. The source of the account belongs perhaps to Jerome.[49] A preceptive verse introduces the lesson: "Now hear of [and understand] the sign of the first day" (872). In *Von den letzten Dingen,* the poet renders the fifteen days before the Last Judgment in six strophes of a total of 110 verses, as compared with the seventeen strophes comprising 160 verses in Frau Ava's account.[50] The greater concentration of strophes in *Von den letzten Dingen,* together with the reduction in amplification, thus accelerates the narrative motion.

As the days proceed toward Judgment, the poet uses the collective *wir* form of address on day thirteen to strengthen the listeners' identification with the vigilant community:

> Als *wirz* habin an der sage
> an dem drizehindin dage
> stant diu greber alliu offin.
> die dar inne warin berochin,
> die habint uf an des grabis munt.
> doch ist *uns* unchunt,
> in welhin bildin sie da habin,
> von diu sul wir des gedagin. (951-58, emphasis mine)
>
> As we hear in the lesson of the thirteenth day the graves shall all be open. They who were enclosed within shall rise up to the edge of the grave. Yet, it is not known to us what form[s] they shall take on, and so we should be silent.

Following the terrors of the fourteenth and fifteenth days (strophe 57), the theme of uncertainty complements the narrative tension already fostered by the rapid sequence of events:

> got hat eine in siner phlihte,
> wanne die vunfzehin dage irgen,
> ob sie sament nach ein ander gescen,
> obe daz gerihte sa irge,
> odir danach kein frist si me. (972-76)
>
> God alone knows in His providence, when the fifteen days shall end, whether they will occur together one after another, [and] whether the Judgment shall take place at once, or after these [days] there would still be a time.

Textual dynamics thus simulate the swift flow of eschatological time. In so doing, they may enable the listeners to experience the rapid approach of the Second Coming and Judgment.

The third part of the poem, *De adventu Christi ad iudicium*, comprises strophes 58 through 68. The testimonies of David and Paul introduce the themes of fire and transformation.[51]

> David sprach alsus "ignis in conspectu eius"
> daz viur inbrinnet vor siner gesihte:

The Call to Judgment

> also beginnit daz gerihte,
> himel unt erde sament brinnit,
> dem viure niut entrinnit. (977-82)

David spoke in this way: "ignis in conspectu eius"—the fire shall begin to burn in His sight; thus begins the Judgment, heaven and earth shall burn together, [and] not escape the fire.

Yet, the world will not be destroyed, but rather transformed by fire: "preterit figura mundi," said Paul as he began to speak of these things: the world must take on another form" (989-92).[52] The testimony of Christ further accentuates the theme of transformation (993-95). As members of the vigilant community the listeners hear the trumpets awakening the dead. The first transformation occurs and the dead arise with their bodies whole. Each will be healthy, never to die again (1018-20). It is the Last Judgment that will decide what the transformation from dead to living will bring to each of the arisen.

The listeners then immediately witness Jesus sitting in judgment (1021-24). In fact, it is in the context of Christ as *rex iudicii* that the poem depicts the open wounds and the tools of his crucifixion (1025-39).[53] The sharp sword of judgment then proceeds from Christ's mouth (1031-32). The poem restrains the saving terror, however, by stressing the reaction of the saved rather than of the damned. Instead of fearing the sword that delivers the verdict, whoever has lived by God's law rejoices (1034-36). From the vantage point of the vigilant community, the listeners experience the separation of the sheep from the goats in the *as if* mode. The learning audience hears that those to be judged comprise four groups (1046-47).[54] The foremost group is already saved before Judgment and comprises the prophets and the saints (1048-50). The lowest group are those already damned prior to Judgment. *Affect teaching* demonstrates their damning error—their neglect of charity through envy and hate (1057-61). The poem then amplifies the error immediately; members of this group lacked the fear of God—the essential element required for purification and the ascent to wisdom (1062-63). Furthermore, they have no good works to their credit: "kein guot sie nie geworhtin" (1064). As a final expression of their *affectus* their erring conduct deters them from saving penance. Exemplary verses then portray *diu nidereste scar* (1056):

> unt umbe swelhe iz ouch so stat,
> daz sie durch ir grozi missetat
> von der cristinheit werdint gesceidin,
> daz selbe sul sie da lidin,
> ob sie an der untriuwe werdint vundin ane riuwe,
> sie werdint der diveli genoze:
> got uns davor bewarin muoze. (1065-72)
>
> And as regards such [a group] it is also true, that they [its members] shall depart from Christendom because of their misdeeds. The very same [misdeeds] they [too] shall suffer there, and if they are found in [their] evil intent to be without remorse, they shall become companions of the devil: may God protect us from this [fate].

As this passage suggests, the poet still provides an undercurrent of saving terror to strengthen the exemplary argument in persuading the learners to heed the lessons of charity and vigilance. Indeed, the desire to remain within the community of the potentially saved may motivate the learning audience more than the fear of being numbered among the damned. And it is this positive learning orientation which continues throughout the final part of the lesson.

The listeners now hear of the third and fourth groups. These stand apart in preparation for Judgment. The audience first learns of the wise group that observes the teachings of the saving lesson: "ir guot vur ir unreht gat: von diu wirt ir guot rat" (1077-78). Because the members of this group repaid good for evil, the verdict brings them consolation and salvation. After this affirmation of the model of saving conduct, the damnation of the other group follows:

> diu ander wirt verkorn.
> owe daz ie wart geborn
> der da wirt verteilit,
> zuo den divelen wirt er ewecliche geseilit. (1079-82)
>
> The other [group] shall not be chosen. Woe that ever was born he who shall be condemned, [for] he shall be chained to the demons forever!

Although the poet does not expressly state this group's error, it is certainly the neglect of the precept of charity as the antithesis of the previous group's conduct. Because the listeners already identify with the vigilant community, they witness the punishment of the erring group as a conformation of their own conduct. Thus, the judgment scene in *Von den letzten Dingen* has the pedagogical function of reconfirming an already correct decision. The listeners no longer require persuasion to choose correctly, but rather the encouragement to adhere to their choice. The poet seeks to provide this motivation in the final depiction of Judgment.

Accordingly, the listeners witness Jesus welcoming those on his right. Because these ones comforted him when he was in need, they receive his kingdom as a reward for their charity (1089-92). The poet then reevokes the theme of pilgrimage. The saved receive the grace granted to the Apostles for following in Christ's path: "sie drahtin rehte in sin phat" (1109). The judgment scene thus confirms the reward that awaits the pilgrim at the end of the journey through life.

Yet, the listeners hear the saved asking Christ how they served him: "herre, wa gedienite wir dir ie? in keinin notin gesahe wir dich nie" (1113-14). Because they exercised charity unselfishly, they are not aware of their service (1115-18). Christ thus reassures them with his answer. The listeners' identification with the potentially saved allows them to experience his response in the *as if* mode:

> do ir iuch die armin
> liezint irbarmin,
> beide siechin unt gevangin suohtint
> unt die beruohtint:
> daz was alliz mir getan. (1121-25)

> Because you have shown mercy to the poor [and powerless], seeking out both the sick and the imprisoned and conforting them: all this you have done to me.

Christ himself confirms the rewards of observing charity and, accordingly, the given lessons of the poem. This pedagogical validation finds its counterpart in Christ's angry response to the other group, those on his left (1129-31). Because of their injustice, they are cursed with the eternal fire that awaits the devil. Yet, the listeners may witness the damning verdict from the perspective of the vigilant community. The punishment of the unjust, then, also serves to confirm the lesson.

Before the poem depicts the reaction of the damned, the learning audience hears that they cannot conceal their sins by deception or lies (1132-36). In fact, it is the angry countenance of Christ that confronts them (1137-39). However, the poem does not amplify their tormenting punishment, but rather their expulsion and separation from the saved. Thus, having desecrated God's temple, they flee from his sight (1140-48). *Affect teaching* highlights the consequences of their error. Their false orientation is evidence of their inability to act in accord with saving reason. They flee from Christ to the devil and hope for safety in hell. The interjection of the poet accentuates their folly:

> *ich* weiz iz den ze jungeist sam irgat,
> ubir die er diu ougin sinis zornis lat:
> von siner bescowede sie vliehint,
> zuo dem divel sie ziehint,
> in der helle druweten samfter genesin
> e sie vor siner gesihte wellin wesin. (1149-54, emphasis mine)

> I know how they shall fare together at Judgment, [they] on whom He casts His eyes of wrath: from His sight they shall flee, [and] proceed to the devil, [for] they would more easily [sooner] expect to find happiness in hell, before they would ever wish to be in his sight [again].

When the separation is complete, "Sa wirt gesundert ubil unt guot" (1155), the listeners learn what each group has to expect. On the one hand, the brief mention of the damned and the suffering they must endure is without amplification: "die verworhtin muozin die hellenot lidin mit sere" (1158-59). And, though the two verses do provide an "empty space" to be filled by common association and each learner's fantasy, the next verse formally ends the account: "kein gewaht wirt ir mere" (1160). On the other, the reward of the saved receives paratactic amplification. Fourteen verses depict the joys of heaven. In particular, the poem stresses the freedom from want and discomfort:

> den seligin iz danne irgat, als iz gescribin stat
> 'non esurient amplius' daz wirt bediutet sus:
> si inhungeret noch gedurstet me, kein hize duot in we
> ir urganc wirt vil guot bi den brunnin stat der bluomin bluot.
> (1161-68)

The blessed shall fare as is written: "non esurient amplius," which means they shall neither hunger nor thirst ever again, no heat shall cause them pain, their coming and going shall be very pleasant by the waterside of the flowers of blood [of the wounds of Christ].

Hate and sorrow will also be absent. All will enjoy spiritual and physical well-being: "dan ist nieman ungesunt, quoniam priora transierunt" (1173-74). Thus, the greater emphasis placed on the saved and their reward, rather than on the damned and their punishment, characterizes the third and final part of the poem.

Strophe 68 provides the peroration. First, however, the author of Apocalypse introduces the theme of renewal; John hears a voice proclaiming: "ecce omnia nova facio" (1176). The vernacular translation follows at once, "niuwe mach ich alliu dinc" (1177), whereby God will renew and remake heaven and earth into eternal paradise. The poet makes no mention of hell. Thus, the poem no longer calls into question the listener's identification with the saved. The eschatological narrative concludes by emphasizing the participation of the servants of God in the process of renewal (1182-85). Indeed, it is the listeners' own group that cultivates the renewed earth.

After the poem has presented the final argument for observing the lesson, the poet makes a common plea to God, "nu bite wir hiute" (1186), for humility and the proper spiritual orientation with which to appear at Judgment.

The teaching strategy in *Von den letzten Dingen* reveals a linear pattern of purification and ascent to wisdom. Textual dynamics, however, slow the forward narrative motion by the use of retarding elements. The paraphrasis of the *discessio* theme, for example, retards the narrative progression towards the day of Judgment without interrupting the sequential motion of the narration, the *ordo naturalis*. The restoration of the narrative momentum may then release and heighten the narrative tension. This technique serves, therefore, to strengthen the force of persuasion of the simplified rhetorical arguments in exemplary form.

The poet also complements the linear pattern by a confrontational teaching strategy. Thus, the poem guides the learning audience to confrontational situations that foster the exercise of vigilance and thereby the application of the lesson.

NOTES

1. Kettler, *Das Jüngste Gericht*, 40. Kettler correctly observes the similarities, "insbesondere eine Parallelität im Aufbau," between the two works.
2. In the major section of the work, *De anticristo, Elia et Enoch*, almost half the strophes (16–39) treat the confrontation between the Antichrist and the two witnesses. The final sections, *De signis XV dierum ante diem judicii* (51–57) and *De adventu Christi ad iudicium* (58–68), extend beyond the theme of the Antichrist.
3. Maurer, *Die religiösen Dichtungen*, 3:361.
4. A manuscript from the monastery of Gleink in Trauntal is now in the Bundesstaatliche Studienbibliothek in Linz, Austria, cod. 33. Bll. 171r–180r. Thirteenth century.
5. 2 Timothy 4:3–4: "Erit enim tempus, cum sanam doctrinam non sustinebunt, sed ad sua desideria coacervabunt sibi magistros, prurientes auribus, Et a veritate quidem auditum avertent, ad fabulas autem convertentur." ("For the time is coming when people will not endure sound teaching, but having itching ears they will accumulate for themselves teachers to suit their own likings, and will turn away from listening to the truth and wander into myths.")
6. Augustine, *De doct. chr.* 4.12.28.
7. Robert Konrad, *De ortu et tempore Antichristi. Antichristvorstellung und Geschichtsbild des Abtes Adso von Montier–en–Der* (Källmunz: Lassleben, 1964), 71–72.
8. Hieronymus's *Commentaria in Danielem* (*PL* 25) is the probable reference. See Hans–Peter Kursawa, 103 n. 99. Kursawa notes that although Jerome's commentary, in particular *In Danielem* 11.37, may have been the given reference, other sources such as Adso von Montier–en–Der's *Antichrist* treatise were used.
9. Konrad, *De ortu et tempore Antichristi*, 76–77.
10. Ibid., 31. See also Horst Dieter Rauh, *Das Bild des Antichrist im Mittelalter: von Tyconius zum deutschen Symbolismus* (Münster: Aschendorff, 1973), 155.
11. Rauh, *Das Bild des Antichrist im Mittelalter*, 156.
12. Adso von Montier–en–Der, *Libellus de ortu et de tempore Antichristi*, ed. Ernst Sackur: *Sibyllinische Texte und Forschungen* (Halle: Niemeyer, 1898), 107 : "Unde et ille homo filius perditionis appellatur, quia in quantum poterit, genus humanum perdet et ipse in novissimo perdetur" (*PL* 101, 1293).
13. Adso, *Libellus de ortu*, 110 (*PL* 101, 1295).
14. Rauh, *Das Bild des Antichrist im Mittelalter*, 57; Konrad, *De ortu et tempore Antichristi*, 29.
15. In analyzing Adso's *De ortu de et de tempore Antichristo*, Rauh observes that the reference to the evil magicians of Bethsaida and Chorosain as teachers of the Antichrist reveals the presence of popular superstitious belief in magic (156). The term "popular," however, requires further clarification in regard to

the specific given sociohistorical context of its usage.

16. Konrad, *De ortu et tempore Antichristi*, 88.

17. Rauh, *Das Bild des Antichrist im Mittelalter*, 386–90; Konrad, *De ortu et tempore Antichristi*, 88. See also Hauck, *Kirchengeschichte*, 4:526–27.

18. Yet, of greater importance than the ideological transfer of Roman authority to the German empire was the immediate presence of Hohenstaufen rule. The listeners hearing the poem around 1170 during the reign of Friedrich Barbarossa lived in the midst of a seemingly durable dynasty. The apocalyptic mood evidenced less than a quarter of a century earlier in Bishop Otto von Freising's *Chronica sive Historia de Duabus Civitatibus* was no longer compelling.

19. Prior to the composition of *Von den Letzten dingen*, the canonization of Charlemagne in 1165 at the behest of Friedrich Barbarossa had already attempted to bolster the Hohenstaufen claim to the Frankish monarch. See Rauh, *Das Bild des Antichrist im Mittelalter*, 397.

20. Rauh, *Das Bild des Antichrist im Mittelalter*, 386. In referring to the *discessio* scene in the *Ludus de Antichristo*, Rauh notes that it may well be a defensive move to counter the Church's claim to imperial authority: "Ja es scheint, als würden in dieser Szene insgeheim jene kurialen Ansprüche auf Oberheit über das Imperium abgewehrt, die auf dem Reichstag von Besançon 1157 im Streit um den Begriff des 'Beneficium' offen zutage tragen." ("Indeed, it seems as if in this scene those curial claims of supremacy over the empire were quietly dismissed, which were made openly at the Imperial Diet of Besancon in 1157 in the contest over the idea of *beneficium*.") Though plausible, caution is advised in establishing a direct correspondence between narrative and historical events.

21. Roman Ingarden, *Erlebnis, Kunstwerk und Wert* (Tübingen: Niemeyer, 1969), 12. Ingarden designates the "empty spaces" as an "Unbestimmtheitsstelle." See also Wolfgang Iser, "Der Archetyp als Leerform. Erzählschablonen und Kommunikation in Joyces 'Ulysses,'" *Terror und Spiel*, ed. Manfred Fuhrmann (Munich: Fink, 1971), 381. Iser uses the term *Leerstelle* (empty space).

22. Marc Bloch, *Feudal Society*, 2 vols. (London: Routledge and Kegan, 1965), 146–47. Also see Rauh, *Das Bild des Antichrist im Mittelalter*, 386.

23. The contextuality of the term "getagit" not only connotes old, "getagit sint die phaffin," but also implies being called before the court of judgment.

24. Rauh, *Das Bild des Antichrist im Mittelalter*, 498; Kursawa, *Antichrist*, 155. See also Matthew 7:15.

25. Apocalypse 9: 1–11.

26. Hennig Brinkmann, *Mittelalterliche Hermeneutik* (Darmstadt: Wissenschaftliche Buchgesellschaft, 1980), 248–49.

27. Franz Quadlbauer, "Die Antike Theorie der Genera Dicendi im Lateinischen Mittelalter," *Österreichische Akademie der Wissenschaften: Philosophische—Historische Klasse, Sitzungsberichte* 241.2 (Vienna: Böhlau,

1962), 59–61. Quadlbauer notes that Conrad von Hirschau, writing around 1100 in his *Dialogus super auctores,* deals with stylistic forms in the section on Virgil. Further, 70. See also Ernest Gallo,"The Grammarian's Rhetoric: The *Poetria Nova* of Geoffrey of Vinsauf," in *Medieval Eloquence,* ed. James J. Murphy (Berkeley: University of California Press, 1978), 68–84.

28. Qualdbauer: "die Tendenz zur kleinen Einheit," 70.

29. Paul Weber, *Geistliche Schauspiel und kirchliche Kunst in ihrem Verhältnis, erläutert an einer Ikonographie der Kirche und Synagoge* (Stuttgart: Greiner, 1900), 27–28.

30. Wolfgang Seiferth, *Synagoge und Kirche im Mittelalter* (Munich: Kosel, 1964), 47; Weber, *Geistliche Schauspiel und kirchliche Kunst in ihrem Verhältnis,* 26. Both authors note the traditional appeal to the Jews during the Good Friday mass in the words of the prophet Jeremiah: "Jerusalem, Jerusalem, convertere te ad Deum tuum."

31. By omitting any *disputatio* in strophe 19 between the Jews and the two prophets, and in strophe 20 between the Jews and the Antichrist, the author avoids the traditional theme of dangerous deliberation found in influential Latin texts. In the text attributed to Pseudo-Augustine, *Sermo contra judaeos, paganos et arianos,* which shares a codex with the *Muspilli,* the recalcitrance of the Jews, their sophistic logic and formalistic argumentation prevents them from recognizing the true testimony of the many witnesses to the wonders of Christ (*PL* 42, 1117–30). The shortsighted argumentation of the Jews is also condemned in another Pseudo-Augustinian work, the *Altercatione de Ecclesiae et Synagogae* (*PL* 42, 1131–40). Both works have been shown to be forerunners of the prophet plays, *Ordo Prophetarum* (see Seifert, *Synagoge,* 133). In *Von den Letzten Dingen,* then, the poet encourages and requires the listeners to exercise positive deliberation according to the precept of charity as a guide.

32. Kursawa, *Antichrist,* 128. Kursawa observes that the *Linzer Antichrist* adheres to the Adso version in distinquishing the three deceptions of the Antichrist.

33. Adso, *Libellus de ortu,* 108.

34. Rauh, *Das Bild des Antichrist im Mittelalter,* 416–527. Contemporary examples are found in Gerhoch's *De investigatione Antichriste* (c. 1160–62); and *De quarta vigilia noctis* (c. 1164); Hildegard's *Liber divinorum operum* (c. 1163–74). In the vernacular literature, the works of (the so–called) Heinrich von Melk are particularly representative: *Von todes gehugede* and *Vom Priesterleben* (c. 1160).

35. On the relationship between rhetorical eloquence and simplicity see Cameron, *Christianity and the Rhetoric of Empire,* 107–11.

36. Seiferth, *Synagoge,* 130. Seiferth refers to the *Ludus de Antichristo.*

37. Seiferth, *Synagoge,* 49–51.

38. Kursawa, *Antichrist,* 128.

39. August Wundrack, *Der Linzer Antichrist* (Ph.D. diss., University of Marburg, 1886), 41–43.

The Call to Judgment

40. Kursawa, *Antichrist*, 128–29.
41. The seven evil spirits contrast with the seven gifts of the Holy Spirit to accentuate the antithetical character of the passage.
42. Kettler, *Das Jüngste Gericht*, 283, 295–98.
43. Kursawa, *Antichrist*, 142. Kettler refers to the Simon Magus saga.
44. Kursawa, *Antichrist*, 167.
45. Kettler, *Das Jüngste Gericht*, 295.
46. 2 Thessalonians 2:8: "Et tunc revelabitur ille iniquus, quem Dominus Iesus interficiet spiritu oris sui, et destruet illustratione adventus siu eum." ("And then the lawless one will be revealed, and the Lord Jesus will slay him with the breath of his mouth and destroy him by his appearing and his coming.")
47. Kettler, *Das Jüngste Gericht,*, 295–97. Kettler notes the following sources: 2 Thessalonians 2:8 and Jerome's *Commentariorum in Danielem Liber*, cap. 11, 44–45 (*PL* 25, 574).
48. Kursawa, *Antichrist*, 182–83.
49. In regard to the difficulty of providing a definitive source, Kettler, *Das Jüngste Gericht*, 402.
50. Kettler, *Das Jüngste Gericht*, 403–17.
51. Kursawa, *Antichrist*, 229.
52. On the placement of the theme of fire in the section *De adventu Christi ad iudicium* as compared with Frau Ava's work, see Kettler, *Das Jüngste Gericht*, 418.
53. Kursawa observes that Christ actively displays the cross and tools of crucifixion as witnesses to the legitimation of his office as judge. *Antichrist*, 233.
54. Kettler, *Das Jüngste Gericht*, 421–23.

CONCLUSION

The examination of seminal Latin treatises in this study has shown that the Augustinian program of Christian culture profoundly influenced the practice of learning and teaching in the early Middle Ages. The central tenet held in common by Augustine, Gregory the Great, and Hrabanus Maurus was the building of Christian charity by scriptural studies and the use of the Bible as the major textbook and literary model for the edification of the Christian community. The examined works of all three Latin authors give evidence to similar pedagogical techniques, namely, the use of biblical models of conduct, affect teaching, the evocation of saving terror and compunction, and paraphrase to move and persuade the learner to imitate models that demonstrate Christian charity, and to reject those that reveal cupidity.

Differences in emphasis between the works of Gregory and Hrabanus are traceable to the historical situation and the pedagogical priorities of each respective period. In the *Regula Pastoralis,* written when disorder and laxity reigned within the Italian bishoprics after the Lombard invasion, Gregory stresses pastoral care and the moral instruction of the Christian community by way of contrasting models of conduct. Yet, Hrabanus, writing *De institutione clericorum* at the monastery of Fulda during a relatively stable period of Carolingian rule, advocates a more balanced transmission of the Augustinian program. This version includes the seven-step *ascensus* pattern, and the study of tropes, the artes, and the Ciceronian categories of style as means of understanding biblical *signa.* By so doing, Hrabanus emphasizes the importance of complementary activities of biblical study and of teaching what is discovered. And, in deference to patristic authority and pedagogical practice, he also presents an abbreviated collection of contrasting models of conduct from Gregory's *Regula Pastoralis.*

The ninth-century eschatological poem, the *Muspilli,* clearly demonstrates the viability of the examined concepts from Latin treatises through their application in German vernacular literature. The use of positive and negative models of conduct together with affect teaching present simplified rhetorical arguments in exemplary form designed to move and persuade the learner to implement the lesson. In fact, the complementary use of exemplary and preceptive verses may strengthen the presentation by confronting the learner with a given course of action and then confirming its consequences at Judgment. The *Muspilli* also evinces a simplified twofold process of purification and ascent to wisdom, culminating in catharsis and *compunctio*.

By focusing attention on the call to Judgment, the teaching strategy aims to persuade the learning audience to implement the lesson through the correct practice of Carolingian judicial authority. The *Muspilli* translates Christian charity, then, into morally sound judicial practice. To achieve this learning outcome, the poet readily evokes the fear of God—and saving (*saluberrimus*) terror—to convert the listener to correct conduct and to promote the exercise of vigilance in maintaining it. In addition, the comparative analysis of the *Muspilli* and the *Sermo de Symbolo* highlights the importance in both works of correcting judicial malpractice.

Finally, paraphrastic intensity and amplification of selected themes may heighten the force of affect teaching and its impact on the listener. The poet then uses the pronouncement of Judgment in an eschatological context to "legalize" and confirm the lesson by assuring the listener that its observance will merit salvation.

As in the ninth-century *Muspilli,* the teaching objectives in the *Memento Mori* at the end of the eleventh century are to convert the listener from error and foster vigilance in observing norms of Christian conduct. Yet, the teaching strategy of the *Memento Mori* contrasts sharply with that of the earlier poem. The purifying ascent to wisdom with its culmination in the cathartic response of the listener is clearly absent in the *Memento Mori,* which stresses, instead, a balanced presentation of rational arguments and controlled emotional intensity. Thus, simplified rhetorical arguments together with affect teaching may predispose the learning audience to imitate or reject exemplary models of conduct on the basis of whether or not the exemplary figure acts in accord with reason, that is, Christian norms of conduct. Consequently, these arguments also promote critical reflection on the part of the listener as opposed to mere conditioned response.

Furthermore, the alternating shift in the listener's identification with positive and negative models of conduct, and the subsequent evocation, release and restoration of narrative tension attests to a balanced and controlled use of textual dynamics as a counterpart to the presentation of rhetorical arguments.

The works of Frau Ava, viewed as one *oeuvre,* show that the poems *Johannes* and *Das Leben Jesu* aim to prepare the listener for the arrival

Conclusion

of the Antichrist and, ultimately, for the call to Judgment. This vital preparatory phase of Ava's overall lesson reveals the influence of the seven-step ascent to wisdom and purification, in particular, in the depiction of the seven gifts of the Holy Spirit.

The correspondence of virtues with the *vita activa* and the *vita contemplativa* fits in well with Ava's religious status as an *inclusa*. Indeed, the *Regula Solitariorum* of Grimlaicus stresses the importance of combining both the active and contemplative life for the religious vocation of recluse. In accord with the ardent "concern for neighbor" in twelfth-century spirituality, Ava's instructional poems are an expression of her concern for the spiritual and personal welfare of others. She thus depicts those who receive the seven gifts of the Holy Spirit in *Das Leben Jesu* as immediately wishing to edify their neighbors. Yet, only after she has sought to predispose her listeners to uphold their identity with the recipients of the gifts and to prepare themselves for the Antichrist's onslaught, does she confront them with the call to Judgment. And, in the final poem, *Das Jüngste Gericht*, she applies saving terror and affect teaching to promote the contemplation of the lesson and its practice.

The inclusion of a catalogue of virtues especially relevant and useful to an aristocratic audience, such as avoidance of bribery at judicial proceedings, attests to the importance attributed by Ava to the active life as an expression of her concern for others, in particular for the spiritual welfare of her fellow members of the nobility. Thus, the teaching strategy provides the first two poems as a preparatory phase to ready the learner for vigilant resistance to the Antichrist, and for the day of Judgment. Ava's work displays a linear ascent pattern, embellished by circular patterns as in the description of the seven gifts of the Holy Spirit from *Das Leben Jesu*, where wisdom begins and ends with the fear of God. The catalogue of virtues in *Das Jüngste Gericht* provides, then, an extension and practical application of the seven gifts for the benefit of both the active and contemplative life.

Almost half a century after Ava had written her poems, the author of *Von den Letzten Dingen* also presents a work with a unified poetic and pedagogical concept. Yet, compared with Ava's work, there is a more striking use of textual dynamics. The employment of retarding elements such as the *discessio* theme varies the sequential narrative motion as an effective means of heightening or releasing narrative tension. And, in comparison with the preparatory phase in Ava's work, which seeks to ready the learner for the encounter with the Antichrist and the ensuing day of Judgment, *Von den Letzten Dingen* intensifies this instructional phase by developing it into a confrontational teaching strategy. The poet thus guides the learner to confrontational situations which provide exercises in vigilance to strengthen the resolve to stay within the community of the saved.

In summary, the continuity of fundamental concepts of learning and teaching in the examined works is also the continuity of strategies of persuasion that shaped religious literature of the German Middle Ages.

BIBLIOGRAPHY

Abbreviations

ABaG	Amsterdamer Beiträge zur älteren Germanistik
CCCM	Corpus Christianorum Continuatio Mediaevalis
CCSL	Corpus Christianorum, Series Latina
CSEL	Corpus Scriptorum Ecclesiasticorum Latinorum
MGH	Monumenta Germaniae Historica
NF	Neue Folge
PL	Patrologia Latina. Edited by J. P. Migne. Paris, 1844-64
SMGBOZ	Studien und Mitteilungen zur Geschichte des Benediktiner Ordens und seiner Zweige
ZDA	Zeitschrift fur Deutsches Altertum und Deutsche Literatur
ZDP	Zeitschrift fur Deutsche Philologie
ZDW	Zeitschrift fur Deutsche Wortforschung

Primary Sources

Adso von Montier-en-Der. *Libellus de ortu et tempore Antichristi.* In *Sibyllinische Texte und Forschungen,* ed. Ernst Sackur, 97-113. Halle: Niemeyer, 1898. CCCM 45.

Alciun. *De virtutibus et vitiis. PL* 101, 613-38.

Ancrene Wisse. Ed. and trans. H. White. London: Penguin Classics, 1993.

Augustine. *De Antichristo Liber Unus. PL* 40, 1131-34.

———. *De catechizandis rudibus.* Ed. I. B. Bauer. Turnhout: Brepols, 1969. CCSL 46, 115-78.

———. *De doctrina christiana.* Ed. J. Martin. Turnhout: Brepols, 1962. *CCSL* 32, 1-167.

———. *De doctrina christiana.* Trans. D. W. Robertson. New York: Liberal Arts Press, 1958.

———. *De sermone Domini in monte Libros Duos.* Ed. Almut Mutzenbecher. Turnhout: Brepols, 1967. *CCSL* 35, 1-188.

[Pseudo] Augustine. *Sermo de Symbolo contra Judaeos, Paganos et Arianos. PL* 42, 1117-30.

Ava, *Die Dichtungen der Frau Ava.* In *Die religiösen Dichtungen des 11. und 12. Jahrhunderts,* 3 vols., ed. F. Maurer, 2:369-513. Tübingen: Niemeyer, 1965.

Beatus Lièbana. *Beati in Apocalypsin libri duodecim.* In *Papers and Monographs of the American Academy in Rome,* vol. 7. Ed. H. A. Sanders. Rome, 1930.

Benedict of Nursia. *Regula Monachorum.* Ed. R. Hanslik. Vienna: Hoelder-Pichler-Tempsky, 1960. *CSEL* 75.

Bernard of Clairvaux. *Sermones in Cantica Canticorum. PL* 183, 1094.

Cassiodorus. *Exposito in Psalterium. PL* 70, 25-1056.

Christ III. The Exeter Book. Eds. G. P. Krapp and E. Dobbie. New York: Columbia University Press, 1936.

Conrad of Hirsau. *Dialogus super auctores sive Didascalion.* Ed. R. B. C. Huygens, Collection Latomus, vol. 17. Brussels, 1955.

Gerhoch von Reichersberg. *De investigatione Antichristi I.* Ed. E. Sackur. Halle, 1897. MG Ldl III, 305-95.

Gerhoch von Reichersberg, *Quarta vigilia noctis.* Ed. E. Sackur. Halle, 1897. MG Ldl III, 503-25.

Gregory the Great. *Liber regulae pastoralis. PL* 77, 13-128.

———. *Dialogi, Liber IV. PL* 77, 149-430.

Hildegard von Bingen. *Liber divinorum operum. PL* 197, 741-1038.

Heinrich von Melk. *Erinnerung an den Tod; Das Priesterleben.* Ed. R. Kienast. Heidelberg, 1946.

Hrabanus Maurus. *De institutione clericorum. PL* 107, 293-420.

The Memento Mori. In *Die religiösen Dichtungen des 11. und 12. Jahrhunderts,* 3 vols., ed. F. Maurer, 2:249-59. Tübingen: Niemeyer, 1964.

The Muspilli. In *Althochdeutsches Lesebuch,* 16th ed., eds. Wilhelm Braun and Karl Helm, 86-89. Tübingen: Niemeyer, 1979.

Otto von Freising. *Chronica sive historia de duabus civitatibus.* Darmstadt, 1980.

Prudentius. *Psychomachia,* 2 vols., ed. E. H. Warmington, 1:274-343. Cambridge: Harvard University Press, 1969.

Sedulius. *Paschale Carmen.* Ed. J. Huemer. Vienna, 1885. *CSEL* 10.

Tertullian. *De anima. PL* 2, 641-752.

Theodulf of Orleans. *Versus contra iudices. MGH* Poet. Lat. I, 493-517.
Vercelli Homilies IX-XXIII. Ed. P. E. Szarmach. Toronto: University of Toronto Press, 1981.
Von den Letzten Dingen (Linzer Antichrist), Die religiösen Dichtungen des 11. und 12. Jahrhunderts, 3 vols., ed. F Maurer, 3:361-427. Tübingen: Niemeyer, 1970.
Walafrid Strabo. *De visionibus Wettini. PL* 114, 1070-79.

Secondary Sources

Anderson, George K. *The Literature of the Anglo-Saxons.* Rev. ed. Princeton: Princeton University Press, 1966.
Auerbach, E. *Literatursprache und Publikum in der lateinischen Spätantike und im Mittelalter.* Bern: Francke, 1958.
———. *Mimesis.* 7th ed. Bern: Francke, 1982.
Baesecke, Georg. "Muspilli II." *Zeitschrift für Deutsches Altertum und Deutsche Literatur* 82 (1948/50): 201.
Ballauff, T. *Pädagogik, eine Geschichte der Bildung und Erziehung,* 3 vols. Freiburg: Alber, 1969.
Bennett, Camille. "The Conversion of Vergil." *Revue des Études Augustiniennes* 34 (1988): 47-69.
Bertau, Karl. *Deutsche Literatur im europäischen Mittelalter.* 2 vols. Munich: Beck, 1972.
Bloch, M. *Feudal Society,* 2d ed. 2 vols. London: Routledge and Kegan, 1962.
Blumenberg, H. "Wirklichkeitsbegriff und Möglichkeit des Romans." In *Poetik und Hermeneutik,* vol. 1: *Nachahmung und Illusion,* 9-27. Ed. H. Robert Jauss. Munich: Fink, 1969.
Bonner, S. F. *Education in Ancient Rome, From the Elder Cato to the Younger Pliny.* Berkeley and Los Angeles: University of California Press, 1977.
Borst, A. *Lebensformen im Mittelalter.* Frankfurt am Main: Propylaen, 1973.
Borst, Arno. *Mönche am Bodensee.* Sigmaringen: Thorbecke, 1978.
Bosl, K. "Potens und Pauper." *Frühformen der Gesellschaft im mittelalterlichen Europa* (1964): 106-34.

Bremond, Claude, Jacques Le Goff, and Jean-Claude Schmitt. *Typologie des Sources du Moyen Age Occidental: L'Exemplum.* Turnhout: Brepols, 1982.

Brinker-Gabler, G., ed. *Deutsche Literatur von Frauen.* Vol. 1. Munich: C. H. Beck, 1988.

Brinkmann, Hennig. *Mittelalterliche Hermeneutik.* Darmstadt: Wissenschaftliche Buchgesellschaft, 1980.

Brown, Peter. *Augustine of Hippo.* Berkeley and Los Angeles: University of California Press, 1967.

———. *The Body and Society.* New York: Columbia University Press, 1988.

Brunner, H. *Deutsche Rechtsgeschichte,* 2d ed. 2 vols. Leipzig: Duncker and Humblot, 1906.

Brunner, O. *Land und Herrschaft.* Darmstadt, 1973.

Burke, Kenneth. *A Grammar of Motives.* New York: Prentice-Hall, 1945.

Bynum, Caroline Walker *Docere Verbo Et Exemplo: An Aspect of Twelfth-Century Spirituality,* Harvard Theological Studies 31 (Missoula, Mont.: Scholars Press, 1979).

Cameron, A. *Christianity and the Rhetoric of Empire.* Berkeley and Los Angeles: University of California Press, 1991.

Chase, Christopher L. "Christ III," "The Dream of the Rood," and "Early Christian Passion Piety." *Viator* 11 (1980).

Cohn, Norman *The Pursuit of the Millennium.* New York: Oxford University Press, 1971.

Curtius, E. R. *Europäische Literatur und Lateinisches Mittelalter,* 7th ed. Bern: Francke, 1948/1969.

De Boor, Helmut. *Die Deutsche Literatur.* Munich: C. H. Beck, 1949.

Deferrari, Roy Joseph, ed. *The Fathers of the Church.* Washington D.C.: The Catholic University of America Press, 1963.

Dickens, Bruce, and A. S. C. Ross eds., *The Dream of the Rood,* 4th ed. London: Methuen, 1954.

Dittrich, Marlies. "Der Dichter des Memento Mori," *Zeitschrift für Deutsches Altertum und Deutsche Literatur* 72 (1935): 58.

Doerr, Otmar *Das Institut der Inclusen in Süddeutschland.* Münster in Westf.: Aschendorff, 1934.

Duchrow, Ulrich *Sprachverständnis und biblisches Hören bei Augustin.* Tübingen: J. C. B. Mohr, 1965.

Eden, Kathy *Poetic and Legal Fiction in the Aristotelian Tradition.* Princeton: Princeton University Press, 1986.

Bibliography

Elias, N. *Der Prozess der Zivilisation*, 2d ed. 2 vols. Bern: Francke, 1969.
Evans, G. R., ed. *Christian Authority, Essays in Honour of Henry Chadwick.* Oxford: Clarendon Press, 1988.
Fichtenau, Heinrich, "The Carolingian Empire." In *Studies in Medieval History*, ed. by Geoffrey Barraclough, vol. 9. Oxford: Blackwell, 1957.
Finger, H. *Untersuchungen zum 'Muspilli.'* Göppingen: Kümmerle, 1977.
Fischer, Wolfgang, and Dieter-Jürgen Löwisch. *Pädagogisches Denken von den Anfängen bis zur Gegenwart.* Darmstadt: Wissenschaftliche Buchgesellschaft, 1989.
Fleckenstein, J. *Die Bildungsreform Karls des Grossen als Verwirklichung der Norma Rectitudinis.* Ph.D. diss., Universität Freiburg, Bigge-Ruhr, 1953.
Freytag, H. *Die Theorie der allegorischen Schriftdeutung und die Allegorie in deutschen Texten besonders des 11. und 12. Jahrhunderts.* In *Bibliotheca Germanica* 24. Bern: Francke, 1982.
Freytag, Wiebke. "Geistliches Leben and christliche Bildung. Hrotsvit and andere Autorinnen des frühen Mittelalters." In *Deutsche Literatur von Frauen*, vol. 1., ed. Gisela Brinker-Gabler. Munich: Verlag C. H. Beck, 1988.
Fritz, Donald K. "Caedmon: A Monastic Exegete." *American Benedictine Review* 25 (1974):351-63.
Fuhrmann, Manfred, ed. *Terror und Spiel.* Munich: Fink, 1971.
Gallo, Ernest "The Grammarian's Rhetoric: The *Poetria Nova* of Geoffrey of Vinsauf." In *Medieval Eloquence*, ed. James J. Murphy. Berkeley and Los Angeles: University of California Press, 1978.
Gardiner, Eileen, ed. *Visions of Heaven and Hell Before Dante.* New York, Italica Press, 1989.
Gentry, F. G. *Bibliographie zur frühmittelhochdeutschen geistlichen Dichtung.* Berlin: Erich Schmidt, 1992.
———. "Noker's Memento Mori and the Desire for Peace." *ABaG* 16 (1981): 25-62.
———. "Vruot... Verdamnot? Memento Mori, vv. 61-62." In *ZDA* (1979): 297-306.
Grau, Gustav *Quellen und Verwandtschaften der älteren germanischen Darstellungen des Jüngsten Gerichtes.* Halle: Niemeyer, 1908.

Greenfield, S. B., and Calder, D. G. *A New Critical History of Old English*. New York: New York University Press, 1986.

Greinemann, Eoliba. *Die Gedichte der Frau Ava, Untersuchungen zur Quellenfrage*. Ph.D. diss., University of Freiburg, 1968.

Grimm, J. *Deutsche Rechtsaltertümer*, 4th ed. Leipzig: Mayer and Müller, 1922.

Haas, A. M. *Todesbilder im Mittelalter*. Darmstadt, 1989.

Hart, Brother Patrick, ed. *The Monastic Journey*. Garden City, N.Y.: Doubleday, 1978.

Hauck, Albert. *Kirchengeschichte Deutschlands*, 5 vols. Berlin: Academie, 1958.

Haug, W. "Das 'Muspilli' oder über das Glück literaturwissenschaftlicher Verzweiflung." In *Zweimal 'Muspilli.'* Tübingen: Niemeyer, 1977.

Haug, W., ed. *Formen und Funktionen der Allegorie*. Stuttgart, 1979.

Hergt, G. "Christentum und Weltanschauung." In *Poetik und Hermeneutik*, vol. 4:357-68. Ed. M. Fuhrmann. Munich: Fink, 1971.

Herzog, Reinhart. "Augustins Gespräch mit Gott." In *Das Gespräch, Poetik un Hermeneutik XI*. Munich: Wilhelm Fink Verlag, 1984.

———. *Die Bibelepik der lateinischen Spätantike*. Munich: Fink, 1975.

———. "Exegesse - Erbauung - Delectatio." In *Formen und Funktionen der Allegorie*, ed. W. Haug. Stuttgart, 1979.

Hintz, Ernst R. "Frau Ava." In *Dictionary of Literary Biography*, ed. Will Hasty and James Hardin. Vol. 148: *German Writers and Works of the Early Middle Ages: 800-1170*. Charleston, S.C.: Bruccoli, Clark, and Layman, 1995.

———. "Frau Ava." In *Semper idem et Novus: Festschrift für Frank Banta*, ed. Francis G. Gentry. Göppingen: Kümmerle Verlag, 1988.

Hofmeister, P. "Mönchtum und Seelsorge bis zum 13. Jahrhundert," *SMGBOZ* 65 (1955):209-73.

Howie, George. *Educational Theory and Practice in Saint Augustine*. New York: Teachers College Press, 1969.

Huppé, Bernard F. *Doctrine and Poetry: Augustine's Influence on Old English Poetry*. Albany: State University of New York Press, 1959.

Illmer, D. "Formen der Erziehung und Wissensvermittlung im frühen Mittelalter, Quellenstudien zur Frage der Kontinuität des abendlandischen Erziehungswesens." In *Münchener Beiträge zur Mediävistik und Renaissance-Forschung* 7. Munich: Arbeo, 1971.

Ingarden, Roman *Erlebnis, Kunstwerk und Wert*. Tübingen: Niemeyer, 1969).

Iser, Wolfgang. "Der Archetyp als Leerform. Erzählschablonen und Kommunikation in Joyces 'Ulysses.'" In *Terror und Spiel,* ed. Manfred Fuhrmann. Munich: Fink, 1971.

Iser, Wolfgang, ed., *Funktionen des Fiktiven*. Munich: Fink, 1983.

Jaeger, W. *Paideia: The Ideals of Greek Culture*. Vols. 1 and 3. Trans. Gilbert Highet. New York: Oxford University Press.

Jantsch, H. G. *Studien zum Symbolischen in Frühmittelhochdeutscher Literatur.* Tübingen: Niemeyer, 1959.

Jauss, H. R. "Alterität und Modernität." In *Gesammelte Aufsätze 1956-1976.* Munich: Fink, 1977.

——— *Alternität und Modernität der mittelalterlichen Literatur* (Munich: Fink, 1977), 20.

———. *Ästhetische Erfahrung und literarische Hermeneutik.* Munich: Fink, 1977.

———. *Nachahmung und Illusion*. Munich: Fink, 1969.

Jauss, H. R., ed. *Die Nicht Mehr Schönen Künste*. Poetik und Hermeneutik III. Munich: Wilhelm Fink Verlag, 1968.

Kaiser, G. "Das Memento Mori: Ein Beitrag zum sozialgeschichtlichen Verständnis der Gleichheitsforderung im frühen Mittelalter." *Euphorion* 68 (1974): 337-70.

Kartschoke, D. *Bibeldichtung: Studien zur Geschichte der epischen Bibelparaphrase von Juvencus bis Otfrid von Weissenburg*. Munich: Fink, 1975.

Käsemann, E. *Exegetische Versuche und Besinnungen.* Göttingen: Vandenhoeck & Ruprecht, 1964.

Kästner, H. *Mittelalterliche Lehrgespräche, Textlinguistische Analysen, Studien zur poetischen Funktion und pädagogischen Intention.* Berlin: Schmidt, 1978.

Keinast, Richard. "Ava-Studien I." *Zeitschrift für Deutsches Altertum und Deutsche Literatur* 74 (1937): 34.

Kennedy, George A. *Classical Rhetoric and Its Christian and Secular Tradition from Ancient to Modern Times.* Chapel Hill: University of North Carolina Press, 1980.

———. *Greek Rhetoric under Christian Emperors.* Princeton: Princeton University Press, 1983.

_____. *New Testament Interpretation through Rhetorical Criticism.* Chapel Hill: University of North Carolina Press, 1984.
Kettler, Wilfried. *Das Jüngste Gericht.* Berlin: De Gruyter, 1977.
Kolb, H. "Dia weroltrehtwison." *ZDW* 18.(1862): 88-95.
Konrad, Robert. *De ortu et tempore Antichristi. Antichristvorstellung und Geschichtsbild des Abtes Adso von Montier-en-Der.* Källmunz: Lassleben, 1964).
Krapp, G. P., and E. V. K. Dobbie, eds. *Christ III.* In *The Anglo-Saxon Poetic Records* 3, *The Exeter Book.* New York: Columbia University Press, 1936.
Krapp, G. P., ed. "The Dream of the Rood." In *The Anglo-Saxon Poetic Records 2, The Vercelli Book.* New York: Columbia University Press, 1932.
Kuhn, Hugo. *Dichtung und Welt im Mittelalter.* Stuttgart: Metzler, 1959.
Kursawa, Hans-Peter *Antichrist, Weltende und Jüngstes Gericht in mittelalterlicher deutschen Dichtung.* Ph.D. diss., University of Cologne, 1976.
Ladner, Gerhart B. *The Idea of Reform: Its Impact on Christian Thought and Action in the Age of the Fathers.* Cambridge: Harvard University Press, 1959.
Lapidge. "Some Remnants of Bede's lost Liber Epigrammatum." *English Historical Review* 90 (1975): 798-820.
Lausberg, Heinrich. *Handbuch der Literarischen Rhetorik.* Munich: Hueber, 1960.
Lämmert, E. *Reimsprecherkunst im Spätmittelalter.* Stuttgart: Metzler, 1970.
Le Goff, Jacques.*The Birth of Purgatory.* Chicago: University of Chicago Press, 1981.
Leckie, George G. *Concerning the Teacher.* New York: Appleton-Century-Crofts, 1938.
Leclercq, J. *The Love of Learning and the Desire for God.* New York: Fordham University Press, 1961.
LeGoff, Bermond C., and J. Schmitt. *Typologie des Sources du Moyen Age Occidental: Exemplum.* Turnhout: Brepols, 1982.
Luhmann, Niklas. "Über die Funktion der Negation in sinnkonstituierenden Systemen." In *Positionen der Negativität,* ed. Harald Weinrich. Munich: Fink, 1975.
Lutz, Eckart Conrad. *Rhetorica divina.* Berlin: De Gruyter, 1984.

Marquardt, Odo. "Kunst als Antifiktion." In *Funktionen Des Fiktiven*, ed. Wolfgang Iser. Munich: Fink, 1983.

Marquard, Odo, and Karlheinz Stierle, eds. *Identität, Poetik und Hermeneutik. VIII*. Munich: Fink, 1979.

Marrou, Henri I. *The Resurrection and Saint Augustine's Theology of Human Values*, trans. Mother Maria Consolata. Villanova University Press, 1966.

———. "Saint Augustin et la Fin de la Culture Antique." In *Bibliothèque des Écoles Francaises D'Athènes et de Rome*. Paris: Éditions de Boccard, 1938.

Maurer, Friedrich. *Die religiösen Dichtungen des 11. und 12. Jahrhunderts*, 3. vols. Tübingen: Niemeyer, 1964.

Mayer, Cornelius "Res per Signa," in *Revue des Études Augustiniennes* 20 (1974).

McKeon, R. "Rhetoric in the Middle Ages." In *Speculum* 17 (January 1942): 1-32.

Mckitterick, Rosamond. *The Carolingians and the Written Word*. Cambridge: Cambridge University Press, 1989.

McMahon, Robert. *Augustine's Prayerful Ascent*. Athens: University of Georgia Press, 1989.

Minis, Cola. *Handschrift, Form und Sprache des Muspilli*. Philologische Studien und Quellen 35. Berlin: Schmidt, 1966.

Mohr, W., and Haug, W. *Über das Muspilli, Zweimal 'Muspilli'*. Tübingen: Niemeyer, 1977.

Moricca, Umberto, ed. *Gregorii Magni Dialogi, Libri IV*. Rome: Istituto Storico Italiano, 1924.

Morrison, Karl F. *The Mimetic Tradition of Reform in the West*. Princeton: Princeton University Press, 1982.

Mottek, Hans. *Wirtschaftsgeschichte Deutschlands*. Berlin: Volkseigener Betrieb, 1974.

Murphy, James J. *Rhetoric in the Middle Ages*. Berkeley and Los Angeles: University of California Press, 1974.

Murphy, James J., ed. *Medieval Eloquence*. Berkeley and Los Angeles: University of California Press, 1978.

O'Connell, Robert, S.J. *Soundings in St. Augustine's Imagination*. New York: Fordham University Press, 1994.

O'Daly, Gerard. *Augustine's Philosophy of Mind*. Berkeley and Los Angeles: University of California Press, 1987.

Ohly, Friedrich. *Schriften zur Mittelalterlichen Bedeutungsforschung*. Darmstadt: Wissenschaftliche Buchgesellschaft, 1977.

Orton, P. R. "Caedmon and Christian Poetry." *Neuphilologische Mitteilungen* 84 (1983): 163-70.
Pannenberg, Wolfhart. "Person und Subjekt." In *Poetik und Hermeneutik. VIII,* eds. O. Marquard and K. Stierle, 407-22. Munich: Fink, 1979.
Payne, Richard C. "Convention and Originality in the Vision Framework of The Dream of the Rood." *Modern Philology* 73 (1975-76): 329-41.
Perrin, Norman *Rediscovering the Teaching of Jesus.* New York: Harper & Row, 1976.
Planitz, Hans. *Deutsche (Germanische) Rechtsgeschichte,* 3rd ed. Berlin: Vahlen, 1944.
Poland, Lynn. "The Bible and the Rhetorical Sublime." In *The Bible as Rhetoric, Studies in Biblical Persuasion and Credibibily,* ed. Martin Warner. New York: Routledge, 1990.
Quadlbauer, Franz. "Die Antike Theorie der Genera Dicendi im Lateinischen Mittelalter." In *Österreichische Akademie der Wissenschaften: Philosophische—Historische Klasse, Sitzungsberichte,* 241.2. Vienna: Böhlau, 1962.
Quitzmann, A. *Die älteste Rechtsverfassung der Baiuwaren.* Nürnberg: n.p., 1866.
Rauh, Horst Dieter *Das Bild des Antichrist im Mittelalter: von Tyconius zum deutschen Symbolismus.* Münster: Aschendorff, 1973.
Riché, Pierre. *Éducation et culture dans l'Occident Paris: Editions du barbare, 6e-8e siècles.* Seuil, 1962.
_____. *Education and Culture in the Barbarian West.* Trans. John J. Contreni. Columbia: University of South Carolina Press, 1976.
Roberts, M. J. *The Hexameter Paraphrase in Late Antiquity: Origins and Application to Biblical Texts.* Ph.D. diss., University of Illinois at Urbana-Champaign, 1978.
Rotermund, Erwin. "Der Affekt als Literarischer Gegenstand: Zur Theorie und Darstellung der Passiones im 17. Jahrhundert." In *Die Nicht Mehr Schönen Künste,* Poetik und Hermeneutik III, ed. H. R. Jauss. Munich: Wilhelm Fink Verlag, 1968.
Rupp, Heinz. *Deutsche religiöse Dichtungen des 11. und 12. Jahrhunderts,* 2d ed. Bern: Franke, 1971.
Sackur, Ernst, ed. *Sibyllinische Texte und Forschungen.* Halle: Niemeyer, 1898.
Schlosser, Horst Dieter. *Althochdeutsche Literatur.* Frankfurt am Main: Fischer, 1980.

Bibliography

Schmidt, Karl. "Über das Verhältnis von Personen und Gemeinschaft im früheren Mittelalter." *Frühmittelalterliche Studien* 1 (1967): 225-49.

Schneider, H. *Kleinere Schriften*. Eds. K. H. Halbach and W. Mohr. Berlin, 1962.

Scholz-Williams, Gerhild. *The Vision of Death: A Study of the "Memento Mori" Expressions in some Latin, German, and French Didactic Texts of the 11th and 12th Centuries*. Göppingen: Kümmerle, 1976.

Schönborn, Christoph. "Die Autorität des Lehrers nach Thomas Aquin." In *Christian Authority, Essays in Honour of Henry Chadwick*, ed. G. R. Evans. Oxford: Clarendon Press, 1988.

Schröder, W. "Grenzen und Möglichkeiten einer althochdeutschen Literaturgeschichte." *Philologischhistorische Klasse* 105/2 (1959): 91.

Schutzeichel, R. *Althochdeutsches Wörterbuch*. Tübingen: Niemeyer, 1974.

―――. *Das alemannische Memento Mori*. Tübingen: Niemeyer, 1962.

―――. "Justitiam vender." *Literaturwissenschaftliches Jahrbuch*, Neue Folge 5 (1964).

Seiferth, W. *Synagoge und Kirche im Mittelalter*. Munich: Kosel, 1964.

Shuger, Debora K. *Sacred Rhetoric*. Princeton, N.J.: Princeton University Press, 1988.

Sieben, Hermann-Josef. "Die <<Res>> der Bibel in <<Doctrina Christiana>>." *Revue des Études Augustiniennes* 21, nos. 1-2 (1975): 74-75.

Singer, J. "Zu Muspilli 90-93." *ZDP* 95 (1975): 449.

Smalley, B. *The Study of the Bible in the Middle Ages*, 3d ed. Notre Dame, Ind.: University of Notre Dame Press, 1978.

Solmsen, Friedrich, ed. *The Rhetoric and Poetics of Aristotle*. Trans. W. Rhys Roberts and Ingram Bywater. New York, 1954.

Spitz, Hans-Jörg. *Die Metaphorik des Geistigen Schriftsinns*. Munich: Fink, 1972.

Springer, Carl P. E. *The Gospel as Epic in Late Antiquity, the Paschale Carmen of Sedulius*. Leiden: E. J. Brill, 1988.

―――. *Sedulius' Paschale Carmen: A Literary Reexamination*. Ph.D. diss., University of Wisconsin-Madison, 1984.

Stein, Peter K. "Stil, Struktur, Historischer Ort und Funktion- Literaturhistorische Beobachtungen und methodologische Überlegungen zu den Dichtungen der Frau Ava." In *Festschrift für Adelbert Schmidt zum 70. Geburtstag,* ed. Gerlinde Weiss. Stuttgart: Akademischer Verlag Hans Dieter Heinz, 1976.

Steindorff, G. ed. *Die Apocalypse des Elias. Texte und Untersuchungen zur Geschichte der altchristlichen Literatur,* vol. 2. Leipzig: n.p., 1899.

Straw, Carole. *Gregory the Great, Perfection in Imperfection*. Berkeley and Los Angeles: University of California Press, 1988.

Swanton, Michael J., ed. *The Dream of the Rood.* Manchester: Manchester University Press,1970.

Szarmach, Paul E., ed. *Vercelli Homilies IX-XXIII.* Toronto: University of Toronto Press, 1981.

Taubes, Jacob. "Die Rechtfertigung des Hässlichen in urchristlicher Tradition." In *Die Nicht Mehr Schönen Künste,* ed. Hans Robert Jauss. Munich: Fink, 1968.

Ullmann, Walter. *The Individual and Society in the Middle Ages.* Baltimore: Johns Hopkins University Press, 1966.

von Montier-en-Der, Adso. *Libellus de ortu et de tempore Antichristi.* In *Sibyllinische Texte und Forschungen,* ed. Ernst Sackur. Halle: Niemeyer, 1898.

Warner, Martin, ed. *The Bible as Rhetoric, Studies in Persuasion and Credibility.* New York: Routledge, 1990.

Weber, Paul *Geistliche Schauspiel und kirchliche Kunst in ihrem Verhältnis,* erläutert an einer Ikonographie der Kirche und Synagoge. Stuttgart, 1894.

Wehri, Max. "Sacra Poesis." In *Die Wissenschaft von deutscher Sprache und Dichtung, Festschrift für Friedrich Maurer.* Stuttgart: Adademischer Verlag, 1963.

Weinrich, Harald, ed. *Positionen der Negativität.* Munich: Fink, 1975.

Weiss, Gerlinde, ed., *Festschrift für Adelbert Schmidt zum 70. Geburtstag.* Stuttgart: Akademischer Verlag Hans Dieter Heinz, 1976.

Wieland, G. R., ed. *The Latin Glosses on Arator and Prudentius in Cambridge University Library MS Gg. 5. 35.* Toronto: Pontifical Institute of Medieval Studies, 1983.

Williams, G. S. *The Vision of Death: A Study of the "Memento Mori": Expressions in Some Latin, German, and French*

Didactic Texts of the 11th and 12th Centuries. Göppingen: Kümmerle, 1976.

Wrenn, C. L. "The Poetry of Caedmon." *Proceedings of the British Academy* 32 (1946).

———. *A Study of Old English Literature.* London: Blackwell, 1967.

Wundrack, August. *Der Linzer Antichrist.* Ph.D. diss., Marburg, 1886.

INDEX

actio concept, in religious poetry, 49, 55, 57–58, 62, 70n.46
active life, Frau Ava on, 104–9
Adalramm (bishop), 47
admonitio characteristics, 24–26, 38n.87
admonitio generalis, 47
Adso von Montier-en-Der, 144, 158, 175n.15
aedificatio concept, Gregory's *aedificatio communis,* 24–26, 28–29; in *Muspilli,* 46–64; purification and wisdom and, 11–13; in religious poetry, 44–46; *timor Dei* and, 20–22
Aeneid, 4
affectus (affect teaching), Augustine's concept of, 11, 13, 17–18, 35n.59, 36n.63; in Ava's *das Jüngste Gericht,* 122–33; Gregory's concept of, 24–26; Hrabanus on, 27–29; in *Memento Mori,* 82–97; in religious poetry, 49, 51–52, 55, 57–58, 62, 70n.46; in *Von den Letzten Dingen,* 140, 143–45, 155–58, 165–66, 170–74
Alcuin, 27, 41n.119, 56, 68n.32, 75nn.86–87
allegory, in *De doctrina christiana,* 43, 65n.1
annunciation, in Frau Ava's *Johannes,* 107–9

Antichrist, in Ava's *Das Leben Jesu,* 117–19; in Ava's *Der Antichrist,* 119–20; plural images of, 145–46; in religious poetry, 51–52; in *Von den Letzten Dingen,* 140–74
Apocalypse imagery, in *Von den Letzten Dingen,* 154–64
Aquinas, Saint Thomas, educational theory of, 5, 30n.8
Aristotelian aesthetics, Christian learning and, 11, 16, 43
ars communis aedificationis, 23–24
as if mode, in Ava's *das Jüngste Gericht,* 129–33; in *Memento Mori,* 84–90, 94–95, 99n.28, 100n.39; in *Von den Letzten Dingen,* 142, 148–50
ascensus pattern. *See also* seven-step ascent to wisdom (Augustine); Christian education and, 179; in Frau Ava's poetry, 103, 106, 117–19; in *Von den Letzten Dingen,* 139
Augustine, Bible as primary learning source for, 15, 34n.45; educational theory of, 4–5; Hrabanus influenced by, 27–29; influence of, on Christian culture, 179; *modus proferendi* concept, 13–22; on scriptural

exegesis, 6–22; on self-instruction, 5–6; *timor Dei* concept, 9–10; writing of *De doctrina*, 4
authority imagery, in religious poetry, 50–51
Ava (Frau), on active and contemplative life, 104–9; on Call to Judgment, 121–33, 168; on charity, 109–19; poetry of, 103–33, 134n.1, 180–81; on practice of vigilance, 119–20
Ava-Studien I, 105

Baesecke, Georg, 68n.32
Barbarossa, Friedrich, 176nn.18–19
battle metaphors, in religious poetry, 47–48
Bede, Venerable, 45–46, 67n.26
Benedictine monasteries, Frau Ava's poetry in, 136n.48; religious poetry during reform by, 58–59
benevoli, Gregory's concept of, 24–26
Bibeldichtung, 45, 66n.20
Bible, aesthetics of, 5; Augustine's concentration on, 43; as prime source for Christian education, 15, 34n.45, 179; religious poetry and, 44–46, 66n.20; scriptural exegesis and, 6–22
Biblepik, 44–46
bishops, Gregory on pastoral responsibilities of, 22–26
blindness imagery, in *Von den Letzten Dingen*, 155–56, 177n.30
Bonner, Stanley F., 34n.44
Borst, 76n.98
bribery, admonitions against, in religious poetry, 56–57
Bynum, Caroline Walker, 103–4

Caedmon, miracle of, 45–46, 68n.27
Call to Judgment (Last Judgment), in Ava's *das Jüngste Gericht*, 121–33; in Ava's *Das Leben Jesu*, 115–16; as legal proceeding, 91, 101n.42; in *Memento Mori*, 84–85, 96–97, 100n.29; in religious poetry, 44–64, 70n.46; in *Von den Letzten Dingen*, 164–74
canonical vocation, 103–4
Cassiodorus, commentaries of, 52
catharsis, Christian learning and, 11, 43; in *Memento Mori*, 89–90, 101n.40; as motif in Ava's *das Jüngste Gericht*, 129–33; in *Muspilli*, 179–80
charity, active life and, 104–9; Augustine's concepts of, 7–10, 21–22, 32n.27; in Frau Ava's poetry, 109–19; Gregory's concepts of, 23–26; Hrabanus on, 27–29; in *Memento Mori*, 84–90; as motif in Ava's *das Jüngste Gericht*, 126–33; in *Muspilli*, 180
Charlemagne, 47, 68n.32; judicial authority under, 60–61
Christ, Augustine's educational theory and, 7–8; figure of, in Ava's *Das Leben Jesu*, 111–15, 136n.42; as "teacher within us," 5
Christ III, 47, 68n.36
Christian education, acquisition and dissemination, 3; *De doctrina christiana* as source of, 15–16; pastoral care theory of Gregory, 22–26, 37nn.74–75; religious poetry and, 59–64
Chronica sive Historia de Duabus Civitatibus, 176n.18
Chrysostom, John, 11, 43
Church, Augustine's concept of, 7

Index

Cicero, Augustine influenced by, 4, 15–17; Christian education theory and, 43; Hrabanus influenced by, 27
cithara image of teaching, 23
clergy, duties regarding learning, 3
communal conduct, Gregory's concept of, 25–26
compunction, process of, 24–26, 38n.88; in *Ava's Das Leben Jesu*, 114–19; in *Muspilli*, 180
Concordia Veteris et Novi Testamenti, 157
Conrad of Hirsau, 152, 176n.27
contemplative life, Frau Ava on, 104–9, 118–19, 137n.49
continual reform concept, in *Memento Mori*, 79
conversio concept, *Memento Mori* as vehicle for, 79, 89–90; in religious poetry, 49, 70n.46

Das Institute der Inclusen in Süddeutschland, 104
Das Jüngste Gericht, 103, 105, 118, 121–33, 181
Das Leben Jesu, 105–6, 109–19, 130, 180–81
De catechizandis rudibus, 4, 9–13
De clericorum institutione, 4, 26–29, 43, 63–64
De die iudici, 47
De doctrina christiana, Gregory's work influenced by, 24, 26; Hrabanus influenced by, 27; influence on Christian culture, 43, 65n.1; *modus proferendi* in, 13–22, 33nn.41–42; overview of, 3–6; religious poetry and, 63–64; scriptural exegesis in, 6–22, 33nn.41–42; *timor Dei* in, 9–10

De institutione clericorum, 179
De magistro, 4–6, 30n.8
De ordine, 4
De Rebus investigandis in Scriptura, 5
De sermone Domini in monte, 106
De Valeriani patricii sepultura, 57
De virtutibus et vitiis liber ad Widonem Comitem, 56–57
De vita pastoris, 22–26
death, as motif in *Memento Mori*, 91–97
delectatio concept, 19–20
Deogratias (deacon), 8
Der Antichrist, 105, 119–20, 130
Dialogorum Liber IV, 57–58
Dialogues (Gregory the Great), 57–58, 63–64
Dialogus super auctores, 152, 176n.27
Die Gedichte der Frau Ava, Untersuchungen zur Quellenfrage, 105–6
Die Sieben Gaben des Heiliges Geistes, 105
discessio theme, in *Von den Letzten Dingen*, 146–48, 176n.20
Docere Verbo Et Exemplo, 103
Doerr, Otmar, 104
Dream of the Rood, 47–48, 68n.36
"dritte Instanz" concept, 137n.51

ecclesiastical influence, expansion of, 3
educational theory, of Augustine, 4–5
Elias and Enoch legend, 52–53, 152–64
Elias Apocalypse, 52–53, 72n.65
eloquence, vs. wisdom, Augustine on, 20
emotions, Augustine on reason and, 17–18, 36n.62
"empty space" imagery, in *Von den Letzten Dingen*, 148, 156–57
eschatological thought, *Memento Mori* and, 83–84, 91–97

Evangelienbuch, 47
Evangelium, 44
exemplary concept, in religious poetry, 49, 70n.46
Expositio in Psalterium, 52

false prophets, in *Von den Letzten Dingen*, 151–60
fortitudo, Augustine's concept of, 10
Frankish kingdom, church reforms, 47; disorder of Frankish Church, 39n.99; Germanic legal terminology and, 50; in *Von den Letzten Dingen*, 147–48, 176nn.19–20
Freytag, Wiebke, 134n.1

"Gattung" literature, 44
Genesis, 47
Gentry, Francis G., 80, 84–85, 99n.28
Gerhoch von Reichersberg, 157, 177n.34
Germanic legal terminology, religious poetry and, 50
Germanisierung, 45–46
Gospel of Luke, Frau Ava's poetry and, 106–7
Greek Christian literature, biblical aesthetics and, 11
Gregory the Great, 4; admonitions against bribery, 57–58; Christian education theory and, 43; Hrabanus influenced by, 28–29; influence of, on Christian culture, 179; manuscripts of, 79–80; on pastoral care, 22–26
Greinemann, Eoliba, 105–9, 118–19, 134n.1, 135n.28
Grimlaicus, 104–9, 181

Haug, Walter, 46, 68n.32
Heliand, 47

hell, fear of, in religious poetry, 50, 71n.55
Hellenistic program, 4
Henry IV, 80
hermeneutics, in *De doctrina christiana*, 43, 65n.2
Herod, as figure in Ava's *Das Leben Jesu*, 108–11; as figure in Ava's *Johannes*, 108–9
Herzog, Reinhart, 11
Hieronymus, 142, 175n.8
Hildegard von Bingen, 157, 177n.34
Hohenstaufen rule, ideological impact of, 176nn.18–19
Hrabanus Maurus, educational theory of, 26–29, 43; influence of, on Christian culture, 179
humilitas, Augustine's concept of, 17
Huppé, Bernard F., 65n.1
hyssop imagery, Augustine's use of, 13, 41n.128

image, Augustine's concept of, 16–17, 35n.53
imitative learning (*imitatio*), Augustine on role of, 14–17; in Ava's *das Jüngste Gericht*, 130–33; Christian learning and, 43; Grimlaicus on, 105–6; Hrabanus on, 28–29; in religious poetry, 49, 70n.46
inclusa concept, in Frau Ava's poetry, 104–9, 118–19, 181
intentio voluntatis, 16–17, 37n.70
Investiture Contest, 79–80, 82, 147
Isocrates, 15, 34nn.43–44, 43
ius talionis, in *Muspilli*, 55–58, 74n.78; in *Von den Letzten Dingen*, 164, 167
iustitia, in *Memento Mori*, 89–90, 101n.40

Index

Jacob's prophecy, in *Von den Letzten Dingen*, 141
Jantsch, 136n.42
Jauss, Hans Robert, 73n.78, 100n.40, 101n.44
Jerome (Saint), 146–47
Jews, conversion of, in *Von den Letzten Dingen*, 154–58, 177nn.30–31
Johannes, 105–9, 130, 180–81
Johannine concepts, in *Von den Letzten Dingen*, 150–54, 158–60, 167–74
John the Baptist, as figure in Frau Ava's *Johannes*, 106–9
judgment, Augustine on, 20–22; in Ava's poetry, 103–33; Gregory on, 24–26, 43; Hrabanus on, 26–27, 40n.117; as motif in *Memento Mori*, 81–97; *Muspilli* as judgment narrative, 47–64, 68n.36. See also Call to Judgment
Juvencus, 44–45, 65n.10

Kartschoke, 66n.20
Käsemann, Ernst, 59
Kettler, Wilfried, 100n.29
Kienast, Richard, 105–6, 134n.1
knowledge, Augustine on use of, 12–13
Kuhn, Hugo, 46, 68n.32
Kunst als Antifiktion, 82
Kursawa, Hans-Peter, 72n.65, 158–59, 175n.8, 177n.32

laity, doctrinal discussion by, 3; *Memento Mori* and, 79–97; teaching and learning of, in medieval church, 14–22
lamentation, in Christian education, 10

language, educational theory and, 5–6, 21–22, 31n.15; religious poetry and, 44–46
Le Goff, Jacques, 49
learner as teacher concept, 5–6
learning, concepts of, 3–29, 30n.1
legal terminology, in Germanic religious poetry, 50–64
Liber regulae pastoralis, 4
libertas ecclesiae, 80
Linzer Antichrist. See *Von den Letzten Dingen*
Literarisierung, 45
liturgy, Frau Ava's poetry and, 106, 135n.28
Louis the German, 47
Luhmann, Niklas, 101n.49

magister interior/exterior concept, 5–6
mahal concept, in *Muspilli*, 54
Marquard, Odo, 82
Marrou, Henri Irénée, 30n.1, 33nn.41–42
Marus, Hrabanus, 4
Mary Magdalene, in *Von den Letzten Dingen*, 160–61
Matthew, figure of, in Ava's *Das Leben Jesu*, 115–16
Maurer, Friedrich, 80
Memento Mori, 64, 79–97, 152; as if motif in, 84–90; judgment motif in, 81–97; manuscript of, 79–80; pilgrimage imagery in, 90–97; teaching objectives in, 180; *Von den Letzten Dingen* compared with, 152–53
mercy, Augustine's concept of, 10
Merton, Thomas, 34n.47
mimesis, *Memento Mori* as vehicle for, 98n.3
modus inveniendi, Augustine's concept of, 13

modus proferendi, Augustine's concept of, 13–22
Mohr, Wolfgang, 46, 68n.32
monasticism, Gregory's educational theories and, 22, 37n.74; sense of vocation in, 103–4
Moralia in Job, 79–80
Morrison, Karl F., 98n.3
Murphy, James J., 23, 38n.87
Muspilli, Ava's *das Jüngste Gericht* compared with, 130; influence on Christian education of, 179–80; *Memento Mori* compared with, 84, 96–97; origins of, 68n.32; persuasion strategy in, 46–64; *Relapsus a baptismo,* 55; *Renuntiare satanae,* 55
mysterium tremendum, 20–21, 36n.69

narrative distance, in *Memento Mori,* 92–93, 101n.44
Nazianzen, Gregory, 23
neighbor, Augustine's concepts of, 7–8; concepts of, in Ava's poetry, 103–4; responsibilities toward, in *Memento Mori,* 84–90
Noker, 64, 80–97, 99n.17
nüziu rede actions, in *Von den Letzten Dingen,* 139–40

O'Daly, Gerald, 5–6, 30, 32nn. 27–28
Old High German literature, 46–47, 68n.32
oration, Augustine on importance of, 17–19
Origen, 11
ornamenta terrestria linguae, religious poetry and, 44–46
Otfrid von Weissenburg, 47

Otto von Freising, 176n.18

paideia concept, Christian education and, 34n.43
paraphrasis, in Gregory's *Regula pastoralis,* 24–26; in *Memento Mori,* 81, 99n.17; in *Muspilli,* 55; in religious poetry, 45–46
Paschale Carmen, 44–45
pastoral care, Gregory the Great on, 22–26
Pauline scripture, Augustinian aesthetics and, 8, 11–13, 18; Hrabanus and, 28–29; *Memento Mori* and, 82–83, 99n.24; *Von den Letzten Dingen* and, 139–40, 142–43, 145–46, 166–67, 170–74
Paulinus of Nola, 4
pedagogical tradition, Augustine and, 15; Gregory's thirty-six characteristics, 24–26, 38n.87; persuasion and, in Frau Ava's works, 103–33
Perrin, Norman, 59
persuasion, Augustine on principles of, 16; Hrabanus on, 28–29; as motif in *Memento Mori,* 88–89; pedagogy and, in Frau Ava's works, 103–33; strategy of, in religious poetry, 46–64
Peter, figure of, in Ava's *Das Leben Jesu,* 112–13, 115–19, 136n.39
piety, Augustine on, 9–11
pilgrimage imagery, Augustine's use of, 6–7, 10; in *Memento Mori,* 90–97; in *Von den Letzten Dingen,* 152–53
poetry, as educational medium, 44–46; influence of *De doctrina christiana,* 43, 65n.1; pagan and non-biblical poetry, 4

Poland, Lynn, 36n.69, 37n.71
Pope Gregory VII, 80
power, exercise of, in *Memento Mori*, 84–90; as legal jurisdiction in *Memento Mori*, 92–97, 101n.42
Praeceptum generale concept, 7
preaching traditions, in Augustine's *De doctrina christiana*, 13
preceptive (*didaktisch*) concept, 49, 70n.46
Proömium, 44
Prudentius, 14, 45–46, 66n.17
Psychomachia, 45, 66n.17
purification, Augustine's concepts of, 8–13
Pyramus and Thisbe, 4

Quintilian, rhetoric of, 34n.44

rahha concept, religious poetry and, 50–51
Rauh, 175n.15, 176n.20
Regensburg Saint Emmeram codex, 46–47
Regula pastoralis, 22–26, 37n.74, 43; Hrabanus influenced by, 28–29; influence of, on Christian culture, 179; religious poetry and, 63–64
Regula Solitariorum, 104, 118–19, 181
reht concept, in *Memento Mori*, 87–88, 91–97, 100n.37, 101n.42
Reichenau, monastery of, 58–59
res concept, Augustine's use of, 6–7
Retractationes, 4, 6
rhetoric, Augustine on importance of, 15–19, 37n.71; in Gregory's *Regula pastoralis*, 24–26; in *Memento Mori*, 89–90, 100n.39; in religious poetry, 44–45
ritual, in religious poetry, 49–50
Roman Empire, in *Von den Letzten Dingen*, 145–46, 176n.18

Saint Ambrose, 18
Saint Basil, 11
Saint Cyprian, 18
saluberrimus terror concept, in religious poetry, 62, 64
salutissimus timor, 50
Satanic imagery, in Ava's *Das Leben Jesu*, 111–12; in Ava's *Der Antichrist*, 120; in religious poetry, 48–49, 51–52, 60
"Sätze heiligen Rechts im Neuen Testament," 59
Schönborn, Christoph, 30n.8
scientiae gradus, 9–10, 17
scriptural exegesis, Christian educational theory and, 6–22, 43; Hrabanus on, 27–29, 41n.131
Sedulilus, Caelius, 14, 44–45, 48
self-instruction, Augustine on, 5–6
self-love, Christian concept of, Augustine's educational theory and, 7, 27, 32nn.25
sensus spiritualis, Augustine's concept of, 4, 12
Sermo de Symbolo contra judaeos, paganos et arianos, 46–47, 55, 60–61, 180
sermon, Augustine on role of, 14–15
seven evil spirits, in *Von den Letzten Dingen*, 160, 178n.41
seven-step ascent to wisdom (Augustine), 9–10, 20–21, 32n.28, 41n.126
Singer, Johannes, 62
spiritus intellectus, in Ava's *Das Leben Jesu*, 117–19
Stein, Peter K., 134n.1, 135n.28, 136n.48

teaching objectives, in Ava's *das Jüngste Gericht*, 132–33; concepts of, 3–29; of

Gregory the Great, 23–26; Hrabanus on, 27–29; in *Memento Mori*, 96–97, 180; in *Von den Letzten Dingen*, 164–65, 171–74
time, as motif in *Memento Mori*, 94–95, 101n.50
timor Dei, Augustine's concept of, 7, 9–12, 20–22, 32nn.27–28; in Ava's *Das Leben Jesu*, 117–19; Hrabanus on, 27–29; in religious poetry, 57–58, 62, 64. See also *salutissimus timor*
tria genera concept, 17–20
tropos, Augustine on concept of, 21

uuenago man, in *Muspilli*, 54–55, 73n.77
uueroltrehtuuison concept, in religious poetry, 51

vernacular, Christian education using, 79
vigilance (*vigilia*) concept, in Frau Ava's poetry, 119–20; *Memento Mori* as vehicle for, 79; in *Von den Letzten Dingen*, 151–52, 155–58
Vom Priesterleben, 157
Von den Letzten Dingen, 139–74, 181–82
Von des todes gehugede, 157
von Melk, Heinrich, 156–57, 177n.34

Walahfrid Strabo, 58–59
Waldo, religious poetry about, 58
wealth, as motif in Ava's *das Jüngste Gericht*, 123–24; as motif in *Memento Mori*, 91–97
Wetti, 58–59, 76n.98
will, Augustine's concept of, 16
wisdom, purification and, Augustine's concept of, 8–13; vs. eloquence, Augustine on, 20

GARLAND STUDIES IN MEDIEVAL LITERATURE
PAUL E. SZARMACH AND CHRISTOPHER KLEINHENZ
General Editors

THE PROTEAN TEXT
A Study of Versions of the Medieval French Legend of "Doon and Olive"
by Kimberlee Anne Campbell

CATTLE-RAIDS AND COURTSHIPS
Medieval Narrative Genres in a Traditional Context
by Vincent A. Dunn

BROTHERS OF DRAGONS
Job Dolens and François Villon
by Barbara Nelson Sargent-Baur

THE *ALEXIS* IN THE SAINT ALBANS PSALTER
A Look into the Heart of the Matter
by Rachel Bullington

TRANSCRIPTION AND VISUAL POETICS IN THE EARLY ITALIAN LYRIC
by H. Wayne Storey

HENRYSON AND THE MEDIEVAL ARTS OF RHETORIC
by Robert L. Kindrick

AUTHORITY AND AUTONOMY IN *L'ENTRÉE D'ESPAGNE*
by Nancy Bradley-Cromey

THE SHORT LYRIC POEMS OF JEAN FROISSART
Fixed Forms and the Expression of the Courtly Ideal
by Kristen Mossler Figg

CHAUCER'S CLERK'S TALE
The Griselda Story Received, Rewritten, Illustrated
by Judith Bronfman

TEXTUAL DECORUM
A Rhetoric of Attitudes in Medieval Literature
by Scott D. Troyan

REWRITING RESEMBLANCE IN MEDIEVAL FRENCH ROMANCE
Ceci n'est pas un graal
by Paul Vincent Rockwell

THE LEGEND OF GUY OF WARWICK
by Velma Bourgeois Richmond

LEARNING AND PERSUASION IN THE GERMAN MIDDLE AGES
by Ernst Ralf Hintz

For Product Safety Concerns and Information please contact our EU
representative GPSR@taylorandfrancis.com
Taylor & Francis Verlag GmbH, Kaufingerstraße 24, 80331 München, Germany

www.ingramcontent.com/pod-product-compliance
Lightning Source LLC
Chambersburg PA
CBHW071355290426
44108CB00014B/1550